India of Shah Jahan

Reshma Umair

ANAMIKA PUBLISHERS & DISTRIBUTORS (P) LTD.
4697/3, 21A, Ansari Road, Daryaganj, New Delhi 110 002
Phones: 011-2328 1655, 011-43708938
E-mail: anamikapublishers@yahoo.co.in

Edition 2021

ISBN 978-81-7975-998-1

PRINTED IN INDIA

Published by Anamika Publishers and Distributors (P) Ltd., 4697/3, 21A, Ansari Road, Daryaganj, New Delhi 110002. Typeset by Aadil Printographics, Delhi 110092 and Printed at Vikas Computer and Printers, Tronica City, Ghaziabad

Contents

Acknowledgment

I must confess that the work on the book ***India of Shah Jahan*** could have been more comprehensive. I therefore, owe a word of apology for the drawbacks, if any, in my work. At the outset of the presentation of this work I would like to put on my gracious acknowledgment to the persons who have played their part in completion of this work.

I want to express my sincere gratitude to my esteemed supervisor Prof. Pradeep Kumar Ghosh, Department of Medieval and Modern History, University of Lucknow, for his benign and skillful guidance throughout the course of this entire work. I have regard for his inexplicable and reliable contributions. It was due to his kindness, keen interest and guidance, that I have been able to complete this academic venture.

My profound gratitude goes to Prof S.N.R. Rizvi, Professor and Ex Head of DDU Gorakhpur University. Dr U. Farahi, Ex head and Dean, Department of Arab culture, University of Lucknow for his kind support and guidance, without which it would have been impossible to complete this work.

I am extremely indebted to my friend Dr. Vineeta Kachar, Associate Professor Lucknow University, whose love, affection and co-operation have been foundation of my success.

My special gratitude goes to my parents and my husband without whose kind support and co-operation, this work could not have been accomplished.

I am grateful to the librarian and staff of Maulana Azad Library, Aligarh Muslim University, Aligarh, Tagore Library Lucknow University, Lucknow, Ameeruddaula Library Lucknow, Acharya

Narendra Dev Library Lucknow, and U.P State Archives.

I am highly thankful to Mr. Raza Abbas (Azmi) who typed this manuscript with the extreme sense of responsibility and due care.

Dr. Reshma Umair

1. Introduction

This present book is a revised and improved version of my thesis which was submitted. The early career of Shah Jahan has been discussed by many writers in their own ways, yet a few important details may be enumerated here. He was born on Thursday, January 5, 1592 at Lahore.[1] His mother was the Rajput Princess (daughter of Raja Udai Singh of Mota in Marwar) variously called Jagat Gosain, or Jodahbai whom Salim had married in 1586.[2]

For Akbar, the birth of his grandson was of more than ordinary pleasure. It was doubly welcomed, it brought him the usual felicity, but more than that, it is reviewed the drooping spirits of his childless wife, Ruqiah Begum entitled Sultan Begum. Her Astrologer, Gobind had predicted to her the happy event and had advised her to adopt the child. Therefore, in accordance with the custom obtaining among the royalty, on the sixth day after the birth of the child, Akbar was invited by his son Salim to give a name to his new born baby, he christened him Khurram or joyous. The same day, he was handed over to Ruqiah Begum, who adopted him; and henceforward until he reached the age of discretion he grew up under the fostering care of his grandmother.

The practice among the Mughals was to put a child to school soon after his circumcision. Accordingly when the prince was 4 years, 4 months and 4 days old his ***'maktab'*** ceremony was performed. The occasion was probably celebrated with the customary pomp and festivity.

His first teacher was Mulla Qasim Beg Tabrezi.[3] He was succeeded by an eminent man Hakim Ali Gilani,[4] a physician of standing reputation and a scholar of sterling merits. In medicine, he was successively a pupil of his maternal uncle Hakim-ul-mulk Shirazi and of

Shah Fatahullah Gilani and in technology a student of Shaykh Abd-un-Nabi. The prince came more in contact with Hakim Ali than with any other of his teachers and seems to have been much attached to him. Later in his life he often remembered with a sense of pleasure and deep gratitude the debt he owed to Hakim Ali for the knowledge he obtained from him during the most impressionable period of his training[5] among the others who were entrusted with the duty of guiding and shaping the intellectual development of the Prince, mention should be made of Shayakh Sufi,[6] a disciple of Miyan Wajihudin Gujarati a delightfull poet, a man of sweet temperament and a libertine. Another was Shayakh Abul Khayr, brother of Shayakh Abul Fazl, "a well-informed young man of regulated mind."[7] He soon acquired knowledge of the Persian language and a command over its expression, but he showed little interest in Turki Jahangir is recorded to have once complained to Ruqiah Begum about the prince's apathy towards the ancestral language[8]; and Akbar seems to have tried to remove this deficiency. In 1601, he appointed Tatar Khan to teach him Turki.[9]

It is doubtful whether the new teacher could create any enthusiasm in his young pupil. But Khurram was not a dull boy. He possessed a sharp wit, a wonderful memory, a love for details and the capacity to master them.

His education was so designed as to make him strong both in mind and in body. Akbar paid a due regard as well to the physical training of Khurram. When in 1597 A.D., he was going for the last time to Kashmir, he left his grandson at Lahore under the guardianship of Mir Murad Juwaini.[10]

The Mir was to teach him archery and to perform daily before him ***taslim-i-qur.***[11] Later when Khurram accompanied his grand father to the Deccan. Akbar appointed Raja Salivahan[12] to train him rifle shooting. Riding and swordsmanship formed a part of his daily exercises and the prince showed more interest in them than in the dry lesson on rhetoric and prosody. Like his father, he became a skilful shooter both with rifle and with bow and arrow, an indefatigable rider, an excellent swordsman and a keen lover of all field sports.

Khurram fell ill of small-pox. His condition became serious and his grandfather grew nervous. He quickly summoned skilful physicians to his bed-side. His prayers had the desired effect and the Prince was soon cured. On the day that the unstinted generosity and set many prisoners free. Thereafter, Khurram went with his grandfather to the Deccan,[13] Akbar's health now began to decline rapidly. One day while he was away from his home he arranged an elephant fight between the animals of Khusrav and Salim. He and Khurram watched the show from the ***Jharokha*** (window).

In the combat Salim's elephant gained the advantage, and moreover his men abused the followers of Khusrav. The latter rushed to complain of it to his grandfather who sent Khurram to Salim with a message to stop the affray.[14] Akbar retired from the scene much exhausted and passed a restless night. In the morning he had an attack of fever, which was complicated by diarrhoea. He was lying at death's door.[15] Khurram was devotedly attached to Akbar,[16] and would not leave his bed side. When his mother tried to persuade him. He firmly replied, No! so long as there is one breath of life in Shah Baba nothing can induce me to leave him.

Exactly one week after his father's death Salim ascended the throne on Thursday October 24, 1605. Soon after this, the even tenure of his reign was disturbed by the outbreak of Khusrav, who on the evening of 6th April 1606, escaped from Agra on the pretext of visiting Akbar's tomb. He took the road to the Panjab and on the way was joined by Husain Beg Badakhshi and Abd-ur-Rahim, Jahangir was disturbed on hearing the report of Khusrav's escape, and ordered Shaykh Farid Bokhari to pursue the rebel. He decided to follow himself shortly. As it was necessary to make some arrangement for the safety of the capital, a council of regency was formed. It included Shaykh Ala-ud-Din grandson of Shaykh Salim. Later Islam Khan was appointed governor of Bengal. Mirza Ghiyas Beg Tehrani, Dost Muhammad Khvaja Jahan and Raja Rao Singh Bhurtiyah. Prince Khurram was appointed its President. This was his first formal contact with public affairs.[17]

Khusrav's rebellion came to an end within less than a months and Jahangir entered Lahore on May 9, 1606. He ordered Prince Khurram to come with Maryam-uz-Zamani and other ladies to Lahore. When he arrived in the vicinity of Lahore, Jahangir went out to Dhar to meet his mother.[18] It was during his father's stay in Lahore that Prince Khurram on March 21, 1607, received his first military rank of 8,000 zat and 5,000 suwar, together with a tuman-u-tugh, a flag, and drums.[19] About a week later he was betrothed to Arjumand Banu Begum, the daughter of I'tiqad Khan, the future Asaf Khan. Jahangir with his own hands put the ring on the finger of his prospective daughter-in-law and the occasion was celebrated with great rejoicings.[20] It was in the month of November of the same year that Jahangir on his return from Kabul assigned to Khurram a ***jagir*** in Ujjain and the ***sarkar*** of Hisar Firoza, and permitted him to pitch a red tent, a privilage generally accorded to the eldest prince only. To crown it all the ***Muhr Uzak*** was placed in his charge and it was ordered that all ***farmans*** and ***parwanas*** should bear his seal.[21]

Jahangir left Lahore on Thursday, 6th March 1607 and after about ten weeks journey entered Kabul on 4th June, scattering gold and silver. The Urtahbagh was assigned to be the residence of Prince Khurram. The existing buildings were not to the Prince's taste liked much by the Prince's, he soon carried out suitable, alterations after which he invited his father to visit the garden. Jahangir was exceedingly delighted with its renovated appearance and with the tastefulness and noble proportions of the new buildings and he passed the whole day in enjoyment and pleasure in the house of his son.

It was on this occasion that to ward off the evil influence of the stars, predicted by the court astrologers, the Emperor contrary to the time-honoured custom, observed the lunar birthday of the Prince. He was weighted against gold, silver, and other metals, which were distributed among the poor and needy.[22] After its suppression to Khusrav he resumed his march, and on the way at several places indulged in his favourite pastime of ***qamurghah.***[23] At Hasan Abdal, both Khurram and Parwez were allowed to participate in the hunt.[24] The party reached Lahore on 23rd November. 1607 and after a little more than six months stay, the journey to Agra was continued. The Emperor entered the capital on the 12th March, 1608.

Four months later he was betrothed to the daughter of Mirza Muzzafar Husain Safavi, a lineal descendent of Shah Isamail of Persia.[25] No doubt, polygamy was more of a rule than an exception in the Mughal household, but this was something quite different. Prince Khurram had not yet been married to his first *fiancee*, what was the need of having another? The plea that he was of marriageable age cannot be advanced because he was not immediately marrying to the Safavid Princess; on the contrary, the celebration of the actual rite was postponed for about a year nor there is any hint in the contemporary records of Khurram having suddenly fallen in love with her, at least his later life does not warrant such a conclusion. Finally no political motive can be seen behind the move. Jahangir celebrated the marriage of the Prince on October 29, 1610. He also presented robes of honour to the most of the *amir* and released many prisoners from the fort of Gwalior.[26]

About after a fortnight when Jahangir was one evening engaged in a *Cheetah* hunt, Anup Ray, who was leading the party, by chance saw a half eaten bullock near a big tree. In another, instant a powerful tiger emerged out a clump of thickets, and rushed past him. He immediately dispatched men to inform Jahangir who rode to the spot in great haste and excitement. He was accompanied by Prince Khurram, Ram Das, Itimad Rai and Hayat Khan. Jahangir's horse shied at the sight of the tiger who had taken shelter under a tree and so he dismounted. Hardly had Jahangir fixed his aim and fired for the third time, when the animal made a furious dash at the party, who losing their nerve fell one upon another. Meanwhile, the tiger turned to the left and desperately charged Anup Ray. The tiger opens its jaws, caught both of his hands, and plunged its sharp teeth through them. Within the twinkling of an eye, Prince Khurram drew his sword, struck the tiger in the lions, and returned the blood-smeared blade to the scabbard. The animal writhed with pain and fell down. None but Hayat Khan could only notice of Jahangir, the latter highly commended his son for his modesty. Anup Ray in recognition of his bravery obtained the title of Ani-Ray Singh Dalan. Prince Khurram on the occasion of the New Year's celebrations was promoted to the rank of 10,000 *zat* and 5,000 *suwar*. Mehrun Nisa or Nur Jahan therefore, had him promoted[27] to the rank of 12,000 *zat* and 5,000 *suwar* on March 27, 1612 and about four weeks later the nuptials of the long engaged pairs were performed. The occasion was celebrated with great pomp and splendour. No amount of expenditure was grudge to make the spectacle as brilliant and joyous as possible. Magnificent processions by day and expensive fireworks by night heightened its charm immeasurably. The entire city of Agra was ***en-fete.***

This gaiety, it seems, lasted for about a month, for at the end of it Jahangir went to the house of his son to participate in the marriage feast. The Prince offered presents to his father, jewels to the ***Begums***, and dresses of honour to the ***Amirs.***[28]

Prince Khurram's third wife was the daughter of Shahnawaz Khan, son of the famous 'Abd-ur-Rahim Khan Khanan, whom he married on 23rd August, 1617, when he was in the Deccan.[29] Matrimonial relationship seemed to be the best way of securing his ungrudging help. Besides this, Shahnawaz Khan, his son, was a promising young genius, and Khurram wanted to include him in the circle of his personal adherents, whose number was now skillfully increasing. By his first wife Prince Khurram had a daughter who was born on 12th August 1611. She was named Parhez Banu and was brought up by Ruqiah Begum.[30] By his second wife, he had fourteen children of whom seven died in infancy. The seven who survived were as follows.

Jahan Ara Begum, born at Ajmer on March 23, 1614.
Dara Shikoh, born at Ajmer on March 20, 1615.
Shah Shuja, born at Ajmer on June 23, 1616.
Roshan Ara Begum, born at Burhanpur on August 24, 1617.
Aurangzeb, born at Dauhad on October 24, 1618.
Murad Bakhsh, born at Rohtas on August 29, 1624.
Gauhar Ara Begum, born at Burhanpur on June 7, 1631.

The history of Jahangir's reign is mainly a record of the brilliant victories won by Prince Khurram. His meteoric rise into prominence thrilled and astonished his contemporaries. He started public life supported by the goodwill of his father and the full favour of his stepmother.[31] Though young in years; he showed signs of mature intellectual level.

His charming manners, his stern rules of conduct, his devotion to duty and his dashing courage, all combined to ensure for him a successful career. Contrast over his brothers and rival, whose failure more than once, gave him superiority and added to his glory. He had never to wait for opportunity; it came to him automatically. Early in 1614 he dispatched Prince Khurram in 'happiness and triumph' to second the efforts of the Khan Azam. A contingent of 12,000 men was placed at his command and Fidai Khan was appointed paymaster of this army. The young general was irritated at the dilatory tactics of his senior and he soon complained against him to his father. Jahangir sent Ibrahim Hussain to impress upon the mind of the Khan Azam the need for loyalty. Prince Khurram placed him under arrest and informed his father of the step he had taken. Jahangir sent Mahabat Khan to escort the prisoner to Ajmer.

This was the first indication of Prince Khurram's aggressive ambition. He was unwilling to share his glory with others, and was eager to succeed by his own resource and his own methods. The subjugation of Mewar enhanced the glory of the Mughul Empire no man was prouder than Jahangir and none happier than Prince Khurram. His reputation as a general of consummate skill and ability was established beyond doubt; and was marked out as the rising star. On his arrival near Ajmer all court ***Amirs*** were ordered to go out to meet him and offer valuable presents. When the Prince appeared before his father, the latter was overwhelmed by his feelings of affection and joy. Prince Khurram gained as a result of campaign was the devoted friendship of a chosen body of men who stuck to him through thick and thin. These included Sundar Das, Mulla Shukur-ul-Lah, saif Khan Barah, Dilawar Khan, Kishan Singh and Mir Hisam-ud-Din. The Prince now stood at the threshold of his pre-destined greatness.

Prince Khurram was now stood on the same level as his elder brother Parwez, and certainly in a more advantageous position. His success gives him prominence, and the united effort of the party recently organized by Nur Jahan pushed him into the forefront. He was now outstanding among contemporaries and rivals.

Though Jahangir was passing a merry time at Ajmer, he was not unmindful of the political situation in the Empire. He was keenly watching the affairs in the Deccan and was disappointed at the failure of his officer there. He thought to go personally and with this idea sent 'Abdul Karim Ma'muri to Mandu to prepare a new building for his private residence and to repair those of the old Emperors.[32] However, he postponed his departure to await the result of the Khan Khanan's renewed activity to retrieve the lost Mughul prestige. He did succeed in achieving the object to a very large extent, but dissensions among his officers retarded his progress. Moreover, rumours of briberies against him were still coming to court and so Jahangir was convinced of the necessity of putting his original plan into action.[33]

Accordingly, the rank of Khurram was increased to 20,000 zat and 10,000 suwar and Parwez was removed from the Deccan on ground of incompetency. He was transferred to Allahabad, and Prince Khurram was nominated to succeed him, "as the signs of rectitude and knowledge of affairs were evident in him."[34]

Prince Khurram was given an opportunity to gain an insight into the Deccan affairs, which Jahangir placed in his exclusive charge.[35] It was about this time that 'Abdullah Khan Firoz Jung was accused of certain misdemeanors, and he was sent far from Gujarat. In great perturbation of mind, he started on foot for Ajmer'. After his arrival there, he secured the sympathy of Khurram, who interceded on his behalf with his father.[36] His fault were forgiven, and he was ordered to accompany his benefactor to the Deccan. He was an experienced officer, and it was really fortunate for Khurram to have secured his services on this occasion. He was going to an unfamiliar region. The officers were unfriendly, if not hostile to him. The help of a man like 'Abdullah Khan, in such circumstances, was of great value'.

Before his departure the prince paraded the pick of his army before the Emperor in the Public Hall of Audience, and Jahangir was so, satisfied that he bestowed on him the title of Shah.[37] This was a unique honour. Never, before had a prince been styled Shah in the lifetime of a ruling monarch. It may be that a sense of vanity, prompted Jahangir to take this step. The Persian envoy[38] was staying at his court, perhaps he wanted to show him that he himself was greater than the Persian's Master, because he could confer upon his own son the same title as was borne by the Persian King, or perhaps this step was a psychological outcome of his own conception which he entertained as a prince at Allahabad.[39]

Shah Khurram left Ajmer on 6th October, 1616, amidst the fervent prayers of his father for success and renown.[40] Besides the valiant Firoz Jang, a host of other officers accompanied him. Of these the most important were Raja Suraj Singh, Dayanat Khan and Mu'tamid Khan was appointed as the paymaster of the army.[41] On the way to Daudpur[42] he was met by Rana Amar Singh, who placed at his disposal a contingent of 1,500 horse under Prince Karan. By rapid marches he reached the Narbada where the Deccan officers, including the Khan Khana Jahan and Mahabat Khan, welcomed him. Without tarrying any longer on the border, he marched straight to Burhanpur.[43] where he arrived on March 6, 1617. His arrival in the Deccan brought about the desired change in the political atmosphere. The Adilshah and Malik 'Ambar found the ground slipping from beneath their feet; and they readily responded to the gesture of peace made by Prince Khurram. They forwarded presents worth one million and five hundred thousand rupees. Malik 'Ambar returned Balaghat and agreed to surrender Ahmednagar and other forts.[44] Thus, a peacefull victory was gained. What arms had failed to achieve so long was won within a short time by diplomacy alone; and the credit of it all went to Shah Khurram.

After making arrangements for the proper administration of the newly recovered territories by placing them in charge of the Khan Khana and Shanawaz Khan[45] he left for the North to meet his father. At Mandu Jahangir was waiting with impatient anxiety to hear the results of his son's activities. Sayed 'Abdullah Barah brought the news of the arrangements and drums were beaten to celebrate the success.[46]

This was followed by a letter from the Prince announcing the arrival of Afzal Khan and Ray Rayan with the ambassadors of the Adilshah who brought jewels, elephant and horses, offering such as had never come in any time. The Prince himself arrived on October 12, 1617. He was received in the Hall of audience and after he had performed the dew rites of salutation and kissing the ground Jahangir called him to the Jharokha and with exceeding kindness and uncontrolled delight rose from his seat and held him in the embrace of affection.

He was given a seat near the thrown and received the unprecedented rank of 30,000 zat and 20,000 suwar together with the title of Shahjahan. Gifts were showered on him by his father in profusion and a magnificent feast was organized by Nur Jahan in honour of the occasion.[47]

It was about a month and a half before Shahjahan could display to his father the rich harvest of jewels and other valuable which he had gathered for him in Shahjahan's the Deccan. On Thursday the 20th

November, 1617, these were arranged in the Hall of Audience before the Jharoka together with the horses and elephant in Gold and silver trappings. To please his son, Jahangir came down to look through them in detail. There were costly pearls, giltering diamonds, fine rubies, and emeralds of beautiful colours and delicacy. But what attracted most the fancy of the Emperor were five elephants of mountainous size and good proportions. All together these offerings aim to 2,260,000 rupees; and out of these, presents worth 200,000 rupees were given by the Prince to his step-mother Nur Jahan.[48]

So, the Deccan problem was solved for the time being. A desire for elephant hunting led Jahangir to make a poor of Gujarat. He dispatched to Agra Maryam-uz-Zamani and other Begums and the people of the ***harem***, and also the baggage and extra establishment, he proceeded towards Ahmedabad. Nur Jahan and Shahjahan accompanied them. The journey was leisurely affair. On the way Dhar and Cambay were visited, and the Emperor ultimately reached his destination[49] on January 5, 1618.

In recognition of his success in Deccan the province of Gujarat was assigned to Shahjahan.[50] On one side of its peninsular portion lies an island called Cutch. This was ruled by a chief, called Bharah; and another descendent of the same branch known as the Jam, held the northern cost line of Kathiyawar. Both of these had temporarily submitted to the Mughals in the reign of Akbar, but latter recovered their independence. Shahjahan now deputed Raja Vikramajit to subdue them. The Jam was first to yield. He waited on Jahangir in March 1618 and was, four months latter, followed by his brother chief.[51] The sojourn in Gujarat did not place Jahangir, and he was soon disgusted with the suffocating heat and dust of the country. Both he and Prince Shahjahan fell ill of fever in May 1618, and the latter became so weak that for 10 days he could not come to pay his respects to his father.[52]

It was impossible to leave the place before the end of rainy season, after which Jahangir started for Agra on the 2nd September 1618, passing through Malwa, he arrived near the capital about the beginning January 1619. The city being still, affected with plague, Jahangir decided to stay in Fatehpur, which he entered on the 7th January. On the same day, the 28 solar birthday of Shahjahan was celebrated. Nine days latter Jahangir took him round the palace and explained to him in detail about the buildings erected by Akbar.

At Burhanpur, Khan Khanan was in miserable plight and appeal to the court for help. In his last dispatched he wrote that it was impossible to hold out any longer. He compared his position that of Mirza Aziz Koka in Gujarat in reign of Akbar, and pathetically called upon Jahangir to save him as his father had saved his foster-brother, otherwise after sacrificing his men, she would perform ***Jauhar*** when the report was placed before Jahangir his heart was moved. He had a great regard for the ***Ataliq*** who had been so tenderly brought up by his father. So far, the Kangra affair had prevented him from sending any effective help to the Deccan. It was now over and the officers were free to go there.

But, who was to lead the campaign? Naturally the only man whom Jahangir could choose was Shahajahan. He was able, he was diligent, and he possessed the necessary experience, and when the Emperor showed him the dispatches of the Khan Kahanan, he readily agreed to undertake the task. But on this occasion, he did not find his position so secure at fort. He noticed a vein jealousy in Nur Jahan, and some ficklemindedness in his father. The party which had so long supported him showed signs of disruption, though apparently he was as much honoured and respected by them as before. Thus, once more by a combination of force and tact Shahjahan patched up a peace in the Deccan. But the success was as unstable as ever, and the Deccan proved a cancer to the Mughal Empire. It ate through its vitality. But to Shahajahan it brought glory twice. It added to his fortunes and established his reputation.

He waded through blood to ascend the throne of Hindustan (at his instance, Asaf Khan killed all the members of the Imperial family). Shahajahan reached the vicinity of Agra on Thursday, January 28, 1628, and stopped in the Dahara Garden for twelve days, waiting for the auspicious hour fixed for his state entry into the capital. On Monday, February 4 at the exact time indicated by court astrologers, the coronation of the new Emperor took place. The ***Khutba*** was read in his name, and he assumed the lofty style of Abul Muzaffar Shihabuddin Muhammad sahib Qiran Sani. Fast couriers were dispatched to distance provinces to proclaim his accession. Sheikhs and Syeds, poets and astrologers, the learned and the pious, all took part of the generous bounty displayed by the emperor. Hakim Rukani Kashi, Sa'idai Filani, and Mir Salih composed felicitous chronograms and were richly rewarded.

From the hall of audience, the emperor retired to the Harem where Arjumand Banu Begum, Jahan Ara, and other ladies flocked round him to tender their congratulation to him. They showered Gold and Silver on him and distributed alms lavishly. This outburst of love and affection delighted Shahjahan, who reciprocated it by bestowing bounteous gifts. To his wife, the empress Mumtaz Mahal, he gave of present ***asharfis*** and four hundreds thousand rupees and fixed for her an annual allowance of six hundred thousand rupees-half of which were to be paid to her in cash from the royal exchequer, and for the other half equivalent jagir were assigned to her. Allowances and gifts for other princes and princess were also set apart. The emperor gave eight hundred thousand rupees to his wife of which four hundred and fifty thousand rupees were to be reserved for Dara, Shuja and Aurangzeb, and the balance was to be distributed among Murad, Roshan Ara and Surayya Begum.

Promotion

It was customary to award distinction and promotions to courtiers and officers on such occasions and Shahjahan followed the practice with greater lavishness than his predecessors. The first to be honoured was Asaf Khan, who was promoted to the Mansab of eight thousand ***zat*** and eight thousand ***sawar du aspa sih aspa,*** the title of uncle and premier empire. Next was Mahabat Khan, who was promoted to 7000 ***zat*** and 7000 ***sawar du aspa sih aspa*** and the title of Khan Khanan. Other names which deserve to be mentioned in this connection are Wazir Khan, Dilawar Khan, Bahadur Khan, Sardar Khan, Raja Vitthal Das and Khidmat Parast Khan. The last named was promoted to the post of Mir Tuzuk.

Administrative Changes

After promotions came the changes which were made in the administration. Loyal officer were confirmed in their post, while the suspect and disobedient were removed to make room for the faithful. In the first category were Asaf Khan, I'tiqad Khan, Khan Jahan, Baqur Khan Najam Sani. Among the latter were Mirza Rustam, replaced in Bihar by Khan Alam, Khwaja Abdul Hasan replaced by Lashkar Khan in Kabul, Fidai Khan, replaced by Qasim Khan in Bengal, Saif Khan replaced in Gujarat by Sher Khan, Muzzafar Khan replaced in Malwa by Khan Zaman, Mahabat Khan, Jahangir Quli replaced in Allahabad by Jan Sipar Khan and Mukhlis Khan replaced in Delhi by Qulich Khan.

Refeerences

1. Abul Fazl, Ain-i-Akbari, Vol. III, p. 921.
2. *Ibid.*, p. 749.
3. Abul Fazl says that he had undergone great sufferings in spiritual contemplation, and many delightful Sufic expressions fall from his lips. A.N., Vol. III, p. 1122. Tabaqat-i-Akbari says that he was distinguished.
4. Both Qazvini and Salih mentioned the name of Hakim Davai as tutor of Prince Khurram, but the only Davai mentioned in the reign of Akbar is Hakim 'Ain-ul-Mulk Shirazi, a descendant of the renowned logician Davvani and a friend of Badaoni. But the Hakim Shirazi died in 1003 A.H., and obviously he could not have been a tutor of Prince Khurram. Tabaqat f. 291; R.B., Vol, I, p. 68, p. 152, p. 154; Maasir-ul-Umars, Vol. I, pp. 568-73.
5. Qazvini, f. 34.
6. Tabaqat, f. 299. Subh-Sadiq f. 100 gives an account of Md. Sufi and says that he died in 1013 A.H. on his way to Lahore where he was going in response to the summons of Jahangir.
7. He was the first tutor of Khusrav. A.N., Vol. III, p. 822.
8. Lahouri. Vol. I, pp. 132-33, Qazvini says that Prince Khurram was familiar only with a few words of Turki because of his association with Ruqiah Begum, f. 134.
9. A.N., Vol. III, p. 1177; he was Bakaval Begi in the reign of Jahangir. R.B. Vol. I, p. 318.
10. He was Bakhshi of Lahore in 1598. A.N., Vol., III p. 1115; Blochmann, pp. 498-99; Qazvini, f. 34b.
11. This was the customary solute among the Mughul sovereigns. It probably meant presenting of 'arms'.
12. Qazvini, f. 35 Salivahan took a special shawl for Abul Fazl from the Court to the Deccan, A.N. Vol. III, p. 1197; Jahangir mentions him as coming from the Deccan with the elephants of Daniyal. R.B. Vol. I, p. 46.
13. Qazvini ff. 36.
14. Maasir-i-Jahangiri, ff. 59b-61.

15. A.N., Vol. III, pp. 1258-62.
16. Maasir-i-Jahangiri, ff. 61-62, Vol. I, p. 32.
17. Iqbalnama, p. 9; Maasir-i-Jahangiri, f. 71; Qavini, f. 42. R.B., Vol. I, p. 76.
18. ***Ibid.***, p. 76; Maasir-i-Jahangiri, f. 73; Qazvini, Rogers and Beveridge f. 43.
19. Rogers and Beveridge The Tuzuk-i-Jahangiri. Vol, I, p. 87 Iqbalnama wrongly gives 20,000, p. 222 Maasir has 8,000 ***zat*** and 5,000 ***suwar***, f. 76.
20. Qazvini, Padshahnama ff, 43-44.
21. During the Nouroz Celebrations of the second year, according to the Tuzuk, Prince Khurram only obtained the rank of 8,000 ***zat*** and 5,000 ***suwar***, a flag and drums and a jagir (R.B., p. 87). The ***Sarkar*** of Hisar Firoza was assigned to him later (R.B., p. 132). Iqbalnama agrees with the Tuzuk (p. 22).
22. Vol. I, p. 115; Qazvini, Padshahnama f. 44.
23. It is a kind of hunt in which the animals are driven towards the center of a circle and the hunters shoot or kill the prey from a very close range.
24. Rogers and Beveridge, Vol. I, p. 129.
25. Rogers and Beveridge Vol. I, p. 159; Iqbalnama, p. 38 Maasir-i-Jahangiri, f. 89b; Qazvini gives a detailed account of the ancestry of Muzzaffar Hussain Safavi, ff. 45-46b.
26. Rogers and Beveridge, Vol. I, p. 180; Iqbalnama, p. 46; Maasir-i-Jahangiri, f. 94.
27. Rogers and Beveridge, Vol. I, p. 256.
28. Rogers and Beveridge, Vol. I, pp 224-25; Iqbalnama, p. 67; Maasir-i-Jahangiri, f. 113; Qazvini, 48b-49b.
29. Qazvini, Padshahnama says that this connection was made to remove the mistrust of the Khan Khanan, f. 72b, Lahouri says that this marriage was due to certain state considerations (Vol. I, p. 390).
30. Rogers and Beveridge, Vol. I, p. 118.
31. ***Ibid.***, Vol. I, p. 256.
32. ***Ibid.***, Vol. I, p. 280.
33. Rogers and Beveridge, Vol. I, pp. 312-14; Maasiri-i-Jahangiri, ff, 140-41; Iqbalnama pp. 85-87; Beni Prasad's History of Jahangir p. 270. Roe, Vol. I, pp. 192-93.
34. Rogers and Beveridge, Vol., I, p. 329; Iqbalnama, 90;Maasiri-i-Jahangiri, f. 147b; Qazvini, f. 69.
35. Ibid., Vol. I, p. 336.
36. Rogers and Beveridge, Vol., pp. 331, 335 and I; Maasiri-i-Jahangiri, f. 144.
37. Rogers and Beveridge, Vol. I, p. 338; Qazvini, Padshahnama f. 69; Iqbalnama, p. 90 Maasiri-i-Jahangiri, f. 148.
38. Muhammad Riza Beg, R.B. Vol. I, p. 336.
39. Jahangir himself, when he was in rebellion against his father, had assumed the title of Shah: this he explained by saying that his father was Shahensha. So it is possible that by conferring the title of Shah on his son he wanted to glorify

himself as much as Prince Khurram.

40. Rogers and Beveridge, Vol. I, p. 339; Qazvini, f. 69; Iqbalnama p. 70; Maasir-i-Jahangiri, f. 147 b.
41. Iqbalnama, p. 91.
42. Qazvini, f. 69b; Iqbalnama, p. 93 Maasir-i-Jahangiri, f.148b; R.B., Vol, I, p. 344.
43. Qazvini, f. 70; R.B. Vol. I, p. 368 Iqbalnama p. 69 Maasir-i-Jahangiri, f., 149.
44. Rogers and Beveridge, Vol. I, p. 380 Iqbalnama, p. 100 Maasir-i-Jahangiri, f. 150: Qazvini.
45. Rogers and Beveridge, Vol. I, p. 393; Iqbalnama, p. 102; Maasir-i-Jahangiri, f., 154. Qazvini, f. 72 b.
46. Rogers and Beveridge, Vol. I, p. 380.
47. Rogers and Beveridge, Vol, I, pp. 393-97.
48. ***Ibid.***, pp. 399-401.
49. For a detailed account of accession see Qawini, ff. 121-32; Lahauri, Vol I, pp. 82-99. Lahauri remarks that Shahjahan adopted the style of Shihabuddin of Asaf Khan (p. 96)
50. Qazvini, f. 88; R.B., Vol. II,. pp. 155-56, and pp. 189-90.
51. Beni Prasad, 'History of Jahangir', pp. 289-300.
52. Rogers and Beveridge, Vol, I. P. 424. at another place Jahangir remarks that the province of Gujarat was assigned to Shahjahan in recognition of his success again the Rana. Rogers and Beveridge Vol, II, p. 261. Qazvini, f. 75b.

2. Theory of Kingship

In its early home in Arabia Islam, people believed in perfect democracy. They claimed equality in social as well as political affairs. Prophet Muhammad declared in his last sermon "Know that every Muslim is the brother of every other Muslim. They all are a fraternity; all equal." At the time of his death he did not nominate a successor, as he did not want to encroach upon the right of the tribe to elect his own leader. Democracy, however, did not last very long practice, soon became widely divergent from theory and even in Arabia it was only during the time of first four Caliphs, as will be shown that real democracy existed.

The democratic institutions of the early Arabs were nowhere evident. The Muhammadan Emperors established autocratic monarchies and discarded the idea of popular government. The same spirit characterized their rule in India.

Abul Fazl in his preface to the Ain-i-Akbari says: "No dignity is higher in the eyes of God than royalty; and those who are wise, drink from its auspicious fountain. A sufficient proof of this, for those who require one, is the fact that royalty is a remedy for the spirit of rebellion, and the reason why subjects obey. Even the meaning of the word ***Padshah*** shows this, for ***pad*** signifies stability and possession, and shah means origin, lord. The title of ***Padshah*** was assumed by Babar in the year 1507 as he tells us in his ***Memoirs.*** "Upto that date people had styled Timur Begs descendants '***Mirza,***' even when they were ruling, now I ordered that people should style me ***Padshah.***"[1]

A belief in the divine right of Emperors was entertained by Timur also, who says in his ***Memoirs***—"whenever, God Almighty exalts any person to the throne of sovereignty, he confers on him special dignity and wisdom, by means of which he renders mankind obedient to him; this virtue is a ray of the Grace of God which shines on the Monarch, and as long as he is grateful for that favour, his fortune and dominion continue to increase."[2] Further he says: Emperor is a shadow of God by means of which shadow a just monarch keeps mankind in subjection, and from the dread of that shadow, the people are obedient, and his power and authority become current over the empire.[3]

In the Mughal system of government the Emperor was no mere figurehead; he personally and actively performed all the functions of government. He was responsible for conceiving plans; and he saw to their execution. He was the head of the civil as well as military administration, and supervised all the State correspondence. No ***farmans*** could be issued without his seal. Even the exchequer was not free from the royal interference, the nature and amount of expenditure being determined by the royal will. The administrator was not left to the community as it was in Persia, (where each town, with its dependencies, administered its own affairs, levied its own taxes, was responsible for its peace, and paid a fixed revenue to the State), or as in Europe (where towns formed so many) independent principalities like the free cities of the middle ages).

The Chaghtai conqueror Babar came to India with ideas that were not quite similar to those of either the early Turkish rulers of Delhi or the Afghans. Claiming the blood of ***Changez Khan*** and Timur in his veins Babar could also claim a system of ideas, which reflected the Mughal, the Turkish and the Islamic culture. By geographical situation, family alliances and political relations the house of Babar could not but imbibe consciously or unconsciously the traditions and beliefs of all those peoples. The Turks, the Iranians and the Mongols all considered the position of a sovereign as something higher than simply a leader. Sovereignty was regarded as their birthright not on the strength of some vague tradition as was the case with Balban's house, but on actual facts of centuries of history. Such was the spell of the house of Changez Khan that even Timur could not venture to break it, and thought it advisable to exercise full power in the name of a descendant of Changez and feel contended with the humble title of Amir or Beg.

It is true that there was sort of election even among the Mughals in determining the Great Khan but the choice was very narrow and had nothing to do with any spiritual or religious connotation. The central point in Timur's conception of sovereignty was that the various offices in an earthly empire are symbols of those in the Empire of God.[4] This idea was imparted to him by or at least had the sanction of, Qutb-ul-Aqtab Zainuddin Abu Bakr, his spiritual guide. Timur believed that 'since God is one and hath no partner, therefore, the viceregent (Emperor) over the land of the lord must be one.'[5] It is significant that the last two Mughal sovereigns and Timur have been linked in the same chain at one end of which appear the names of the Umayyad and Abbasid Khalifas. It is also said that both Timur and Shahrukh Mirza read the Khutba in their own names in the mosque like some previous Khalifas.[6]

The principles defining the role and standing of monarchy in a polity may be referred to as the theory of Emperorship, peculiar to that particular power structures distinguishing it from others, (study of these principles is important for understanding the basic character and inter-war Emperor of a monarchial states).

R.P. Tripathi argues that the Timurid notions regarding Emperorship were derived chiefly from Turkish Turani, and Mongol traditions, in all of which a sovereign was considered 'something higher than simply a leader.' He points out that in the Mongol tradition, which is recognized as the most significant influence shaping the Timurid polity, the ruler was a political sovereign pure and simple; and unlike the caliph there existed sacred law limiting his powers. The crux of his interpretation lies in the thesis that Babur's victory over the Afghans 'further strengthened the trend of centralization in the state structure.'[7] It seems that by implication R.P. Tripathi endorses Rushbroack Williams view that Babur's was the very embodiment of absolute Emperorship based on divine sanction.[8] The assumption behind such an understanding would be that the Timurid political structure was essentially oriented towards a highly centralized state capable of holding together a vast empire and that in this respect it was far superior to the structure of the Afghan power which had reduced the Sultanate into a confederacy of tribes holding different regions. R.P. Tripathi has termed the principles of Emperorship current at the time of early Timurid rulers as Turko Mongol theory of Emperorship on the understanding that these principles were evolved as a result of the blending of the Turkish and Mongol traditions, both oriented towards greater centralization which facilitated their blending.

For example, it is yet to be fully established that the impact of Turkish tradition on the Timurid institutions was really as great as it is sometimes made out to be.[9] No doubt Babur claimed Turkish identity,[10] and a large number of the nobles serving under him consisted of Turkish Emperor Turanis of Mongol descent, with owing to their cultural background were categorized vaguely as Turks,[11] but there is no firm evidence that the Mongol upheaval had been revived to any appreciable extent by the Timurid princes, including Babur himself.[12] From a study of the relations between the nobility and the Emperor, during the time of Akbar, it would seem that the growth of the autocratic features of the Mongol Emperorship was directly related to the erosion of the Chaghati complexion of the polity.[13]

That the acceptance of Malfuzat-i-Timuri as a source for the ideas prevailing in the time of Timur may lead to certain untenable conclusions can be gauged from the following example. Relying on Malfuzat, R.P. Tripathi has attributed to Timur the idea that since God on earth is one and hath no partner, therefore the viceregent over the land of the Lord must be one.[14]

Timur himself never used any title higher than Amir.[15] Although Timur's successor, Shah Rukh did assume the exalted Turkish titles of ***padshah*** and ***sultan-ul-Azam,***[16] the idea of the nominal over lordship of the Khans remained alive down to the time of Abu Saeed Mirza.

Throughout this period the ***farmans*** were issued in the name of the Khan and the latter regarded the Timurid Princess as his vassals.[17] Even after the formal discarding of the suzerainty of the Khan, the Timurid rulers did not adopt the title of ***Khaqaan***[18] which according to the Mongol tradition would have given them a right to claim over lordship over all those territories and peoples that had been ruled by Chaghtai khan. The Timurids claimed descent from a distinguished chief of Chaghtai ulus[19] and a vast majority of their officers also belonged to the Chagtai khans settled in Central Asia.[20]

The first Timurid prince to assume the supreme Mongol title was

Babur who incidentally, was also most critical and contemptuous towards 'the Mughals' and called himself a 'Turk'.[21]

The diffidence of the Timurids in assuming the title of ***Khaqaan*** could be construed as indicating their growing alienation from the Mughal tradition and the degree of influence that they accepted from the early Turkish institutions of royalty. Repeated references in the contemporary records, particularly the Babur-Nama, to the Timurids and the officers serving under them as 'Turks', and Emperor a clear distinction between them and the 'Mughals', would further reinforce such an impression. It would, however, be a misleading idea. The categories of 'Turk' and 'Mughal' as used in Babur-Nama and other contemporary Timurid records have little racial implication.[22]

Hence the claim of Timurid rulers of Central Asia and their nobility to Turkish identity and their contemptuous attitude towards the 'Mughals' should not mislead on to think that in the Timurid polity the absolutist traditions of the early Turks had a greater role as compared to those of the Mughal origin. Although they had abandoned the Mongol language and certain social etiquettes in favour of Turkish language and Central Asian customs, the position of the Timurid royalty and its relation with the nobility continued to be governed by the traditions evolved under the early Mongol Khaqaans which are variously referred to in the chronicles as Yasa-i-Chingizi, Yasa-i-Chaghtai, Tura-i-Chaghtai etc.[23]

In this respect the Timurids of Central Asia resembled the Indian Afghans in the cases of cultural transformation,[24] failed to bring about a corresponding change in the polity. The fact that the Mongol tradition exercised a strong pull not only in Kashgher and other parts of Mughalistan but also among the Timurid chiefs of Trans-Oxiena, who otherwise were always at pains to demarcate themselves from the 'Mughals' is amply borne out by the account of Babur-nama itself. In his account of 1506 Babur makes the following significant observations:

> "My fore fathers and family had always sacredly observed the rules of Chingez. In their parties, their courts, their festivals, and their entertainments in their sitting down and rising up, they never acted contrary to the ***tura-i-Chingezi.*** The ***tura-i-Chingezi*** certainly

possessed no divine authority, so that one should be obliged to conform to him; every man who has a good rule of conduct ought to observe it. If the father has done what is wrong, the son ought to change it for what is right".[25] From this statement it is obvious that while the ***tura-i-Chingezi*** had not remained as powerful force for governing the conduct of the Turkicised Muslim 'Mughals' settled in Central Asia as it was for the nomads of Mughlistan and their chiefs, yet it was recognized by the former as one of the chief source of their tradition. Babur's claim to the title of Khaqaan after 1526 [26] is further indicative of a tendency on the part of Timurids to resuscitate certain Chingezi institutions that had been put into the shadow Timurid's time.

Regarding the Chingezi tradition of Kingship it must be noted that despite the divine origin of the power of the sovereign, the tribal character of the Mongol polity did not permit the rise of absolutism comparable to Turkish monarchy. As Barthold observes in the empire founded by Chingez Khan the principle in force was that 'the empire belonged not to the ruler, but to the ruling family.[27] And according to Mughal code all those who claimed descent from Changez Khan would be included in the royal family. This would naturally make the circle of state very large. The law was that Khan would be elected by the Princes and high officials from amongst the descendants of Changez Khan .[28]

Another important feature of the Mongol polity, discouraging absolutism was the prevalence of hereditary privileges among a large section of the nobility. According to the Mongol tradition all those claiming to be the off-springs of Bukhu Khatagi, Bukhatu Salji and Boduanchar, the three mythic figures whose birth was attributed to supernatural inspiration, had a special standing sanctified by divine origin.[29] For their position and statutes they did not have to depend upon the sweet sill of a Emperor, moreover three of Changez Khan's chief lieutenants were also allowed certain hereditary privileges which could not be withheld by any ruler without going against the code of the Mongols.[30]

If all the nobles serving under Babur who traced their ancestry to the above figures, mythical or real are taken into account it would appear that a vast majority of his nobles would be claiming a special statute by virtue of their birth.

There is sufficient ground to assume that the privileges of different sections of the nobility sanctified by Chingezi tradition were respected among the Timurids till Babur's time. For instance Babur's advice to Kamran not to choose his ***wakil-i-mutlaq*** outside the circle of nobles belonging to a particular 'Mughal' tribe suggests the prevalence of conventions recognizing hereditary claims to certain positions and offices. [31] The tribal nature of the Mongol polity was further highlighted by the absence of slave bureaucracy from its state organization. The large-scale employment of slaves as imperial officers was a characteristic feature of all the Turkish sultanats including those of Samanis, Ghaznavides, Seljuqs and Ottomans and the Delhi Sultanate. [32]

Among the Timurids down to Babur's time such a bureaucracy was conspicuous by its absence. It was introduced into the Mughal state organization by Akbar who in 1561 not only gave a high office to a slave (***I'timad Khan***)[33] but also introduced the concept of ***banda-i-dargah*** a noble regarded as slave of the Emperor notwithstanding his legal status, direct consequence of this significant change in the theoretical basis of the Emperor's relationship with the nobility.

It was in the Kabul period of his life that Babur realized the necessity of a strong and highly centralized system of administration with a view of maintaining control over the nobles and people alike by this time he had developed a distinct personality of his own by attaining the title of Padshah, he attempted to rise above his contemporaries; but in effect he was hardly in a position to formulate any plan or undertake any campaign without the consent of his nobles, who undoubtedly, on the whole, were more loyal to him and their counter parts in Fanghra. The assumption of the title of Padshah 1507 at Kabul was not without significance. It marks the definite stage in the development of his idea about the Emperorly dignity. Though according to B.P. Saxena much has been made of the assumption of the title of Padshah. It has taken to a new theory of Emperorship and also an exhibition on his part of a desire to assert himself as the best representative of the house of Timur. But the designation of Amir or Sultan added to that of the Mirza would have completely served the purpose even Timur was addressed, as Amir and the absence of the title of Padshah did not detract his position or authority as sovereign. Babur was simply imitating the Persian e.g. and to escape the charge he changed the word Shah into Padshah both of them conveying the same meaning.[34] At Kabul, he found that there was sovereign over the Afghan under tribal leaders. They neither feared nor obeyed any authority that's why Babur realized the necessity of asserting his position as sovereign. Following the Persian and Timurids Tradition he claimed it on the ground of heredity. Mrs. Beveridge in a short note has clarified the circumstances, which might have impelled Babur to take this step.

She writes–"various gleanings suggest motives for Babur's assertion of supremacy at this particular time he was the only Timurid ruler and the man of achievement he filled Husain Baigera's place or Timurids headship; his action shared that he aimed to fulfill Timur's place. (P. 401) Babur was proud of his ancestry and believed in the inherent right of the Timurids to rule.[35]He was a firm believer in the hereditary right of sovereignty. He assumed the little of Padshah in 1507; it is difficult to say whether Babur believed in the Turko Mughal Theory of Emperorship.

Like the Safavids, the Timurids did not consider minority a disqualification for attaining sovereignty. Babar was himself a minor, though the eldest son of his father, when he got the throne. The Mughals of Farghana supported even the claim of Jahangir Mirza, who was younger than Babar. They did not show any reluctance to recognize a minor as their sovereign like the early Turks and the Afghans in India.

In the time of Babar, the nobility was very powerful. The nobility and religious classes both exercised great power in Central Asia. Babar own outlook was more practical and political than religious. [36] Although he had unbounded faith in the will of God and had versified the Islamic law for the guidance of his second son, his memoirs do not show any superstitious and morbid regard either for the schoolmen or the details of the law. The ease with which he could adjust his actions to the wishes of Shah Isma'il Safavi is a good example of his general outlook. In his letter to Humayun written in 1529, almost at the end of his career, he summed up his final opinions regarding sovereignty; retirement matches not with rule. He advised him to 'take counsel and settle every word and act in agreement with well-wishers. Personally, however, so far as the sovereign power (***Padshah***) was concerned. Babar did not like the idea of the division of authority.

The Timurids were free from any belief in the legal superiority of the Khalifa, dead or living. The position of the first four Khalifas was however different. They had come to enjoy an extraordinary place in Muslim thought. They had acquired a semi-religious and sanctified position never attained by any Khalifa of any dynasty.

Babur

Babur believed in the hereditary right of kingship, which had been adopted by Changez Khan and the undivided authority of the monarch asserted by Amir Timur. Babur's faith in superiority of his blood was so great that he was not afraid of losing his prestige by freely mixing and participating in the social life of his officials.

Babur was essentially a soldier and a practical man, he hardly bothered about the theories. Even the advice that he gave to the mind of his son the duties of a king. The gist of his advice may be summed up as follows:

1. The king should court danger, hardship and show velour in arms;
2. He should slum indolence and ease;
3. He should consult Begs and ministers, should avoid private parties; and call the court to public twice every day;
4. No should keep up the strength and discipline of the army.[37]

Babur did not want to reduce his ministers to the position of mere puppets. He believed that the exercised the functions entrusted to them with energy, responsibility, honesty and tact. So long as they did not act in a way prejudicial to the interests of the state and people or the general policy of the Emperor. They were allowed to have their way and take credit or discredit for their actions, when the ministers seemed to falter or fail, the emperor stepped in just to set things right by pulling him up or removing him from office or by adding strength to his elbow."[38] Thus Babur acted as a supreme judge of the state. He believed that it was not his duty to govern, but to see that his government was carried on well and his subjects could look up to him for sympathy and justice even against the government.

Humayun

Humayun was unanimously recognized by the Mughals as the successor of Babar to the sovereignty of Delhi; and the ***Khutba*** was read and coins were struck in his name. The practical question, however, was the way in which the empire was to be divided between the brothers.

The ***Khutba*** was read in the name of Humayun in Delhi, Kabul and Ghazni. Humayun had a mystic bent of mind, and as such probably believed that the phenomenal world was only a shadow of the reality that the human eye cannot ordinarily see. He had also faith in astrology like shadow of God on earth and therefore was expected to do within his sphere what God did in relation to his creation.

The early Turks believed in the theory that the Emperor was shadow of God on earth. But no one seems to have given so much emphasis to it as Humayun. His first official historian, Khwand Mir, calls him a personification of the spiritual and temporal sovereignty (***Jam ai Sultanati Haqiqi va Majazi***)[39] and his Majesty the Emperor, the shadow of God (***Hazrati Padshah Zill-i-Ilahi***).[40]

He was believed to receive in situations and inspiration from God (***Ilhamati Rubbani va Varidati Subhani***).[41] His rival Sher Shah also appears to have believed that his mind received special suggestions and directions from God.[42] Abul Fazl in his exuberance uses the word is hardly anything more amusing and significant than the transfer of sovereign power for a few hours.[43]

Humayun did not realize that Shah Isma'il had enjoyed a religious status and a national position that no Timurid could claim from his subjects. Not long after he was made to realize the differences when his officers objected to go with him to Kashmir on military and political grounds. When they found Humayun determined they deserted him so completely that he was compelled to abandon his intention and return to Kabul.[44]

Like his father and the Surs, Humayun was not willing to recognize any power politically superior to him. He however, did not assume the title of Khalifa. Although in Mecca and Medina the Khutba was read in the name of the Ottoman Sultan, he like his father, did not attach any importance to it. Humayun recognized that sovereignty was hereditary and it was indivisible and it was not subordinate to any foreign power.

As Humayun had mystic trials in his disposition, he considered that a sovereign was like the sun in the solar system. He just believed that as in the solar system the planets move round the sun, the state also moved in a similar manner round the sovereign. Humayun circular canopy with twelve segment of the zodiac was believed to be the symbolical expression of his conception of sovereignty. He also believe that monarchy was a personal property, which testifies his hold experimental when the temporarily transferred the sovereign power to the water carrier, Nizam, who had saved his life in battle of Chausa.[45]

When Askari Mirza rebelled against Humayun he is said to have exclaimed one night while he was drunk Emperor wine, "Am not I a Emperor, God's representative on earth?" every Mughal Emperor regarded himself as the wise regent of God.[46]

There was no differentiation of the functions of the Legislature, the Executive, and the Judiciary. All the functions were performed by the Emperor. He was the supreme Legislature, the head of the Executive, and the highest Court of Appeal. He needed the counsel and consent of none though he might ask for it. As one proud of his ancestry and believing in the inherent right of the Timurids to rule, Babar was a believer in the hereditary right to sovereignty. In his letter to Sultan Sa'id regarding the succession to the authority in Badakshan he, laid emphasis on the 'hereditary rights' of the heir.[47] Akbar carefully fostered the inherited advantages of his own personality. A complex mixture of acute intelligence, great sensitive and warmth, and an easy, yet never abandoned dignity marked his over-whelming appeal as a political leader. His open style was remarkable for an Indo-Muslim autocrat. As father Monserrate observed:[48]

> It is hard to exaggerate how accessible he (Akbar) makes himself to all who wish audience of him. For he creates an opportunity almost every day for any of the common people or of the nobles to see him and converse with him; and he endeavours to show himself pleasant-spoken and affiable rather great an effect this courtesy and affiability has in attaching him to minds of his subjects.

Akbar

Akbar (or his advisers) established a degree of paramount spiritual authority for the Emperor unprecedented in previous Indo-Muslim experience. Abul Fazl explicitly states the core of his ideology in the introductory Akbar-Nama passages describing Akbar's ancestry and descent.[49] Beginning with Adam, the ancestor of all men, Abul Fazl in 52 human generations traces the passage of the hidden Divine resurgence until it reaches and illumines the spirit and intelligence of Akbar, its intended recipient.

Akbar's 'heaven descended forefathers' from the seven planet all come to earth as 'Emperors, Emperor of Emperors, Emperordome bestowers and Emperor makers (who) governed the world by God-given wisdom and true insight'. Adam, born 7000 years ago, was the first ancestor (as, of course, he is for all men).[50] Thereafter, Abul Fazl briefly lists five biblical prophets before reaching Ikhnush[51] or Enoch, who, among his other accomplishments 'guided men to the reference of the Great Light (the sun)'[52]

The continuing line of male descent leads through Joseph to his son Turk, ruler of Turkestan, thus shifting from biblical Prophets (common to Islam and Christianity) to the first Turko-Mongol figure[53] Akbar inherited a complex theory of sovereignty. Besides sharing the views of the Turkish and Mughal rulers, Akbar believed that the king was superior to all other human beings and was the shadow and vicar of God on earth.

The enunciation of Akbar's theory of kingship made by Abul Fazl on behalf of his sovereign for the first time in 1567, was revolutionary in character in as much as it repealed the Islamic Theory of sovereignty by a secular sovereignty. Akbar believed in the principle of 'Sulh-i-Kul,' which he learnt from his famous teacher Mir Abdul Latif. Abul Fazl says the emperor must give paternal love to his subjects and in his wisdom he must understand the spirit of the age and shape his plans accordingly the remark of Abul Fazl in (Ain-i-Akbari Vol. III) that his sovereign should keep himself in touch with the spirit of the age, is a veiled reference to the limitations of his power.

Akbar rejected the religious bigotry and no longer remained the commander of the true believers–"Amir-ul-Moninin' he became the king of all his subjects, irrespective of religion and race. Thus, the enunciation of a new theory so radically different from the Islamic concept of sovereignty made it necessary to clip the power by the Ulema and remove the check, they had exercised on the royal authority; in 1579 Akbar issued a proclamation at the instances of Shaikh Mubarak, called 'Mahzar' it gave the emperor the dignity if Imam-i-Adil or Lord just, a title which no one be he a Sunni or Shia, could object to, the document-'Mahzar' gave Akbar no power until and unless the Ulema failed to agree even then the emperor had the power to interpret Muslim law and not to make it. The authority exercised by the Ulema was incompatible with the new theory of kingship, which was based on the principle of a common and uniform citizenship and equality of all human being and toleration for all faiths.

Mughal Khan, the son of a Turk, is the first eponymous ruler in an unidentified series of nine Mughal (or Mongol) Emperors. The last, or ninth generation of the dynasty, is defeated, massacred and dispersed by an enemy. The survivor's retrite in confusion to a mountain valley, Mughalsitan, hidden far to the east. After 2000 years in seclusion, a most important natal event occurs. Alanquwa (Alan-qo-q) a Mughal princess married to Zubun Biyan, Emperor of Mughalsitan, becomes a childless widow[54] when her royal husband dies pre-maturely. But Alanquwa is a woman of the utmost purity from whose forehead shone the 'lights of theosophy' (***anwar Khuda shinasi***) and the 'divine' secrets' (***asrar ilahi***). As the princess lay sleeping in her tent one night a ray of light miraculously entered her body and impregnated her.[55]

The progeny born from this conception were triplets, three brothers, who collectively were called 'nairum' or 'light-produced'. Abul Fazl describes the-introduction of the divine illumination into the body of Alanquwa, and its Transmission to her sons as the 'first manifestation' (aghaz zahur) of the divine origin of Akbar. From the eldest of the three brothers, who possessed the illumination of his mother to the greatest degree, the hidden light passed through generation after generation until the Shahanshah of mankind, Akbar was born in 1542[56]

Following short notices of nine Turko-Mongol rulers, members of the chain of descent, Abul Fazl arrives at Chingez Khan (Temuchin), who, somewhat surprisingly, he does not glorify. In an apologetic passage he concedes the prevailing Islamic view of Chingez Khan as a destructive.[57]

Jahangir

Jahangir continued Akbar's concept of kingship, of course with some modifications but the reactionary trend had started in the Mughal polity during the reign of Jahangir.

More than three decades later, at considerable expense and effort, he ensured complete recognition as true Muslim Emperor: 'In the pulpits of Mecca, Medina and other holy places, the ***Khutba*** was read in his name.[58] Babur, in a practice followed by his son, grandson, and all subsequent Timurid rulers, began his dynastic genealogy with Amir Timur (or Sahib Qiran, the posthumous title). The magnificently calligraphed, etched iron seals and ceremonial gold coins of the dynasty invariably bear this official statement of dynastic authority.[59] Surviving manuscripts of histories of Timur, profusely illustrated, also demonstrates that these were not merely formulaic expressions, but represented a deep and continuing interest in Timur (and one suspects in measurement against his achievements) on the part of Emperors such as Shah Jahan (1627-58), reigning in the period of the Empire.[60]

The Twelve Ordinance of Jahangir and the Fatawa-i-Alamgiri were the work of the monarchs themselves generalissimo of the army and the guardian of peace and nobody else had any hand in them. The Emperor was not only the Supreme Executive, but also the supreme judge. In his capacity as supreme Judge, he was in theory accessible to every one, high and low.

The entire administrative machinery derived its momentum from those who, besides, being the highest temporal authority, had also a religious sanction behind his power. He was regarded as the shadow of God.[61] He was the source of entire administrative law, and even in religious controversies his decision was held final and it did not conflict with the shari't (common law).[62]

The absence of written law in the Mughal period not only appear to us strange but leads us to imagine that the sovereign must have exercised his will in an arbitrary manner. This is given by European traveller. The Mughal Government was essentially a paper government.[63] Every administrative detail was recorded with scrupulous care and minuteness not at one place but at several places. In a way this absence of written law was a blessing because it saved litigants from the extortion of venal lawyers and it secured to them swift justice.[64]

Shahjahan

Shahjahan gave up Akbar's theory of kingship and reversal to the Islamic theory, became evident. The orthodox section received greater encouragement, because in the outlook of the emperor, they could see a definite learning towards orthodoxy. His tendency towards Islamic characteristics of the state became more pronounced.

The entire administrative machinery derived its momentum from the emperor, who, beside being the highest temporal authority, had also religious sanctions behind his power Abdul Hamid Lahori (Padshahnama) writes that he was regarded as the shadow of God on earth and as such his commands deserved unquestioning obedience. He was the source of entire administrative law, and even in religious controversies, his decision was held final, provided it did not conflict with the "Shariat". There is no doubt, that the Mughal government did secure conditions in which peaceful life was possible and as such it may be termed as "enlightened despotism". Tavernier (Travels in India by V, Ball) remarks that Shahjahan ruled over his subjects as a father over his family. The emperor held the main strings of policy, but the details were carried out by his 'officers', who were responsible to him. In theory they were his servants, but in actual practice they were his advisers. It lay with the emperor to ask for advice for his officers, but to accept or reject it, was his choice. However, the officer enjoyed a fair amount of independence in their respective department. J.N. Sarkar remarks that the Mughal government was essentially 'a paper government'. Every administrative detailed was recorded special care and minuteness, not at one place but at several places.

Shahjahan's reveals a noticeable change in government religious attitude. B.P. Saxena observes: "The pendulum had now definitely swung to the other side; and court historians bestowed lavish prays on Shahjahan for the revival of Islamic Traditions (Sunni Orthodoxy)". He abolished the practice 'sejdah' and 'paibos'. He revised the practice of desecrating and destroying Hindu Temples, though it was revived in the reign of Jahangir; became systematic under Shahjahan. The Hindus were forbidden to dress in the Muslim style, to sell or drink wine openly or privately, to cremate their dead or burn Satis near Muslim graveyards and to purchase Muslim slaves of war. In some parts of the empire, especially in the Punjab, Kashmir and Gujarat the Hindus and Muslim mixed together freely, even enter married. In 1634, Shahjahan forbade this practice. He revives the pilgrim tax upon the Hindus systematic efforts were made at the instance of the emperor to convert the Hindus both by persuasion and by force.

In his policy, the Ulema found a positive encouragement to religious fanaticism. He was considered as the champion of Islam, but the emperor did not allow the orthodox Ulema to interfere in his administrative policies. Shahjahan was a great diplomat on the one hand, he tried to assert the Islamic character of the state and on the other hand, he tried to make a compromise between Muslim orthodoxy and Akbar's liberalism. He is therefore, known as 'half Akbar and Half Aurangzeb'.

Shahjahan felt that the introduction of the 'Ilahi Era' ley Akbar had led to the neglect of the Hijri Era, which had certain religious sanctity attached to it. The emperor reinstated the Hijri Era in the court life and in official documents. The emperors love of 'Nazars' or offerings accorded sanction to a pernicious custom of guilded bribery, which caused a great deal of corruption in the administration.

Aurangzeb was too jealous of power to share even the semblance of it with another. He kept everybody at a distance. Even the princes of the blood royal were treated with suspicion which on more occasions than one very nearly proved fatal to the empire. It was this policy of keeping everything concentrated in his own hands that as mainly responsible for the tottering condition of the empire during the last days of this mighty Emperor's life. Over centralization, which was the distinguishing feature of the whole of the Mughal period, was carried to its utmost limit under Aurangzeb.

Tavernier bears testimony to the great and uncontrolled power of the Mughal Emperors. The great Mughal is certainly the most powerful and the richest monarch of Asia; all the Emperordoms which he posses constitute his dominions, he being absolute master of all the country, of which he receives the whole revenue.

Mandelslo, the German Traveller says:–"The Great Mughal was the heir-general, to all the officers in his service." No such thing existed as "inheritance of estates belonging to great persons." The Emperor was the absolute owner. No wonders that in India, more than elsewhere, men worshipped the rising sun; under such a system the nobles were a 'time-serving military aristocracy.'

Bernier, the French physician, in his Travelling in the Mughal Empire says:–"It should borne in mind, that the great Mughal constitutes himself heir of all the Omrahs; or lords, and likewise of the ***Mansabdars***, or inferior lords, who are in his pay; and, what is of the utmost importance, that he is proprietor of every acre of land in the Emperordom, excepting, perhaps, some houses and gardens which he sometimes permits his subjects to buy, sell, and otherwise dispose of among themselves,[65]

These views of European travellers are to be discounted a good deal in the light of our knowledge of the actual state of the country as derived from other sources. To a western mind political despotism was naturally repugnant even when it was of a benevolent type. Concluding this discussion it may be suggested that the administrative and military difficulties of Babur and Humayun partly stemmed from the Mongol characteristic of the Timurid polity.

While the task of holding together vast territories in Hindustan required a highly centralized administration, there was little scope of building such a state organization on the basis of the Timurid tradition of Emperorship. Such dichotomy in the nature of the political aim and the organization through which it was sought to be achieved would naturally result in breakdown and raptures. This would partly explain the crisis in Humayun's relations with his nobility during the periods, 1538-41, and 1543-53. in fact Humayun's defect at the hands of Sher Shah (1540) and the protracted civil war in Afghanistan (1545-53) were essentially the manifestations of a breakdown in the relation of the Emperor and the nobility. But the gradual elimination of the senior Chaghtai nobles and corresponding erosion of the Chaghtai features of the Timurid nobility, in due course, resolved this crisis and facilitated the transformation of the Mughal Empire into a highly sophisticated absolutism under Akbar. While rejecting the Mongol heritage, the Indian, Timurids, from Humayun onwards, drew heavily on the traditions and practices evolved under Turkish rulers of thirteenth and fourteenth century.

If is true that the efficiency of the Mughal government depended upon the strength of the monarch, but its continuance and crystallization into a permanent system could only be secured by the skill and loyalty of the officials. Exceptional qualities were required to ensure the smooth Emperor of the governmental machinery.

Shahajahan reign makes a reaction against the liberal policy of Jahangir. The contemporary Muslim chronicles describes him with pleasure as SHAHANSHAH DIN-I-PANAH and speaks with approbation of his measures against Hindu Orthodoxy in 1632 he got the news from Benas what the wealthy people desired to complete the idols temples. An order was issued that in Benaras in (476) other parts of the empire the temples whose construction has commenced should be raised to the value ground. It was said completely demolished.

As an orthodox Sunni forbade to Tabarra or the abuse of the first three Khalifas in the dominions of the Kutub Shah. Tabarra liberally means complete dissention from something that in bad or highly objectionable. The Shias were in the habit of abusing first three ***Khalifas, Abu Bakr,*** Omar and ***Usman*** of introducing the name of the Persian Emperor in the Khutba. The Emperor as a champion of Sunni Orthodoxy strongly objected to this aspect the Deccan Sultans etc. give up the practice and clause etc. their effect was added in the treaty.

The Emperor with his Court was not merely the center of government, but he was the whole government itself. The Emperor was not only the head of the law-man Emperor machinery, but his will was the law. That will drove forward the machinery of government. He was the cause of its unity and vigour. The Emperor was the original source of every department of administration, and there was no necessity to distinguish between the part of the administration which was personally administered by the Emperor and the part administered by those to whom he had delegated his authority for convenience's sake.

The office of the Prime Minister, who is always a most powerful personage in western countries, was never allowed to develop under the Mughals, as the sovereigns were unwilling to entrust much power to any individual whatsoever. As a result the monarch had to bear the whole burden of sovereignty. A monarch who was not able or willing to bear this burden had no place in the Mughal system. The poor talents of weak rulers would have been supplemented by those of the ablest men in the empire and the head that wore the Mughal crown would have felt less uneasy. Under these powerful ministers who were rightly called the ***vizir-i-mutelak***, the Emperors were not only relieved of all burden of sovereign but also power. They became mere puppets in the hands of their wazirs, who except in name exercised all the powers of royalty. This preserve the integrity of this personal system of government the Mughal Emperors maintained a tight hold over their Viceroys.

The seal was an instrument by means of which the sovereign could keep his hold over all affairs of government. When Akbar worried of Bairam Khan, who on several occasions had behaved as if he was independent of the young Emperor, the later took the reins of government in his own hands and advertised this fact by requiring that no orders issuing from the court should be obeyed unless issued under the royal seal.[67]

"The royal seal was circular in shape with the name of ***Timu-i-langn*** and other Emperors of the Mughal dynasty. Below was the impression of the hand in saffron. The ***farmans*** which bore the royal seal with the impression of the hand in saffron colour were sent by the Emperor to other Emperors, Princess, Rajas and other potentates for an assurance of peace or other binding promises. By these ***firmans*** he made a gift of provience or land. Some ***firmans*** were attested by the seal only but bore the counter mark of the chief vizer. They served as evidence for villages, lands, houses, and so forth, of which the Emperor made a grant to anybody."[68]

At another place Manucci says:–The Mughal attests all the ***firmans*** and the grants that he accords. Usually the seal is stamped in ink, and below it the Emperor, dipping his hand into a red liquid, impresses its shape upon the document to be dispatched. The Mughal Emperors could exercise almost complete control over the administration inspite of the great bulk and intricacy of business. The one central fact which looms large in the politics of those times is that the executive was entirely in the hands of the Emperor. The Emperor enjoyed real sovereignty which was indivisible and inalienable.

He could delegate a part of it to any one but he could share it with none. Two sovereigns could not live in one domain. The Emperor's position was further strengthened by his financial freedom from any external control. Payments were frequently made out of the royal treasury on the Emperor's word of mouth. It was not an executive body independent of the Emperor like the English cabinet. Only men of the highest rank were admitted to this court, and most of these had to obtain previous permission to attend. (All business concerning the State government declaration of war, and conclusion of peace was done here).

References

1. A.S. Beveridge, Babar's Memoirs, Vol., II, p. 344.
2. Timur's Memoirs. Translated by Stewart, pp. 6-7.
3. ***Ibid.***, p. 7.
4. Malfuzat Institutes, Political and Military, written originally in the Mogul Language by the Great Timour improperly called Tamerlane, first translated into Persian by Abu Tauleb al-Hussaini and thence into English with marginal notes by Major Davy, Oxford, Clarendon Press, 1773.
5. ***Ibid.***
6. ***Ibid.***, 9, 11, 15 Malfuzat Institute ... .f. 3v.
7. R.P. Tripathi. ***Some Aspects of Muslim Administration***, Second Edition, Allahabad, 1959, pp. 91, 92, 105, 106.
8. Rushbroack Williams, An Empire Builder of Sixteenth Century reprinted S. Chand & Co., Delhi, p.161.s
9. Ikram, ***Muslim Civilization in India***, Columbia University Press, 1964, p. 136, who maintains that the Mughal dynasty was Turkish in origin.
10. ***Babur-nama***, tr. by A.S. Beveridge, London, 1921, pp. 4, 158 n 1, 529.
11. The Chagtais of Farghans were a 'Turkish' spea Emperor group. Babur himself was ignorant of the 'Mughal' dialect his mother tongue being Turkish. He has referred to his Central Asian nobles and troopers in a blanket manner as Turks to distinguish them from the local soldiery of Bhira. ***Babur-nama***, pp. 4 155, 389.
12. One instance of the revival of Turkish institution was the use of the titles, padshah and sultan-i-azam by the Timurid Emperors. Apparently, these titles came into vogue during the reign of Shah Rukh Mirza whose coins carry both the titles, See,

Rodgers, ***Catalogue of the Coins***, part II, Calcutta, 1894, pp. 141-147, of. A.S. Beveridge, ***Babur -name***, pp.1 n 3, 34n 2, whose observation that the title padshah was not part of the style of any, Timurid until 913 H. (1507A.D.) is obviously based on a chance but inaccurate remark of Babur (***Babur-nama***, p. 344).

13. Iqtidar Alam Khan, 'The Nobility under Akbar and the Development of his Religious Policy, 1560-80', the journal of the Royal Asiatic Society, 1968.
14. Malfuzat Institute, Political and Military, written originally in the Moghul language by the great Timur, first Translated into Persian by Abu Tauleb al-Husaini's hence its English with marginal notes by Major Davy, Oxford, Clarendon Press-1733, for similar ideas see Hafiz Abru, Oriental and Indian Office Collections, London.
15. For the legends inscribed in the coins issued by Timur Cf. Rodgers, ***Catalogue of the Coins***, pp. 140-141. Compare, Bounvat, the Encyclopedia of Islam, ed. By Wensinik and others, Vol.IV Leyden, 1934, p. 777, who asserts that in 790 H. (1388A.D.) Timur 'definitely took the title of Sultan' but has not specified the source.
16. Rodgers, ***Catalogue of the Coins***, pp. 141-144.
17. Tarikhi -i- Rashidi, 83-84, 172.
18. Catalogue of the Coins, pp. 145, 149,150. Rodgers has read the title al-Khaqaan al-adl in the legend inscribed on a silver coin of Ulugh Beg's successor; Abdullah, dated 845H, but it would appear that Rodgers' reading of partly broken legend is erroneous. The expression al-khaqaan al-adl does not correspond with the standard formula which carries the word' adil and not adl.
19. For the Timurid claim of descent see, Rathhold, ***Four Studied on the History of Central of Central Asia***, Vol. II, tr. By Minorisky, Leyden, 1963, p. 14
20. According to Barthold (Four Studies, Vol. II, p. 31) the Chaghtai Emperordom in the fourteenth century was not regarded as Muslim.'Timur's warriors wore pigtails like heathen Mongols. When during the siege of amascus (1400-1401) Timur's grandson Sultan-Husayn betrayed his people and went to the besiegers, they first of all cut off his pigtails and made him change clothes.
21. It would appear that Babur assured the title of Khaqaan after his victory over Rana Sanga in 1527. This is borne out by the fact that Babur's claim of being a ghazi is registered in the legends of coins, which include the title of Khaqaan. Nelson Wright, ***Catalogue of the Coins in the Indian Meseum***, Calcutta, Vol, III, Oxford, 1908, pp.1-2.
22. From ***Babur-nama*** it appears that 'Mughal' and 'Turk' were purely cultural categories. Sometimes two persons claiming affinity to the same clan would be differently identified as Turk and Mughal in keeping with the region from where they hailed and the language they spoke. While a Chagtai Mughal settled in Samargand or Andijan and having Turkish as his mother-tongue would be called a Turk, a man with similar affiliations but hailing from Kashghar or from some area further in the interior of Mughalistan, where some Mongol dialect was

spoken, would be categorized as a 'Mughal'. A specific example illustrating this is as follows: while Hindu Beg of the Quchin clan was regarded as Turk, the people of Mughalistan claiming to be of the same clan were regarded as 'Mughal' subjects of the Khan. Cf. ***Babur-nama,*** 25, 26, 301, 389. For Hindu Beg's identification as Quchin, see Haft Risalah-i-Taqwim al-Buldan, f. 125 b.

23. For interesting references to the yasa' or tura see the ***Secret History of the Mongol Dynasty*** tr. By Wei Kwei Sun, Aligarh, 1957, pp. 164-166n-15; ***Rashid Al-Din Fazlelah Tarikh-i Mubarak-i Ghazani,*** ed. By Karl Jahn London, 1940 A.D. pp. 30, 58-69, 67-68; Tarikh-i-Ghazida, MS in Leningrad State Museum, No. 153, 472, quoted by berthold, Turkistan, G.M. S.N.S., London, 1958, p. 461n5; ***Juvaini, Tariki-i-Jahangushai,*** ed. By Mirza Mohammad Qazvini, Vol. I, 1912, p. 24; ***Babur-nama,*** pp. 59, 155, 298-299; ***Tarikh-i-Rashidi,*** pp. 69-70; ***Badauni, Muntakhab-ut-Tawarikh*** ed. By Ahmad Ali and Co., Bibliotheca Indica Series, Vol. II, p. 216; Abdul Fazl, ***Akbar-nama,*** vol. III, Calcutta, 1877 A.D., Vol., p. 63.
24. ***Muntakhab-ut-Tawarikh,*** Vol. II, pp. 389-390, it would appear that the Afghan chiefs in Islam Shah Sur's service used to converse with each other in Hindi. Apparently, they looked down upon their homeland as a barren and unproductive territory. For them the ruler of Kabul was no more important than a muqaddam or an ordinary local chief.
25. ***Memoirs,*** tr. John Leyden and William Erskine, ed. By Emperor, Vol. II, Oxford University Press, 1921, p. 7 A.S. Baveridge's ***Babur-nama,*** pp. 298-299.
26. Supra.
27. Berthold, ***The Encyclopedia of Islam,*** ed. By Winsinik and Co. vol. I, Leyden, 1913, p. 861.
28. The Secret History of the Mongol Dynasty, pp. 164-166n 15.
29. Among these Boduanchar was Chingiz Khan's ancestor. But the two others also had a divine origin. Their descendants would naturally claim higher statutes as compared to ordinary Mongols. Compare, the Secret History of the Mongol Dynasty, pp. 50-51 and Abul Fazl, ***Akbar-nama,*** Vol.I, p.65.
30. For the positions and privileged assured by Chingiz Khan to Shigi Khutukhu, Munlik and Mukhdi . ***The Secret History of the Mongol Dynasty,*** pp. 143-144.
31. Beveridge's translation of Babur's letter to Kamran, dated, May-April 1526, ***Journal of the Asiatic Society of Bengal,*** New Series, Vol. XV, 1919, pp. 330-333.
32. Compare, notes by D. Sourdel, C.E. Bosworth, P. Hardy and Halil Inalcik, ***The Encyclopedia of Islam,*** ed. By. B. Lewes and others, Vol. II, Leyden, 1965, pp, 1079-1091.
33. ***Akbar-nama,*** Vol. II, p. 79, Cf. Muntakhab-ut-Tawarikh, Vol. II,p. 65.Mir Abdul Hai's comment quoted by Badauni goes to suggest that the rise of a eunuchs (Khwaja Sara) to a position of importance in the administration was considered a sharp break from Timurid Tradition.
34. (Dr. B.P. Saksena Article, "Ideal of the Mughal Sovereigns" ***The Journal of the United Princes Historical Society,*** July-1941).

35. (Dr. M.L. Roy Choudhary, ***The State and Relegion in Mughal India***, Pub. in Calcutta in 1951, p. 798).
36. Mirza Haider Dughalat, ***Tarikh-i-Rashidi,*** English translation by E. Dension Ross, p.172.
37. ***Some Aspects of Muslim Administration in India*** (R.P. Tripathi, pp, 58-59).
38. ***Ibid.,*** p. 59.
39. ***Khawaja Mir Humayun Nama*** Or., 1762 f., 126 r.
40. ***Ibid.,*** f. 133 r.
41. ***Kh. Mir Humayun Nama*** f. 133v. Also see Akbar Nama, I, 120.
42. This can be clearly inferred from the anecdotes given in Abdullah's Tarikh-i-Daudi, British Museum, Ms. Nos, Or, 1701 and 197, ed, I. H. Siddiqi, Aligarh, 1929.
43. Gulbadan, 140 says two days, Jauhar Aftabchi Tazkirat-ul-Waqiat, British Museum Ms. 16711, English tr. Charles Stewart, reprint, Delhi, 1970, f. 25v. Stewart 19 says two hours (Sa't). Whatever be the duration the fact of transfer is there. The sovereign according to Muslim theory cannot transfer his sovereign right to any man or assembly, B.D. Macdonald, ***Development of Muslim Theology, Jurisprudence and Constitutional Theory***, London, 1903.
44. 330 Tabaq, Akb., p. 165 r. Jauhar, Charles Stewart, ***Private Memorirs of the Moghul Emperor Humayun by Jauhar*** (English tr.) London 1832, reprint, Delhi 1970, 107.
45. (U.N. De, ***Mughal Administration***, pp. 7-8).
46. ***Ferishta's History of the Rise of the Mahomedan Power***, Vol. II, p.81. Translated by J.Briggs.
47. Tarikh-i-Rashidi 389; Abu'l Fazl, Akbar Nama, i. 115-16.
48. Antonio Monserrate, Commentary, tr. and ed. J.S. Hoyland and S.N. Banerji (London, 1922), p. 197. Monserrate also noted that Akbar 'is especially remarkable for his love keeping great crowds of people around him and in his sight and thus it comes about that his court is always thronged with multitudes of men of every type, though especially with the nobles, p.198.
49. To substantiate these points Levine analyses a number of well-known paintings. See, for example an incident at the siege of Chitor, the great Rajput fortress in the painting. 'Akbar Uses Sangram to Shoot Jaimal at the Siege of Chitor' Levine, I, pp., 63-4.
50. Abul Fazl, Akbar-Nama, I, p. 143.
51. At this juncture, Abul Fazl engages in a lengthy digression in which he explains the Hindu and Jain views on the age of the Universe. These essentially cyclical cosmologies suggest that countless Adams may well have begum each of innumerable ages of man, p. 154.
52. Ikhnush is also Hermes, a key figure in the philosophy of Suhrawardi Maqtul.
53. Ikhnush is also Hermes, a key figure in the philosophy of Suhrawardi Maqtul. p., 168.

54. According to Blochmann, this withdrawal to Mughalistan derives directly from the Mongol traditions, p. 175n.
55. ***Ibid.***, p. 179; Abul Fazl, Akbar-Nama. 3 Vols. (Lucknow edn.), I, pp. 51-2. I have used this edition of the Akbar-Nama text to veryfiy key passage and phrases from the translation because the Bibliotheca Indica edition was not accessible at the time of writing.
56. ***Akbar-Nama***, (trans.), I, p. 180; (text) I, p. 52.
57. ***Ibid.***, p. 179. Abul Fazl, ***Akbar-Nama***. 3 Vols (Lucknow edn.), I, pp. 51-2. I have used this edition of the Akbar-Nama text to verify key passage and phrases from the translation because the Bibliotheca Indica edition was not accessible at the time of writing.
58. ***Ibid.***, (trans.), I, p.212; (text), I, p. 62. The term used for Monarchy is ***farmanrawai.***
59. For a seal of Babar see Momin Mohiuddin, The Chancellery and Persian Epistolography Under the Mughals (Calcutta, 1971), p. 77. For a more elaborately decorated seal of Akbar, bearing the ***tughra*** see the picture, text and translation in B.N. Goswamy and J.S. Grewal, The Mughals and the ***Jogis of Jakhbar*** (Simla, 1967), pp. 57-61. (The tughra was a square, etched, vermilion rendition of the Emperor's titles placed besides the official seal at the head of all formal rescripts.)
60. See Khan Sahib Abdul Muqtadir, 'Note on a Unique History of Timur and his Descendants in Iran and India..', ***Journal of the Bihar and Orissa Research Society*** III, 175-263. the handsomely calligraphed and illustrated 'Tarikh-i-Khandan-i-Timuriyah' was compiled by an unidentified author in Akbars' reign. It bears an autograph note of Shah Jahan describing
61. Its contents as 'the history containing an account of the circumstances of Hazrat Sahib Qiran, the "world seizer" and his descendants' (p. 268).
62. In p. 2; A.H. Lahouri, Vol. I, p.7, Monucca relates the Story of Khan Khanan's (ought to be khan Alam) Mission to Persia where he said to the Shah that his Emperor was God upon earth, Vol. 11, p. 46 1.
63. Char Chaman , f. 27b; ***Lahouri Styles the Emperor as Pillar of Shara***; Vol.I, p. 7, Qazvini, f. 1887.
64. ***Mughal Empire Administration*** by Sarkar Published in 1924, p. 11.
65. Berneir, p. 236; ***Manrique***, Vol. I, p. 354 and Vol. II p. 268; ***Manucci***, Vol. I, pp. 197-204.
66. ***Manucci's Storia Do Mogor.*** Translated by W. Irvine. Vol. III, p. 232.
67. Abdul, Hamid Lahori, ***Badshah-nama*** tr., Vol 1. p.402.
68. ***Fersihta's History of the Rise of the Mohammedan Power***. Translated by J. Briggs. Vol. II, p. 198.

3. Central Structure

The theory on which Babur organized his central government did not seek to centralize all powers and departments of the states in the hands of the Emperors, or to reduce the Ministers to the position of mere puppets. According to this principl, Babur considered that the duty of the emperor was to see that the Ministers exercise the functions entrusted to them with energy, responsibility, honesty and tacts. So long as they did not act in a way prejudicial to the interest of the state and the people are, as to the general policy of the emperor, they were allowed to have their own way and take credit or discredit for their actions. When the Ministers seemed to faulter or fail the emperor slepped in just to set things right by pulling him up or removing him from the office or by adding strength to his elbow.[1] Thus, the emperor acted as a Supreme Judge of the State. Thus, Babur considered that it was the duty of the emperor not to govern but to see that his government was carried on well. People could look upon to him for sympathy and justice even against his own government this as precisely the theory even his illustrious grandson Akbar.

This is not in keeping with the Mughal methods of government, because they had solemn delegated authority, which they could keep in their own hands. Besides, they kept a careful watch upon the doings of their servants who were not independent in any sphere of their authority. The Mughals did not possess any equivalent of a cabinet; the highest incumbents of office under them were heads of departments, rather than ministers. They were consulted severally as well as in undefined groups in matters for which they were responsible or even, if the monarch so desired, in matters of state generally on some occasions, but they had no right to tender advice, nor there were any institutions, the membership of which would entitle them to express views, whether accepted or not. Such views could be sent for to tender advice as the emperor wanted to consult. It was, however, customary to consult some of them on important occasions; besides, in matters pertaining to their departments, they did express their views because they were experts, their opinions carried weight.

It is not surprising, therefore, that the Mughals designated only the higher officers of the departments of finance as ministers; the others were considered to be just high dignitaries and servants of the state. The question of mutual consultation or of joint responsibility simply did not arise. Each one was responsible to the monarch.

The imported foreign elements in the Mughal administrative system

The Mughal system of government took its colour from the race and creed of its sovereigns. They were a foreign Muhammadan dynasty, who settled in India eight centuries after Islam had been developed in those countries.[2]

The Mughal Sovereign's legal position and powers

According to the theory of the Quranic law, the sovereign is only the commander of the true believers (***amir-ul-mumnin***) and is responsible to the general body (***jamait***) of the Muslims for the proper discharge of his duties. But no constitutional machinery for controlling or judging him, such as a Parliament or Council of Ministers responsible to the people, was in existence in any Muhammadan country or even conceived of.

No doubt, it was open to a number of theologians (***ulema***) to issue a decree disposing the sovereign as a violator of the Quranic law and therefore, unfits to reign. The Mughal Emperor had no regular Council of ministers. The ***wazir*** or ***diwan*** was the highest person below the Emperor, but the other officers were in no sense of his colleagues. They were admittedly inferior to him and deserved rather to be called secretaries than ministers, because nearly all their work was liable to revision by the wazir, and royal orders were often transmitted to them through him.

The Emperors : Position in the State

The theory of State in India, both under the Hindu and Muslim rule, is the theory of monarchy. All the political ideas functions of state one centered around the person of the monarch. Shahjahan in his letter to Shah Safar on the occasion of his succession to the throne, expressed his views about the qualities of monarch.[3] Both Shahjahan and Jahangir regard themselves at least in theory, as Muslim Emperors. They do not think themselves above Islamic Law. The Emperor is the khalifa of God. He rules by virtue of divine right sovereignty is a gift, and the Emperor is elected by the God. The robe of kingship fits him is supported to be the head of the government, the commander of the State forces, the fountain of Justice, the chief legislature and the final authority in the country.

Jharoka-i-Dastan

Shahjahan gave considerable attention to every sphere of state activities. Lahori says that 'this institution was the innovation of Hazrat 'Arsh-i-Arshyani and it has been continued by his majesty above, so the people might get the blessing and could see the Emperor before the beginning of their daily work. Shahjahan usually sat in the Jharokha (nearly 48 Minutes) as the business required people submitted their petitions and presented their cases. They were dealt in the Daulat Khana-i-Khas-i-khas-o-Am, or khilavat khana. Thus it is clear from the above passage that Shahjahan did not deal with cases on the spot.[4]

Some other business was also transacted at the Jharoka, Montserrat saw elephant bought under Akbar. The same practice was continued under Shahjahan. He did not hold elephant fights on Thursday, which was his coronation day. The most famous case under him was one in which Aurangzeb showed his courage and presence of mind when he was attacked by one of the furious elephant during the contest and he got the title of ***Bahadur*** from his father Shahjahan.[5]

Diwan-i-Khaso-o-Am

After the morning work of four and a half hours Akbar returned and appeared again in the afternoon and held a full ***Darabar.***[6] Jahangir continued the afternoon meetings Shahjahan made certain alterations in this programme and he did not retire from Jharokha of the ***Diwan-i-Khas-o-Am*** (***also Daulat Khan-i-khas-o-Am***) and held the full Darbar. The nature of the work was nearly the same as under Jahangir. From the Jharokha window, the Emperor proceeded to the ***Diwan-i-Am,*** which was the hall of public audience. It was a beautiful building of red sand stone plastered white with lime and contained 40 pillars. Mohammad Saliah accounts it as follows:

> This auspicious place is honoured by the emperor who takes his seat in it early every day. In front of this, there is a magnificent and lofty halls supported by 40 columns and measuring 67 (qaz) by 24 (qaz .....). On three sides of the hall there was a silver railing with three gates. Outside this railing at a short distance was another railing of wood with three gates. Red colour. (Ibne Hasan). Shahjahan horses and elephants are here brought before him and are tested by certain servants to see if they are in good health. On Wednesday the emperor did not go to Jharokha-khas-o-Am and went straight to the Daulatkhana from the Jharokha-Darshan and dispensed justice.[7]

From the hall of public audience, the emperor passed to the ***Daulat Khan-i-khana*** miscalled ***Ghusalkhana*** between the ***Diwankhana*** and the harem it was a place where the emperor used to take his bath. It was a secluded place and was chosen for this reason by the emperor for transacting business of an important nature (by Muhammad Saliah's accounts) GHUSALKHANA was the recognized constituents of the Mughals. It was Akbar who started the practice of transacting public business in the ghusalkhana, which was situated between the harem and Diwan-i-khana only the chief officers of the crown and the monarch's personal attendance were allowed to be present.

Distinguished visitors, ambassadors, and rulers from other countries, were received at first in the public darbar, and later on admitted into private audience in the private chamber, if so desired. Montserrate gives an account of his first appearance before Akbar, and other interviews with him.[8] Chandra Bhan has given a very vivid account of the reception of Khusrau, son of Nazar Muhammad Khan, the ruler of Balkh by Shahjahan.[9] Shahjahan received Jagat Singh, after his defeat and surrender, with the bag of money, which he had brought to present, hung round his neck.[10]

Procedure

Abul Fazl has left no record of the procedure followed in the darbar for the transaction of state business, though the state machinery, by the time of the completion of the 'Ain-i-Akbari had been fully established. He gives an account only of the seating arrangement followed in the darbar, and only casual references are found to put before Akbar by officers concerned, and those who had the privilege to stand near the throne, or who were entitled to speak before the Emperor. Similarly no such account is available under Jahangir. Pelsaert, who lived at Agra and had chances to know all about such matters, has left nothing definite in his records on that point. De Laet simply says: 'The Emperor daily comes forward to this place between three and four p.m .... He stays here till evening, hearing cases and listening to dispatches from the various provinces, which the vazir reads to him.[11] But Shah Jahan's chroniclers have left a complete account of the procedure of business transacted in the darbar and in other meetings. The elaborate arrangement under him must be regarded as the development of the procedure, which must have been followed in the previous two reigns.

Shahjahan in the Jharokha of Diwan

He entered Jharokha-i-Diwan immediately after retiring from the Jharokha-i-Darshan. Here as under Akbar and Jahangir, Princes, Amirs and officers assembled and stood left and right, according to their ranks. The secretaries of various departments stood by the Jharoka, where the Emperor took his seat, and read out their notes on various subjects. The affairs connected with the mansabdars were put before the Emperor by the bakshis. Their increments were sanctioned and posting made. Mansabdars and other officers, proceeding to provinces, or coming back to the court, were also presented at that time. The bakshis, standing on the ***right,*** put forward all such cases of mansabdars and took down brief notes of orders passed on them.

Amin

The daroghah, or the superintendent, was assisted by an expert staff. The sarafi, with a staff of sarrafs, under him, determined the purity of the coins. The Mughal coinage succeeded in achieving a very high standard of purity; the older Iranians standard of purity known as dah dahi, that is, ten out of ten, was changed by the Mughals into twelve out of twelve; the methods of judging the purity of the species were improved; in adition to the sarrafs, the mints employed banwaris for testing the purity of gold. The Amin was the authority who decided the issue of purity if any differences of opinion arose among the other experts in the mint. Then there were the usual accountants and clerks; on the technical side, there were workers in metals, assayers, die makers and others.

Sadr-i-Kul

Sadr-i-Kul (the chief sadr of the dominions) presented the reports of the sub-ordinate sadr, and placed before the Emperor any other matter connected with his department. He also recommended the case of deserving persons and obtained the royal sanction for their stipends.

The Daily Life of a Mughal Emperor

In the Persian histories, we find full description of the way in which the Mughal Emperors used to spend the day. After doing his morning prayer and devotional reading, and appearing at the balcony of the salute (***darshan***), where he looked at elephant-combats and the parade of cavalry, the Emperor held his public audience in the ***Diwan-i-am*** hall for two hours. The Paymaster-General reported to him the petitions of the military officers and immediately received His Majesty's orders on them, giving promotions to some, new posts to others. Officers who had come from the provinces and those newly appointed to some province or post were then presented by the heads of their departments ... Next came the clerks of the department of the Crown-lands or the Emperor's privy purse. Through their chiefs, they submitted their various proposals and received orders.[12]

The Chief Departments and their Heads

The chief departments of the Mughal administration were as follows:

1. The Exchequer and Revenue (under the High ***Diwan***).
2. The Imperial Household (under the ***Khan-i-saman*** or High Steward).
2. The Military Pay and Accounts Office (under the imperial ***Bakshi***).
3. Canon law, both civil and criminal (under the Chief ***Qazi***).
4. Religious endowment and charity (under the Chief ***Sardar***).
5. Censorship of Public Morals (under the ***muhta-sib***).

Inferior to these, but ran Emperor almost like departments, were:-

6. The Artillery (under the ***Mir Atish*** or ***Darogha-i-topkhana***).
7. Intelligence and Posts (under the ***Darogha of Dak Chowki***).

The innumerable ***karkhanas*** (i.e., factories and stores), each under a darogha or superintendent, were not departments. Most of them were under the ***Khan-i-saman.***

Wakil

The head of the administration was the wakil, who was considered to be "the Emperor's lieutenant in all matters connected with the realm and the household." As such, he was the Emperor's chief adviser; he was also especially responsible for advising the Emperor upon "appointments, dismissal, promotions and demotions. The financial offices were not under his immediate superintendence, yet he received the returns from the heads of all financial departments and kept abstract of their returns."[13]

In practice however, such an office depends for its authority upon personal equation. These powers were exercised by ***Bairam Khan*** in the days of Akbar's tutelage; when the emperor grew up; he began to resent the wakil's authority and brought about his downfall. No other wakil was so powerful until the decay of the monarch's authority in the later days of the empire; mostly the office was ornamental; sometimes it was not even filled. Even when the wakil did not have much power, he was influential as the highest official of the realm having access to the monarch and often his confidence. He could not exercise the final authority because of the monarch's interest in the details of the administrative matters, but he was useful as a check Emperor authority, because papers were submitted to him and he might be called upon to account for any irregularities or mistakes.

The Wazir or Chancellor

Wazir in the Mughal Empire meant the prime-minister. It was an honorific title, without necessarily implying the charge of any particular branch of the administration. He was, no doubt, always the head of the revenue department, but it was in his capacity of ***Diwan.***[14] The wazir's office received all revenue papers and returns and dispatches from the province and the field armies. He also acted as the Emperor's representative on many ceremonial occasions. He wrote letters "by order" (***hasb-ul-hukm***) in his own person though under the Emperor's directions. All orders for payment, except for small sums or money previously allotted, had to be signed by the ***Diwan,*** and the payment (except to the field army and the workman of the State factories) was made through his department only. The ***wazir,*** also called the ***diwan-i-kul*** or ***diwan-i-a'la*** to distinguish him for the subordinate and provincial ***diwans,*** was the head of the fiscal administration of the empire. In theory, he was subordinated to the ***wakil***; actually, however, he had independent authority.[15]

The wazir had to be strict with the highest officers in their financial dealings with the State and sometimes had to perform unpleasant duties by calling them to account. Once Dara Shikoh violently rebuked the famous wazir Sadaullah Khan for turning down his request for the grant of certain sums as irregular; when the matter was reported to Shah Jahan by the appropriate authority, he censured the favourite prince and mollified the wazir by expressing his appreciation and sending him valuable presents.[16] ***Sadaullah Khan*** and ***I'timad-ud-Daulah*** were the greatest Diwans in the history of the Mughal Empire and contributed considerably to its wealth and sound administration.

He kept a strict control over the provincial diwans and their offices and received for scrutiny detailed statements about the income and the expenditure continuously from the provinces.[17] The imperial treasuries also were under his control.[18] At the centre he was assisted by three high officials; they had direct access to the monarch and were present in the diwan-i-am as well as the diwan-i-khas. They held almost independent charge of their departments and were directly responsible to the monarch.

The Mir Saman was dependent upon the wazir in financial matters only; he took all matters up to the monarch directly.[19] His associate, the ***diwan-i-buyutat***, however, was really subordinate to the wazir; he too had direct access to the monarch and, in all probability, represented the point of view of the diwan's office of the financial aspects of the administration or expansion of the buyutat.

He was also responsible for the proper administration of the internal finances of the buyutat. He also made out the estimates of the expenditure twice a year and obtained the sanction from the wazir and the monarch.[20] The Mir Saman was not only responsible for the efficient working of the buyutat but had other important duties as well.

The Bakshi or Paymaster

Bakshi was one of the most powerful officials of the state under the Mughals; his subordination to the wakil was only nominal. In importance he can be compared to the wazir; he corresponded to the '***arid***-i-***mumalik*** of the Sultans of Delhi; the Bakshi was even more important because of the monolithic organization of the services in the mansabdari system of the Mughals.

Mir Bakshi was himself a highly placed ***mansabdar*** and was responsible for the smooth work Emperor of the mansabdari system. It was his duty to see that able men were appointed as ***mansabdars.*** Though the appointments were made by the Emperor, yet the candidates had to pass the bakshi's security, because it was mostly he who presented candidates to monarch.[21]

The MIR BAKSHI was assisted by two other bakshis at the centre; he himself was also called the second and the third bakshis respectively. In the beginning, one bakshi was considered adequate to deal with the work, but in Shahjahan's reign, the number was increased to three. Mostly all the three bakshis were in attendance in the various audience of the monarch.[22] The work among them was divided in accordance with the ranks of the mansabdars.[23]

The bakshis have sometimes been described as paymasters general of the army; this is not correct, because the payment was made by the office of the diwan-i-tan; only in exceptional circumstances, like a long campaign, did the bakshi make payments mostly ad hoc sums to the mansabdars.The Mir Bakshi was kept informed of the main happenings in the province of the provincial bakshis; important items of the news received from them and the ***sawanih nigars*** were reported to the emperor.[24] The bakshis were responsible for assigning the duty of mounting guard on the place to the different mansabdars.[2] In the evening when the emperor inspected the guards and the royal ensigns were brought out, the bakshis were in attendance.[3] There was a separate bakshi for the ahadis.[25]

The accounts of the empire were divided into three categories. The first, called 'abwab-u'l-mal,' dealt with all the income, which accrued through the revenues or other sources. The record was not only kept up-to-date, but any departure from the normal, like an increase or a decrease, was explained, citing the cause. The second was called 'arbab-u't-tahwil'; this section dealt with the amounts spent in the household; the name came from the fact that it was dealt with the accounts of the people who had sums of money in their custody (tahwil) for meeting contingent expenditure, of which they had to render account. The third was called '***tawjih***'; which is dealt with the sums of money spent on salaries or the income of the assignment given in lieu thereof. The record was kept in the form of loose leaves in all these sections; this was technically called a ***daftar*** and was a collection of ***sandas***, or vouchers showing payments. Thus, a voucher could be taken out easily in case of doubt for inspection and examination.[26]

No money could be drawn from the treasury even by an officer authorized to keep impress cash without a muqasa, which was a certificate from the mustaufi that the sums of money previously advanced had been spent correctly.[27]

Mir Bakshi

The bakshi of the shagird pasha is found under Shahjahan as well.[28] Thus by the reign of Shahjahan the number of the bakshis was fixed at three. They were attached to the central office and worked together.

The other two bakshis noted above were distinct from them and as they dealt with a particular class of servants only, they cannot be regarded as members of the central department.[29]

List of the Prominent Mir Balshis

AKBAR	Lashkar Khan....	No definite period of service of each as Mir Bakshi can be determined		
	Shahbaz Khan Kamboh			
	Asaf Khan Qazivini			
	Shaikh Farid.....			
JAHANGIR	Shaikh Farid	1st year to	2nd year	=1 year
	Vazirul Mulk	2nd year	7th year	=5 year
	Khwaja Abdul Hasan	8th year	16th year	= 8 year
	Sadiq Khan	16th year	18th year	= 2 year
	Iradat Khan	19th year	22th year	=3 year
SHAHJAHAN	Iradat Khan (Continued for a short time)			
	Sadiq Khan (Second time till death).....	1st year to	6th year	=5 year
	Islam Khan	6th year	8th year	= 2 year
	Mir Jumla	8th year to	10th year	= 2years
	Mu'tamad Khan	10th " year	13th year	= 3 year
	Salabat Khan	13th year	17th year	= 4 year
	Asalat Khan	17th year	20th year	=3 year
	Ja'far Khan	20th year	23rd year	= 3 year
	Khalilullah Khan	23rd year		

The Mir Bakshi was thus an equal sharer in power, status, and influence with the chief divan. The powers held by the vazirs of other Muslim monarchies were divided between them. The Mir Bakshi was the head of the military department and as such, the chief representive of the mansabdars, but the position did not give him any influence with the army.

He was not the commander in-chief of the forces of the Empire nor he was entitled to lead an expedition by virtue of his office. In most cases separate bakshis (called bakshis-i-askar or lashkar) neither selected by the chief bakshi nor necessarily taken from his department. They only worked under his supervision. The Mir Bakshi is generally regarded as the paymaster of the army, but it was not a part of his regular and permanent duties.

Mir Saman

Mir Saman, was the in-charge of the state karkhanahs, and put before the Emperor any matter he thought worthy of the Emperor's attention. In the same manner, the diwan of the same department placed before the Emperor the papers and financial matters connected with his duties. He was followed by the bakshis of the Ahadis, and the Mir Atish (Commander of the Artillery at the Capital), who put forward the cases of their respective departments and obtained the necessary sanction.

The Daroghas (Superintendents) and mushrifs of elephants and royal stables kept a fixed number of horses and elephants ready in groups for inspection, and passed them by the side of the red parapet (of the second and the outer apartment of the divan), and the Emperor inspected them from a distance, noticed their condition and passed orders for deductions to be made from the salaries of their keepers, in case they were found lean or in bad condition. As this, the officers in charge of the ***dagh*** and ***tashishah*** (branding and verification) presented the soldiers and horses of amirs. In spite of the heavy work transacted in this meeting, Shahjahan read all important papers himself, and at times wrote on the spot replies to urgent inquiries with his own pen.[30]

The Diwan and bakshi were admitted for sate business, and gradually certain nobles of the court were also allowed in. Thus, state business came to be transacted there, and the chamber, by its proximity to the bathroom, came to be known as the Ghusalkhana (or bathroom). Shahjahan gave it the name of Daulat Khana-i-Khas, and it became popularly known by this name under him.[31]

Shahjahan held the private assemblies twice everyday. One was held immediately after his retiring from the Diwan-i-Khas-o-Am in the morning. Here the vakil and the vazir had the chance of private conversation with the emperor, and they reported the cases and put before him matters, which could not be discussed, in the full darbar.

Divans presented the affairs of the khalsa and the jagirs.

Reports received from provincial governors were handed over to a few of the trusted nobles, who went through them and put the text before the Emperor. Orders were passed on them and sent through the vakil or the vazir to the clerks, who drafted the farman. Drafts of such farmans were placed before the Emperor in the same assembly, and he went through them personally and made necessary alteration or corrections.[32]

The chief sadr presented needy persons, who could not be presented in the Divan and obtained orders for land or cash allowances. After the transaction of this business, some time was devoted to the inspection of work done in the different branches of the karkhanahs. The daroghas of the building department, in consultation with the engineers and architects, presented maps and models for proposed royal buildings. The Emperor went through them step by step, and made most suitable alterations, and often criticized them. The vakil, Yamin-ud-Daula, took down notes and details of alteration which were handed over to the officers of the department of necessary action and future references. Some time it was also spent in inspecting the birds and other animals trained for hunting, and the fine horses, which were paraded in the courtyard.[33] Shahjahan usually, spent four to five gharis (nearly two hours) in this assembly.

Shah Burj

After finishing the work in the Ghusal Khana, he retired to a still closer apartment, called the Shah Burj. This was peculiar only to Shah Jahanabad, Lahore and Akbarabad. This place was originally reserved for conferring with the princes, but a selected few were admitted on business for a short time, and they always retired after finishing it.

The Emperor himself summoned the chief minister at times to confer with him an important and confidential matters, which could not be expressed in other assemblies for reasons of state. Sometime the wazir was allowed to present to the Emperor in the gathering of any urgent business concerning the khalsa or the jagirs, which was not attended to for lack of time at the last meeting of the Daulat Khana-i-Khas. Usually two to three gharis were spent here. From the Shah Burj the Emperor retired to the female apartments, offered his afternoon (zuhar) prayers took his luncheon and after a short nap, resumed his work there.[34] First the affairs of the ladies, presented by Empress Mumtaz Mahal during the few years of her life after Shah Jahan's accession to the throne and later on by her daughter, Begam Sahib. Satiun-Nisa, a refined and learned lady of the court, acted as a secretary to both the mother and the daughter till her death. The Emperor stayed in these apartments till 'asar prayers, after which he appeared in the public hall of audience, took the salute of the guards, and received the kornish of the 'fortunate ones' present there, and entered the Daulat Khana-i-Khas, where state business of the same nature as transacted in the morning was attended.

The Emperor sat till sunset and rose for prayers, which he always offered in congregation. Here the ulamas and sheikhs joined accompanied him to the private chambers.[35] After the prayers the Daulat Khana-i-Khas was beautifully lighted, and scented candles, in gold and silver candlestick studded with precious stones, added to the lusture of the beautiful hall. The lighting time also formed an institution under Akbar and it continued under his successors. Jahangir composed a couplet himself, which was recited at the time. Shah Jahan was always present. Praises to God and verses of thanksgiving, followed by couplets of prayers for the long life of the Emperor and the continuance of the empire closed the ceremony.[36]

Chandra Bhan says that Shahjahan resumed business again after the prayers.[37] He did his work at this hour cheerfully and never seemed tried or uninterested, but rather refreshed. He spent four to five gharis, or nearly two hours, in the work after prayers.

Duties of the High Steward

The Khan-i-saman or High Steward, was the second highest officer in the realm and stood immediately below the Diwan.

The duties of a Khan-i-saman are thus enumerated in Dastur:-

1. Attestation [of the salary bills] of the workmen and menials from the monthly, yearly and daily rolls [of attendance] of those newly appointed as well as increment [in the salary] of the old ones.

2. First appointment, dismissal and posting of ***daroghas, amins, mushrifs*** and ***tahsildars*** [of the various ***karkhanas***].
3. Laying down rules for the work of the karkhanas and treasuries [of the household department].
4. Writing slips for hire and wages of labour.
5. Replying to the prayers of the managers of the ***karkhanas.***
6. Issuing permits for the granting [of state houses] as reward and for allowing [nobles to lodge temporarily in] them.
7. Inspection of ***nim-gosht*** and ***pao-gosht.***
8. The Emperor bonds for money security from the menials and managers [of karkhanas].
9. Considering application from the workshops and stores.
10. The Emperor care of the ***nazar,*** charity-fund, and present.
11. Fixing the daily rations of cattle.
12. Permits for the distribution of food [from the royal kitchen], its increase or decrease, and the letters of order (***ahkam***),-except the letters of the female apartments. These were to be signed first by the Khan-i-saman and then by the ***Buyutat.***
13. Permits for the loan of articles from the ***karkhanas.***
14. Reply to the final presentation of accounts (***muhasibat***) concerning the recovery of State advances (***mutalibat***).
15. Escheat of property. if the order is to restore [to the officer under audit], then send a copy of the order to the office [of diwan], so that his ***tankha*** may be paid according to it.
16. Things made to order (***farmaish***) of the Emperor in the provinces.
17. The Emperor, the income from the gardens and the rent from the shops and residential houses [belonging to the State].
18. Long sheets of letters from the ***karkhanas.***
19. The diaries and ***awarija*** of the ***subahs*** as well as the ***awarija*** of the imperial camp are to be sealed without change.
20. Initial the petitions from the officers as Emperor for advances and the granting of residences for alighting in, etc.
21. Attestation of the attendance of the daroghas, amins, ***mushrifs*** and tahvildars of ***larkhanas.***
22. Appraising the different articles of ***peshkash*** (tribute and present)

and ***amual*** (escheated personal property of dead mansabdars).

23. Attestation of the cash reward which appertains to the commanders of squadrons (***sahib-i-risalaha***)?
24. Distribution of porters among the different ***karkhanas.***
25. Arrangements for the marriages of the princes.
26. The ***tumars*** (registers) of the cash realization of the amounts due on audit [***musahibat***], should be sent by the auditors to the office of the Khan-i-saman, and copies of them should be given to the office of the Buyutat.
27. Plans of lodging and buildings [belonging to the State].[37]

Duties of Buyutat

Buyutat is the double plural of the Arabic word ***bait*** meaning 'house'. In Mughal India ***Diwan-i-buyutat*** popularly always shortened into ***Buyutat,*** was the title of an officer who registered the property of deceased persons, in order to secure the payment of the dues of the State as well as to safe-guard the property for the heirs of the deceased. In addition, he was in some respects under study of the Khan-i-saman, as the following list of his duties [Z. 21b; D. 84a] is enumerated as follows:–

1. To allot money to the various funds or cash balances out of the treasury of general expenditure and of the ***karkhanas.***
2. To escheat the property of deceased nobles in co-operation with khan-i-saman.
3. To make provisions (***saranjam***) for the ***karkhanas.***
4. [To fix] the prices of articles.
5. Estimating the [necessary] treasury of the karkhanahs. Send the estimate to the monthly expenditure to the Diwan's office.
6. Daily accounts of the ***karkhanas*** accompanying to the Emperor during his marches.
7. Endorsement of receipts, (***qabuz***).
8. The Buyutat should write the date on the descriptive rolls (***chihra***) of the menials.
9. On the report of branding of cattle, he should write, "Brought to the branding."
10. [Rejection or sale of] old articles in ***karkhanas*** according to the

suggestions received from the different ***karkhanahs***.

11. Fixing halting-days for the cattle.
12. Siaha of ***tankha*** from the expenditure treasury. The advances to the menials, barqandazes and cattle should be paid in the presence of the Buyutat himself.
13. The slips [***chithi***] granting articles [***jins wa ajnas***] should be kept in the office of the Buyutat.
14. The rooms of the ***karkhanahs*** should be saled with the Buyutat's seal.
15. Grants [to] petty officials for food store [***zakhira***].
16. Ascertainment of the prices of the things in purchase and other departments and their cash, under the seal of the Buyutat.
17. The requisitions of the ***karkhanahs*** to be signed first by the Buyutat and then by the khan-i-saman.

The ***siaha*** of the expenditure and the summary grant (***sarasari tankha***) for food of the cattle should go to the Buyutat's office, and thereafter be signed by the khan-i-saman.

Every officer of the Mughal government was enrolled as a commander of so many horsemen. This title was only a convenient means of calculating his salary and status. It did not mean that he had actually to maintain so many horsemen in his service. Thus, theoretically, even the civil officers belonged to the military department and therefore, the salary bills of all officers had to be calculated and passed by the paymasters of the army.[38]

The Treasury and Household Department

1. *Diwan or Chancellor of the Exchequer*

The Exchequer was presided over by the High Chancellor (***Diwan-i-ala***), who bore the courtesy title of wazir, and had two assistant called the ***Diwan-i-tan*** (or Diwan of Salaries) and the ***Diwan-i-khalsa*** (or Diwan of Crown lands).[39]

We can get a clear idea of the High Diwan's office work and method of transacting business from the recorded practice of some of the famous diwans of the middle of the 17th century. (D. 101a-102a). Sadullah Khan (the most famous wazir of Shah Jahan) used to proceed in the follwing ways:

> First he read the letters received and replied to them. Then he selected the applications of the ***tankkha*** department which were fit to be accepted, and submitted them to the Emperor with reasons for their acceptance, after signing his name at the bottom. Next the papers of the departments of rent-free land grant (***aima***) were signed. Thereafter, the abstract memos (***yad-dasht***) of the amin's office were signed by him. Finally he gave a hearing to the plaintiffs. Before leaving office he used to listen to the agents (of the princes, governors and other nobles) who pressed their requests.

The distribution-list of the ***chawki*** (i.e., mounting guard round the place on different nights by different nobles), was signed by him in the morning before all other work. He used to draft the royal letters in private, but urgent ones were composed by him in his office room. Jafar Khan's office-procedure was the following:

> First, he drafted the farmans and urgent letters. Then he read the paper of the ***tankhwah*** office, applications (arzi) and orders (parwanahs). Next he immediately took into consideration any paper of the ***Khalsa*** department, or any ***naqdi*** or abstract-memo, etc., that any one submitted to him, disposed of it, and then applied himself to other business.

Between the death of Sadullah Khan (7th April, 1656, O.S.), and the installation of Mir Jumla as his successor (7th July, 1656), and also during 1657-1663 Rajah Raghunath acted as officiating ***diwan***. He used to conduct the work of the Exchequer thus, he reported to the Emperor the purport of the petitions received, in the same manner as the High Diwan, and then placed the papers before His Majesty. After drafting the royal letters (***farmans***) he submitted them to the Emperor, after whose approval they were written. On the attested copies (***tasdiqat***) of the mandates (***risalah***) of the diwan, according to which the abstract memos were drawn up, he used to write, 'Incorporate with the report of events (***waqiah***)' On the abstract-memos of the waqiah he wrote 'Bring to His Majesty's ears a second time (***arz-i-muqarrar***, for confirmation) and compare with the original ***waqiah.***[40]

The Diwan of Khalsa was to be submitted to the Emperor in writing a summary of the dispatches of the lower diwani officers and clerks (***amal***) that were fit to be reported, and to reply according to the regulations. The other prayers were to be verbally reported, or, if worthless, to be intiated by him without reporting to the Emperor. [41]

The duties of the Diwan of Khalsa include–investigating into the notes (***muskha***) of the revenue departments,correction of the ***tumar-i-jama*** (record of the total standard assessment) of the Crown lands, estimating (***barawardan***) the expenditure of the troops and the Emperor's personal staff and retinue. The High Diwans office kept of all sheets signed by the Emperor.

Duties of the Diwan of Tankha

The Diwan-i-tan dealt with the following matters [Z. 34b-36a; D. 89b-90b]

A. Requiring submission to the Emperor
B. Orders (***parwanahs***) relating to the granting (***tankha***) of jagir, cash, salary, fixed salaries of workmen and the people of the ***tahvil.***
C. Sheets to be signed the ***siah*** of jagirs, the grant of aid (***musa'idat***), sheets of the demand for the restitution of advances requests.
D. Permits (***dastaks***) for grant (tankha) of cash and grant of aid.
E. After the Emperor had signed the rolls (***tumars***) of arrears and of officers whose pay was due (***talbdar***), the High Diwan should attest with his signature the copy of the Emperor's writing on these papers.
   The ***daul*** of cash payment should be signed by the Diwan-i-tan. On the sheets of branding and verification of cavalry, he should write approved.
F. ***Aima*** and other things farmans, memos, parwanahs for grant of subsistence allowance (***madad-i-mash***).
G. The writing office farmans in terms of the Emperor's dictation, parwanahs 'by order' (***hasb-ul-hukm***).[42]

Asaf Khan continued in his office under Shahjahan. As father-in-law of the Emperor, and the chief person to whom Shah Jahan owed his throne he held every honour, which could be bestowed upon a minister. He was given the rank of eight thousand, the highest up till then held by amir of the state. He was styled 'amvi (uncle) in farmans'.[43] At the request of his daughter, Queen Mumtaz Mahal, the royal seal was also entrusted to him.[44]

Asaf Khan dies in the fifteenth year of the reign and after him, no vakil was appointed under Shahjahan. The rest of his ministers were divan-i-kul (chief divans) and not vakils. Under Jahangir, Asaf Khan was definitely ordered to sit in the Divan and to look the political and financial affairs.[45] This order was necessary under the conditions in which the appointments was made, but Asaf continued to sit in the divan under Shah Jahan as well. Chandra Bhan says that he sat with Afzal Khan in Divan-i-A-la and their relations were most cordial.[46]

The Mir Bakshi reported the proceedings of the ***kachehri*** to the Emperor every day in the open court.[47] The author of the ***Tarikh-i-Shakir Khani*** considers it a special privilege granted to Asaf Khan that he sat in the Divan and he has included it in the list of honours conferred upon him, like the privilege of Naubat and coming in his palki up to the gate of the ***Divan-i-Khas-o-Am***. But, in spite of Asaf Khan's privilege, the position of the ***divan-i-a'ala*** remained unaffected so, far as the affairs of his department were concerned and there is no trace of his influence in it.[48]

Divan under Shah Jahan

The Divan (Abul Hasan), the Mir Bakhshi (Iradat Khan), another Bakhshi, the (Mu'tamad Khan) a man of no less influence than (ministers)–and the Mir Saman (Mir Jumla), were all loyal supporters of the vakil whom they had helped in securing the throne for his son-in-law.

A reference in ***Chaharchaman,*** shows that on the whole Abul Hasan had not been a convenient colleague to Asaf Khan. But his nominee did not enjoy the position long and the following year he was sent to the Deccan, as a governor, and the learned scholar 'Allami Afzal Khan, the most trusted Divan and Counselor of the Emperor in his days as a Prince, was appointed in his place.

Afzal Khan continued in the office for ten years till his death in the twelfth year of the reign. Afzal Khan remained with the Emperor in all his tours, and besides his administrative work, he had charge of the drafting of farmans; during this period all-important farmans, particularly those addressed to other rulers, were drafted by him.[49] His position, ascendancy over the vakil in state affairs, is further revealed in the tenth year of the reign, when Shahjahan fell ill and was in bed for nineteen days. Afzal Khan was admitted to the bedroom for state affairs.[50] Afzal Khan appears to have been very modest and assuming and like I'timas-ud-Daula a man of peaceful nature. Shah Jahan himself said that Afzal Khan never spoke a word against anyone in his presence. [51]

Islam Khan, who held the governorship of Bengal was appointed the Divan-i-kul. He was also attached to the Emperor in his days as a Prince, and had for some time been his representative at the court. Since his accession to the throne, he had acted as a second Bakshi. Mir Bakshi rendered good services as a governor of Gujarat and Bengal.

Diyanat Rai (Rai Rayan), who held charge of the khalsa section of the department, was appointed as acting Divan, and the order was issued that (a) all affairs of the divan should be put before the Emperor and Diyanat Rai should deal with matters of detail and routine (b), Jafar Khan should take charge of the register of mansabdars salaries, put all matters connected with it before the Emperor and sign it according to orders, (c), sanads (certificates) of jagirs should also be signed and sealed by him.[52]

Brahman supplied further details in the same connection. He says; Diyanat Rai signed the registers of jagirs and put his seal upon the parvanas of divans and kroris, which is the work of the Divan-i-a'la, but according to royal instructions, the place reserved for the ***Divan-i-s'la's*** seal and signatures was left blank. As the draft of answers to the settlement of accounts [53] was solely the function of the Divan-i-a'la, Rai Rayan several times tried to do it, but he was checked by Rai Subha Chand[3] who was in charge of that section and noted for honesty and selflessness and he did never let him do it.

Sa'dullah Khan was first made an acting Divan and a few months later was confirmed in his post as Divan-i-kul.[54] Sa'dullah Khan was decidedly the most learned, the most efficient and the best Divan of Shah Jahan. He combined in his person the highest literary accomplishment of his age with an extraordinary capacity for the management of officers placed under his charge.[55]

Sa'dullah Khan was not only the best Divan of Shah Jahan but can also be regarded as the best of long line of the Mughal vazirs. The author of ***Irshad-ul-Vuzara*** writing under Aurangzeb, selected only four names[56] from the list of the ministers of Akbar, Jahangir and Shah Jahan and among them Sa'dullah Khan occupies the highest position.

A sketch of the duties of Divan in his department is given below.

The Assistant Divans Of Shah Jahan

Divan-i-Khalsa:		
Diyanat Rai	from	Ist Year to the 14th
Bhara Mal	from	14th Year to the15th
Jasvant Rai	from	15th Year to the 23rd
Raghunath Rai	from	23rd Year to the 30th
Divan-i-Tan:		
Rai Man Das	from	Ist Year to the 5th
Mir Abdul Latif	from	5th Year to the 9th
Diyanat Rai	from	9th Year to the 14th
(combined with the Khalsa)		
Jasvant Rai	from	14th Year to the15th
Mukand Das	from	15th Year to the16th
(made the Diva-i-buyutat)		
Abdul Malik	from	16th Year to the 26th
Rai Raghunath Rai	from	26th Year to the 30th
(combined with the Khalsa)		

The Divans Department and Office Work

The department of the divan included besides the divan-i-a'la or vazir.

1. Divan-i-Khalsa (for khalsa lands).
2. Divan-i-tan (for salaries).
3. Mushrif (chief accountant).
4. Mustaufi (auditor).

The office of the divan is concerned with all the affairs of the Empire. Paper and orders issued by the Divan, which did not require Emperor's sanction or signatures:

(a) Papers relating to the quarries made by amils and answers given to them by the department.[57]
(b) Certificates of sanctioned appointments, and of cash salaries of Princes, and orders for payments of the same in parganas.
(c) Orders for the payment of salaries of subordinate officers and of commissions granted to treasury officers and kroris.
(d) Orders demanding the payment of the pending balances due to the government.
(e) Orders for rendering necessary help.[58]
(f) Orders for confiscation for pending balances of account.
(g) Orders for dispatch of balances in the provincial treasuries to the central government.
(h) Orders on matters particularly brought to his notice by the Emperor.
(i) Communication of all royal orders issued to provinces and regarding the army.
(j) Orders issued on the basis of reports received from the ***vaqi'h navis***.
(k) And on any other matter ordered by the Emperor.

They were counter-signed by the ***Divan-i-khalsa***, who wrote the words 'examined the mark and noted the signatures'[59] his office received copies of all royal orders, and they were forwarded by him to the office of the Bakhshis and khan saman (Mir Saman). The Divan's office was divided into different sections for the proper discharge of these duties, and the work allotted to each section was clearly defined:

Section (a) dealt with the reports and papers received from provinces;
Section (b) dealt with pending balances of revenues;
Section (c) was concerned with ***parvanajat*** issued by the department.
Section (d) dealt with dastaks ; and
Section (e) with papers forwarded to the Emperor.

In the departmental routine, it appears that the Divan-i-khalsa had greater importance and responsibility than the Divan-i-tan, and that he was not confined to khalsa lands only

As all papers requiring the Emperor's signatures, are forwarded to him for information, necessarily required the chief Divan's signatures, similarly all matters connected solely with the department passed through the Divan-i-khalsa, though in most cases, he had only to write the words 'mulahza shud' (seen) which showed that in such matters he had no discretion or power of action.[60]

In the same way all papers relating to cash salaries passed through the Divan-i-tan, and in this connection he kept a record of the following papers:

a. List of mansabdars received from the bakshis.
b. List of revenues collected year by year.
c. Forms of sureties taken from officers and other servants.
d. Register of branding and verification.
e. Salary accounts of mansabdars.

Office of the Mustaufi

Like the office of the Divan, the Mustaufi's office was also divided into several sections, which dealt separately with 'amils' pending balances, capital, revenues treasuries jagirs, conversion of jagirs into cash salaries, loans and arms.[61]

The Kotwal and his Duties

In connection with the public peace, it may be more conveniently discussed the kotwal and his functions. He was essentially an urban officer, being the chief of the city police.

The ideal KOTWAL is described as a man who follows the regulations in his outward actions and fear God inwardly. He should attend when the sovereign or provincial viceroy holds a court of justice or grants public audience. On taking over charge, he should satisfy himself by a personal inspection that horse and foot attached to his post are really upto the fixed strength and have their proper equipment arms and store, and that the appurtenances of his office such as long rods, fetters and lashes,[62] are really of the number entered in the official list. He should check the number of the persons in the prison and ascertain (their) answers to the charges against them. Then he should report to his official superior the cases of those prisoners whom he considers innocent and secure their liberation. In the case of the guilty persons who can pay, he should take orders for exacting suitable fines from them and then releasing them. In the case of penniless prisoners, the kotwal should report and take action as commanded. A statement of the cases of those deserving to be kept in prison should be sent to the kotwal. In the case of those deserving death, the kotwal should, through proper officers, freely state their cases to the judge (in writing) on the day of trial receive the Qazi's signed sentence of death and execute the sentence.

Summoning the watchman and sweepers, he should take bonds from them that they would daily report to him the occurrences of every ***mahalla*** (ward of the city) without suppression or exaggeration. He should enlist a foodman (***piada***) singly from each ward and post him there as a spy to report all news, so that he may compare the reports from these two sources and thus, know the truth and do the needful in the case.

At places of sale and purchase, at places of entertainment (***shaadi***) where spectators assemble, keep watchmen to seize the pickpockets and the snatches up of things and bring them for punishment.[63]

Mannuchy (ii, 420-421) gives a more valuable account of the kotwal's work from actual observation. It is his business to stop the distillation of spirits. He has to see that there, were no public women in the town, nor anything else forbidden by the Emperor (Aurangzeb). In a sanad of appointment, the kotwal said that there may be no theft in his city and that the people of the place may enjoy security and ply their trade peacefully. He is to carry out the Qazi's written orders and not to act at his own discretion in keeping men accused of peculation in prison or in releasing them. If there is a ferry at the city he should take care not to collect any toll on the ferries (as they were abolished by the Emperor), to prevent the boatman from charging more than the proper hire, and to stop lawless men and oppressors from crossing the ferries.[64]

News Reporters

The agency by which the Central Government learnt the news of the country consisted of (1) the ***waqai-navis,*** (2) the ***sawanih-nigar***

(3) the ***khufia-navis***,–all three of whom sent written reports and (4) the ***harkarah***, literally brought oral news, and at time also sent news letters.

The term Waqai-navis (some time written as ***waqi-nigar*** also) and sawanih-nigar mean something, viz., a writer or surveyor of occurrences. There was a difference between them in this that the ***waqi-navis*** was the more regular and public reporter of the two, while the ***sawanih-nigar*** was of the nature of a secret reporter on important cases only. There was a Waqi-navis attached to every field army, province and large town and a sawanih-nigar at special places and time only. The latter was intended to be a spy and a check on the former! The ***Mirat-i-Ahmadi*** (Sup. 175) makes the point quite clear as follows.

"In former reigns ***waqai-navises*** were employed (to report provincial occurrences); but owing to the suspicion of their entering into collusion (with the local officers), ***sawanih-nigars,*** who are also called ***khufia-navies,***were appointed to reside secretly in the subhas and report news. At last when the latter was entrusted with the duty of supervising the postal arrangements within the province, the matter became public." I believe that it was then that a third or most secret class of reporters, i.e. ***harkarahs*** or true ***khufia-navises*** were posted to the provinces, Manucci [ii, 331] implies the same thing.[65]

According to the contemporary history of Jahangir the Baharista-i-Gaibi, the practice of appointing public news writers to each province and reading their reports openly in the Emperor's court was introduced by the monarch, to make a display his greatness before the expected Persian ambassador. Secret news reporters in the province were an important element of the Abassid administration.

The public intelligence of a province example (***waqai nawis***) appointed agents in most of the small parganas to report him the occurences of these places, out of which he selected was fit for the emperors and incorporated it in the provincial newsletter. In the officers of the subahdar, the diwan, the faujdar of the environs of the provincial capital the court of justice, the Kotwals Chabutara, Shahajahan stationed his clerk to brought him every evening a record of what had occured there during the days. In many of the important parganas separate reporters were appointed directly from the imperial court to send to the provincial diwan.[66]

In Hidayat-ul-Qawayed the waqai nawis is charge to send his reports of occurences once every weak, and the Sawanih Nigar eight times in a month.The Khufiya Nawis or secret agents was the most confidential agent he reported secretly on events without any communication with the local authority, who often did not even know his name. All people were in mortal dread of these secret intelligence officers and their offices.

The news-letters were sent to an officer of the court named the Darogha of Dak Chauki, i.e., Superintendent of Post and Intelligence, who handed them unopened to the wazir for submission to the Emperor. These four classes of public intelligencers acted under the orders of this Darogha who was their official superior and protector. Sometimes an irate governor would publicly insult or beat the local news-writer for a report against himself, and then the Darogha would take up the cause of his subordinate and get the offending Governor punished.

Waqai should be sent once a week, sawanih twice, and the Akbar of harkarahs once [a month] and the dispatches in cylinders (nalo) from the ***nazim*** and the diwan twice every month, in addition to urgent matters (which are to be reported immediately.)"[67]

Sadr

The term sadr-ul-sudur (the chief of the sadur) used by the Mughals was very accurate. According to Muslim jurists, the sadr is the connecting link between the Emperor and the people the upholder of shara and the spokesman (***naqib***) of the ulama. He is indispensable to the State and the Emperor. The Emperor should show him every possible mark of respect and consult him in all matters of law and religion.

All civil and military officers of the state should carry out the orders passed by him in his capacity as a sadr, and if any opposition is offered even by a noble or a pillar him, so that the position of the sadr be upheld and his respect increased in the eyes of the people.

The Duties of the Sadr

The Sadr should keep a close watch over the ulama of the state, inquire into their condition and capacities as teachers and instructors, and exercise full control over the teaching of all sorts of knowledge in the state. Thus, while exercising a sort of censorship in this matter, he should be in touch with teachers and students, and discourage and if necessary prohibit the teaching of subjects, which might affect the religious idea of the Muslims.

The Qazis and the muftis should be appointed from, this class of teachers and students, and deserving cases recommended to the Emperor for award of stipends and lands. All three emperors utilized other occasions also for charities, the most common being the birthday of the Emperor and his sons, Hindu and Muslim festivals, the entry of the Emperor into a city during his tours, and on his return to the capital; illness on the part of the Emperor or of his children and their recoveries also formed occasions for the benefit of the poor.[68]

Besides these occasions, which were usual under Akbar and Jahangir, Shahjahan allotted Rs. 72,000 to be distributed every year on five occasions connected with his faith as a Muslim.[69] The chief feature of those charities is that they proceeded from the conception of the Emperor's duties towards his subjects, and as far as the poor were concerned Muslims nowhere made any differences between caste and creed.

Darogha

The creation of the post of the darogha of the ghusal khana who acted as a private secretary to the Emperor in the private chamber, and of the post of 'arz-i-mukarrar, who had the duty of revising royal orders and presenting them a second time for the Emperor's sanction, and the placing of both these officers directly under the Emperor and appointing trusted persons known to him, further created a check upon all the first three ministers, who by the nature and importance of their duties remained near the Emperor. The darogha of the ghusal khana, the ***arz-i-mukarrar*** and the ***musavvada navis*** (officer in charge of the draft of the farmans), divided among themselves the duties of the dabir of other Muslim monarchies, and these officers enjoyed the respect which is attributed to that office in the ***Chahar Maqala.***

Judicial System

The duties of a Muslim Emperor in an Islamic state which require him to rule in accordance with Quranic law and to enforce Shara. Thus, a Muslim Emperor besides performing the ordinary duties connected with his office, has also to uphold the dignity of his religion through defined channels and to rule according to Islamic Law.

The Emperor is the shadow of God and the gift of Divine mercy is common to both believers and non-believers (kafiro mu'min).[71] A Emperor must curtail the hand of oppression (zulm) upon the weak of injustice even if he be a kafir is never rejected by God.[72] The law of inheritance, marriage and divorce, are so closely related to the religious beliefs and faith of Muslims that they could not be altered or amended in any form. Hence, civil law admitted no scope for any change and it remains substantially the same even today in British India. Islamic law applied to Muslims in all civil cases. Criminal law was the same both for the Hindus and Muslims. Similarly, the Muslim law of evidence and contract applied to the Hindus as well. In cases of inheritance, marriage and the like, Hindu law also admitted no scope for any modification.

Accordingly no effort was made by the Mughals to disturb the corporate life of the villages or encroach upon their ancient institutions or to bring them in line with other centralizing agencies; as a result of this, they retained their autonomy and 'throughout the country the village assemblies are still administrating village finance and justice'. [73]

Mufti

The existence of a mufti does not appear to be compulsory. If the qazi is capable and qualified to give fatvah, he can decide the case himself, otherwise he will refer the case to the mufti and ask fatvah from him.

Muhtasib

The Islamic state includes a muhtasib also who besides his police duties of examining weights, measures and provision and preventing gambling and drinking of Emperor, performed the duties of a religious censor. The duties defined by Al-Mavardi give an idea of the scope of his activities.

1. He was to see that Muslims offered their prayers kept fasts in the month of Ramazan and abstained from drinking etc.
2. It was his duty to stop begging in the streets and to forbid a beggar from begging if, he possessed means of livelihood.
3. He was to examine the credentials of a physician and to stop him from practicing if, he was not qualified or worthy.
4. He was required to supervise the condition of slaves and to see that they were not harshly treated by their masters.
5. He was required to see that, when leaving the shore, boats were not loaded beyond capacity.

It appears that ordinary cases were attended by the Emperor in the open darbar every day, and important cases requiring the evidence of witnesses and their cross-examination were attended by him on the day in the week fixed exclusively for the administration of justice.

According to Lahori, Shah Jahan retired on Wednesday from the ***jharokha-i-darshan*** to the ***daulatkhana-i-khas*** and on that day none was admitted there, except the officers of justice (***mutas-saddiyan-i-adalat***), theologians qualified to give fatvah (***arbab-i-fatvah***), a few learned noted Qazis for their highest rank together with the post of the vakil, but the office carried no power.

The ministers under all three monarchs Akbar, Jahangir and Shah Jahan, enjoyed the absolute power among them the highest respect which a minister in any state can expect or enjoy. Muzzafar Khan, Raja Todar Mal and Mir Fataullah Shirazi under Akbar; I'timad-ud-Daula and Khwaja Abdul Hasan under Jahangir; 'Allammi Afzal Khan and Sa'dulla Khan under Shah Jahan deserve special mention in this court.

Justice

All the three monarchs had set apart a day for personally attending to judicial cases. Akbar had fixed Thursday, [74] Jahangir reserved Tuesday[75], On that day, he retired from the Jharoka of the darshan direct to the private chamber, and no one, except the officers of the judicial department and persons entrusted with the duty of giving the fatwah, and a few ulemas noted for learning, piety and honesty, were admitted. The rules and regulations laid down by Akbar, followed by Jahangir and developed by Shah Jahan, shows the attitude of these monarchs towards their responsibilities and position in the state. Hence there are only a few occasions under each monarch on which he absented himself from one or the other.

References

1. R.P. Tripathi, ***Administration of the Mughals***, p. 59.
2. Jadunath Sarkar, ***Mughal Administration*** by p. 5.
3. A.H. Lahori, ***Padshahnama*** I, pp. 284-85.
4. ***Ibid.***, I, 130 (pt. 11).
5. ***Ibid.***, I, p. 489, 6 year. The Elephant name was sudhkar, Aurangzeb's age was 15 years, Hawkins also mentions the case of persons thus injured, p. 1087.
6. ***Ain-i-Akbari***, p. 155, AN. III, p. 257.
7. ***Mughal*** (Ishwari Prasad) Chugh Publications, Allahabad, p. 503.
8. ***Monserrate***, pp. 28, 37, 50, 64, 133-4.
9. ***Brahman***, pp. 127-31.
10. A.H. Lahori, I, p. 256 fifth year.
11. De Laet, pp. 98 and 99.
12. H.K. Naqvi, ***History of Mughal Government and Administration***, p. 72
13. Abu-'l-Fazl, ***Ain-i-Akbari***, Vol I, p. 4.
14. Sir Jadunath Sarkar, ***Mughal Administration***, p.20.
15. Ashraf Khan, f. 31a.
16. For details vide ibid., ff, 31b-36b; also ***Dastur-ul-Alamgiri*** f. 31b.
17. Abu-'l-Fazl, A'in-i-Akbari, i. p. 4.
18. Abdul Hamid Lahauri. p. 146.
19. ***Ibid.***, also Abu-'l-Fadl, ***A'in-i-Akbari***, ii, I Dawabit-i-Alamgiri ff. 22b, 23a.
20. History of Mughal Government and Administration by H.K. Naqvi, 1990, Kanishka Publishing, House, New Delhi, p. 77.
21. Abd-ul Hamid, i. pp. 146, 147, 153; ***Dastur-ul-'amal-i-agahi***, f. 8a; Kazim, p. 1099.
22. For details of the division of work, vide, ***Dawabit-i-Alamgiri***, ff. 17-20.
23. Ashraf Khan f, 34b; Ali Muhammad Khan, Supplement, p. 175.
24. ***Dawabit-i-Alamgiri***, f. 18a.
25. Kazim, ***History of Mughal Emperor***, p. 1105.
26. Abu'l-Fazl, ***Ain-i-Akbari***, ii p.11
27. ***History of Mughal Government and Administration***by H.K. Naqvi, 1990, Kanishka Publishing, House, New Delhi, p. 84.
28. Abu'-l-Fadl, ***Ain-i-Akbari***, ii, p. 11.
29. A.H. Lahori, p. 91. Haji Ashor appointed in the eleventh year.
30. Abul Fazl has included all the bakshis in his list in the Ain-i-Akbari, p. 232, which also shows that there was no such distinction in that reign.
31. ***History of Mughal Government and Administration***by H.K. Naqvi, 1990, Kanishka

Publishing, House, New Delhi, p. 85.

32. A.H. Lahori, I, pp. 146-8. ***Saliah***, pp. 244-246, ***Brahman***, pp. 11-23 and 35-39.
33. A.H. Lahori, I, p. 148. Saliah uses the term Khilvat Khana, I, p. 247, and elsewhere he constantly uses the old term, Ghusal Khana. Brahman uses the same throughout. The term thus survived. Saliah, I, pp. 249-50, and II, p. 512; Br, Mus. MS, 486.
34. Saliah, I, p. 248. Lahori, p. 148..
35. Brahman, pp. 26-8. Lahori, pp. 148-149. Shahjahan had very fine taste in architecture. The case in which he criticized plans and buildings, and ordered alterations, are throughout recorded in his chronicles, immediately after the midday meal is common in Northern India.
36. Saliah, I, p. 249. Lahori, I, p. 152. Brahman, pp. 35-39. Brahman is not very accurate in his arrangement.
37. According to Brahman, he finished this work before the Emperor (pp. 34-35), but a little
38. ***Ain-i-Akbari***, p. 43; Bloch, p. 49; Brahman, p. 38.
39. A.H. Lahori, p. 380, Seventeenth Year.
40. ***Mughal Administration*** by Sir Jadunath Sarkar, IVth Edition, Published by M.C. Sarkar and Sons, Ltd., Calcutta, 1952, pp. 43, 44.[Z. 20a-21b; D. 83a-84a].
41. ***Mughal Administration*** by Sir Jadunath Sarkar, IVth Edition, Published by M.C. Sarkar and Sons, Ltd., Calcutta, 1952, p. 21.
42. ***Mughal Administration*** by Sir Jadunath Sarkar, IVth Edition, Published by M.C. Sarkar and Sons, Ltd., Calcutta, 1952, p. 27.
43. ***Mughal Administration*** by Sir Jadunath Sarkar, IVth Edition, Published by M.C. Sarkar and Sons, Ltd., Calcutta, 1952, pp.32, 33, 34.
44. ***Mughal Administration*** by Sir Jadunath Sarkar, IVth Edition, Published by M.C. Sarkar and Sons, Ltd., Calcutta, 1952, p. 36.
45. ***Ibid.***, p. 39-40.
46. A.H. Lahori, I, p. 114.
47. ***Ibid.***, I, p. 180. In the fourth year when he was sent to the Deccan, it was given to Begam sahib and thereafter remained with her (p. 406).
48. ***Tuzuk***, p. 412.
49. MS. Add, 1892, pp. 94-5.
50. MS. Add, 6585, F. 54a..
51. ***Ibid.***, Fs. 54b and 55.
52. In the Punjab Tour: seventeenth year, Lahori, I, Tenth year, Lahori, II, p. 234. With Daftar and his staff, Lahore, twelfth year Lahori, II, p. 91.117.
53. Letter to Nazar Muhammad Khan, Ruler of Balkh, sixth year, Lahori, II, p. 466.
54. Brahman, pp. 94-5. He also records his famous sayings, which give an idea of his conception of vizarat. (1) 'There are two kinds of vazirs–one who listen to the Emperor carefully, understand him act upon what is told to them; the others are those upon whose word the Emperor acts and upon whose considered opinion he relies. We who are vazirs in this age cannot understand correctly or carry out

what we are told by the Emperor according to his will and pleasure. How can we attain the other position?

55. A. H. Lahori, II, p. 132.
56. Brahman, pp. 100-1. This would mean the settlement of accounts due from jagirdars and passing orders in the same connection, a work of great responsibility, made Divan of Lahore in the thirteen year.
57. Sa'dullah Khan's reputation as a scholar had come to the notice of the Emperor during his visit to Lahore in the fourteenth year of the reign. He was presented before the Emperor by Sadr Musavi Khan and was enrolled in the personal staff of the Emperor as rozina dar (on cash salary, literally on daily allowance). Thus he was not given any grade nor included among the mansabdars. During the course of one year, he got the grade of 1,000 zat-200 horse and was given the post of arz-i-mukarrar, usually given to the most trusted person known to the Emperor and the following year was made the darogha-i-ghusl khana (Superintendent of the private chamber), an office of still greater confidence. In the seventeenth year he was made Mir Saman with 2,000 rank, and in the eighteenth year given the rank of 3,000. In the nineteenth year he was made the divan-i-khalsa and put in charge of the drafts of farmans. The same year he became the divan and after it the divan-i-kul in the grade of 5,000. In the twentieth year he was given the rank of 7,000, in recognition of his service in the Balkh expedition; and an allowance of krore dams annually (Rs 2 ½ lacs), in the twenty-third year. Besides Persian and Arabic, he knew the Turkish language. He was a pleasant conversationalist and a fluent speaker and was considered superior to the scholars of Iraq and Ajam. (Brahman, p. 195) Brahman worked as his assistant and was his favourite companion; he writes about him as he judged him from personal contact, not as a mere subordinate official but as a friend connected with him in all other activities of his life as well. He says, 'at times I remained with him from evening till midnight'.
58. MS. Or. 233, Fs 64-5. Abul Fazl, I'timad-ud-Daula, Asaf Khan Abul Hasan Sa'dullah Khan, besides Mir Jumla who is to be included under Aurangzeb. in case of technical difficulties the collectors used to draft their quaries and forward them to the central government for necessary orders; special forms were prescribed for the purpose of ensuring brevity and lucidity cases. Such orders required the revenue officer's sanction to justify the action of his subordinate.It would mean help given to amils by faujdar in collecting rents in difficult and troublesome
59. MS. Or, 1,641, F. 30b and Add, 6,599, F. 151b.
60. The divan wrote a word or two on papers placed before him and terms were fixed for each kind of work. The form given below gives an example of such terms added with signatures (Or. 1,641, F. 151).

Asnad

(Entered in the Diary)	(Forward for Revision)	(Seen)
Tasdiq	Yad Dasht	Roz Namcha
(Granted)		

61. The facts of this section of the chapter from pp. 204-209 have been collected from MS. Or 1,641, Fs 31-6 and MS. Add 6,59, Fs. 38, 112, 151-2 and 156, and various forms of appointments given in Add. 6,598, 6,599. and Tarikhi-i-Shakir Khani.
62. Mughal Administration by Sir Jadunath Sarkar, IVth Edition, Published by M.C. Sarkar and Sons, Ltd., Calcutta, 1952, p. 57.
63. ***Ibid.***, p. 58.
64. Mughal Administration by Sir Jadunath Sarkar, IVth Edition, Published by M.C. Sarkar and Sons, Ltd., Calcutta, 1952, p. 60.
65. ***Ibid.***, p.61.
66. Mirat' Ahmadi. p. 174-175e
67. ***Mughal Administration*** by Sir Jadunath Sarkar, IVth Edition, Published by M.C. Sarkar and Sons, Ltd., Calcutta, 1952, p. 63-64.
68. A.N., III, p. 717.
69. De Laet, p. 93; Hawkins, p. 16; Finch, p. 184.
70. Cases of absence from state business.
71. Adab-i-Saltanat, F. 14
72. A.N. III, p. 257, and p. 477, and p. 722; Advice to qasim Beg Tabrezi Mir 'Adl-i-Urdu (army).
73. Mukerji, Democracies in the East, p. 207.
74. Lahori, II, pp. 472 and 632. The arrangement continued for one year.
75. Lahori, II, p. 354, 394, 395, 400.

4. Provincial Structure

The thirteenth century of the Christian era opened with the establishment of the historic throne of Delhi, of Turkish invaders from beyond the north-west frontiers of the country, who seriously set out to build up an empire.

The following century and a half, after their conquest of Hindustan, was marked as much by the zeal for reconstruction as for expansion and destruction, though not by a far-sighted statesmanship. This period of an utmost century and a half of a steady decay and decline. The Mughal Empire was divided into provinces, called subahs. Each subah consisted of several sarkars, which were further sub-divided into mahals or parghanahs. A convenient number of villages called mawda's or dihs were included in each mahal.[1]

In Mughal administration, jargon a village was not only the conglomeration of houses where the peasants lived but also the land surrounding it. Hence the boundary of each mawda' was clearly demarcated. Each one of these was an administrative unit. Smaller hamlets called nagalahs were included in mawda's in Shah Jahan's time wazir Sa'd-u-llah Khan established a new unit called a Chaklah,[2] which included a number of parghanahs. The sarkar was not abolished, so that the chaklah did not replace it.

A province was under a governor who, in the beginning, was called a sipahsalar or commander of armed forces.[3] As his title signifies, his main duty was the defence of the area and the maintenance of the peace and order. However, from the very beginning he was also the head of the civil administration. The Ain-i-Akbari says that "the forces of the province and its habitants are under his order". On the civil side his duty was to encourage and expand cultivation. He was required to extend all, help to the peasants and to appoint the Amils and keep himself informed about their work. He was also to undertake the construction of tanks, wells, canals, sarais and other building of public utility. He had also taken interest himself in laying orchard and gardens.[4]

Four provinces of the Deccan were grouped into a viceroyalty, which was generally conferred upon a son of the emperor. The charge was termed Ayalat.[5] Sometimes the provincial governor was assigned a Naib. This was done if a minor prince was appointed as a governor. In such instances the prince was really in training and the naib carried out all the duties of a governor.[6] The Mughal governors were all appointed with defined powers. Only the hereditary tributary chiefs had a different status. According to the classical Muslim definition, the Mughal governorships were Imarat-ul-Khassah or imarat-ul-tanfidh.

A governor with defined powers was traditionally entrusted with the supervision of the troops, the punishment of criminal and rebels and home defense. He was not allowed to intervene in the administration of justice or the levy of taxes. Nor was he given the right to lead prayers or act as the spiritual leader of the people,[7] the Mughals believe in the centralized government and were generally averse to delegate too much authority.

Even hereditary Hindu rulers like the rulers of Rajputana States, found that their traditional independence was being circumscribed in many ways. One method was to enroll them as mansabdars and treat them like ordinary servants of the state. However, their autonomy within their states was not seriously affected.

Under Shah Jahan the entire empire was divided into twenty-two subas[8] or provinces, each under a subehdar or sipahsalar. Of these Delhi and Agra had governors only during the absence of the Emperor[9] Kandhar was recovered by the Persian; Balkh and Badakh Shan remained only for short time in the Imperial possession; and the four subahs of the Deccan were sometimes held by a single officer.[10] The rest were administered by governors. With the exception of Avadh[11], we get a connected account of appointments of governors and transfers from one province to another in the Empire. It is only in the twenty second year that Itiqad Khan is mentioned as having replaced Mirza

Khan as governor of Avadh.

Provincial governors[12] were chosen from amongst capable military officers who were also gifted with executive ability. They were expected to be men of character and integrity. Shah Jahan did not tolerate incompetence or abuses in provincial governments and never hesitated to remove even his favourite officers from their charge if their conduct was found to be unsatisfactory, complaints against them reach to the court. He dismissed Azam Khan and Shaista Khan[13] from the governorship of Gujarat on the ground of their incompetence and Tarbiyat Khan from the governorship of Kashmir,[14] because the people complained of him.

On the other hand, Zafar Khan was appointed governor of Kashmir because the inhabitants liked him. [15] Another instance of the dismissal of a governor is that of Wazir Khan who was removed from the Punjab on the ground of oppression. [16]

The administration was concentrated in the provincial capital. It was city-government, not in the Greek sense of the term, but rather as a government living and working in the cities and mainly concerning itself with the inhabitants of the cities and their immediate neighbourhood. The Mughals-after due allowance has been made for their love of hunting and laying out pleasure gardens and their frequent marches.

The villages were neglected and despised, and village-life was dreaded by them as a punishment. No doubt, the villages were the place from which their food and income came. Life in a village was intolerable to them as residence on 'the Getic and Sarmatian shores' cultured poet of imperial Rome. This feeling comes out very clearly in a Persian couplet:

Zagh dum su-i-shahar wa sar su-i-deh.
Dum-i-an zagh az sar-i-u beh*

The Subahdar and his duties

The term SUBAHDAR comes from the Arabic word '***sub***' meaning direction or point of the compass. In very early times the provinces into

* Surely the tail of a crow was turned towards the city and its head towards the village; Surely the tail here was better than the head!(better', i.e. nobler or happier).

which every large kingdom was necessarily divided, named in accordance with their bearing towards the capital, such as the viceroyalty of the north, of the south, of the east and of the west, in which ever of these directions there was enough territory to compose a separate province. Similarly, the provincial governors of the Bahmani Empire were styled ***tarf-dars*** from the word ***tarf*** meaning direction.

The country was covered by an immense number of small geographical units, each occupied by different tribes and the tribes often migrating from place to place, it was at first, impossible to give any single historical or tribal name to a province, which was the aggregate of several such tribal settlements and socially unconnected districts. It was more convenient to designate the viceroyalties as the northern, the southern, etc. hence, the origin of the terms ***subahdar*** and ***tarafdar.***

The ***subahdar*** was officially called the ***nazim*** or regulator of the province. His essential duties were to maintain order, to help the smooth and successful collection of revenue and to execute the royal decree and regulations sent to him. When a newly appointed subahdar went to the High Diwan to take his leave before setting out for his province, the Diwan was to deliver the following charge to him, "Experienced men have written concerning a subahdar's work that he ought to keep all classes of men pleased but his good behaviour, and see that the strong may not oppress the weak". He should keep all oppressors down, etc. A long string of good counsels (40 in number) as to what subahdars should do and what they should avoid doing, is given in Akbar's Farman.[17]

A distinction has been made between deputies of princes, who acted as Governors on behalf of the princes (the latter holding appointments as Governors from the Emperor), and deputies of ordinary Governors. The names of the Farmans have been recorded, while the latter have been ignored. In analyzing the main Table, again the Princes who governed through deputies are not treated as Governors at all (generally such Princes governed another province directly in person). [18]

Record shows 466, years during which provincial Governors are known to have held office. The number of appointments known is 166 and the number of persons serving as Governors 81, in other words, on average each a single term of a Governor lasted for less than three years.[19]

This compares with an average of a little more than two and a half years that we have found for Aurangzib[20] so that, in this respect one can see little change during the two reigns. Jahangir's reign also displays the same tendency towards frequent transfer.[21]

In actual fact the range of variations was very great. There is record of single terms of office as Governor extending to 12 to 9 and 8 years. At the same time single persons serving as Governors in different provinces, held office of totals of 17, 16, 15 years. In both these respects, Aurangzeb's reign records higher figures. In that reign the maximum period a person held office as Governor of the same province was 23; and the maximum period a single person held office of governors in different provinces was 41.[22] The later figure, however, can be ascribed to the much longer period during which Aurangzeb ruled. On the other hand, in Shah Jahan's reign, just as in the reign of Auranzeb, officers were appointed and dismissed or transferred within the same year. We can thus infer that the Mughal court did not approve of long terms for Governors, and generally transferred or recalled them after two or three years. A table giving the duration of average terms of office held by Governors province-wise during the reign of Shah Jahan is given below.

Provinces	*Total Number of years for which appointments are known.*	*Total Number of actual appointments as Governors.*	*Average tenure of Governors*
Bengal	32	7	4 Years 6-3/4 months
Orissa	32	9	3 Years 6-1/2 months
Bihar	32	12	2 Years 8 months
Allahabad	32	10	3 Years 2-1/2 months
Avadh	6	4	1 Year 6 months
Agra	18	10	1 Year 9-1/2 months
Delhi	28	12	2 Years 4 moths
Lahore	32	10	3 Years 2-1/2 months
Kashmir	32	8	3 Years 2-1/2 months
Kabul	32	14	4 Years months

Multan	32	14	2 Years 1-2/3 months
Sind	32	9	2 Years 1-2/3 months
Ajmer	30	12	3 Years 4 months
Gujarat	30	12	2 Years 8 months
Malwa	32	13	2 Years 5-2/3
Deccan	32	11	2 Years 11 months

It does not seem that any particular policy regarding a province was behind the longer or shorter terms there. It may be said, in general, that the provinces where conditions were more stable like Bengal, Kabul, Orissa and Ajmer were allowed to have Governors serving for terms longer than elsewhere. It is interesting to note that Bengal and Kabul also enjoyed the same position under Aurangzeb, where too the longest average tenure was found in Bengal, Kabul, Gujarat, Delhi (in that order).[23] The total number of years in which appointments are known during the reign of Shah Jahan is 466, out of which Iranis held appointments for 210 years i.e. 45% Turanios 104, i.e. 22% Afghans 11, i.e 2 %; other Indian Muslims 48, i.e. 10%: race not known 18, i.e. 3.8% During the reign of Aurangzeb the total number of years in which appointments are known is 833, out of which Iranis held the appointments for 536 years, i.e. 64% and Turanis 105 years, i.e. 12.5% Afghans 7 (slightly less than 1%) other Indian Muslims 84 (10%), Rajputs 10 (1.2%) others including race not known 35 (4.2%).[24] Thus the Iranis during the reign of Aurangzeb were far more numerous among the Governors than they were under Shah Jahan. On the other hand the Turanis under Shah Jahan held a much better position. This might have been due to a conscious policy on the part of the Shah Jahan since he was very proud of being a descendent of Timur, the Qiran-i Sani, and always emphasized the fact that he was a Turani. It appears that during the reign of Jahangir the Iranis had practically monopolized all the important posts in the Empire.[25] From the table no. 1, it will be seen that their number continued to be very large during the first five years of Shah Jahan' reign. But then he appears to have deliberately promoted the Turanis, so as to remove the imbalance in the composition of the nobility. The proportion of Indian Muslims was about the same as during the reign of Aurangzeb. The Rajputs and the Afghans were not appointed as Governors in numbers commensurate with their numerical strength in the higher nobility. This again was also to be found under Aurangzeb. It is interesting to note that the Princess appear as Governors very prominently during the last phase of Shah Jahan's reign, just as was later the case during the last years of Aurangzeb. Their number, even when cases where they governed through deputies are excluded from consideration, was very large. Out of the 10 persons known to have held office, in the 32nd Regnal Year of Shah Jahan, as Provincial Governors, as many as 5 were Princes; and out of 14 provinces in which appointments are known as many as 9 were under the Princess (including those governed by them through deputies).

The general picture that emerges from the above study is that, in fact the system of appointments and transfer of Governors remained the same during the 17th century. It can be ascertained that in respect of transfer of Governors, the Mughal administration revealed no tendency towards either reducing or increasing their frequency. A question evolves that why certain provinces like Bengal and Kabul held longer tenures in store for their Governors than others. But here the trend in the reigns of Shah Jahan and Aurangzeb is the same which is quite obvious. Almost the same may be said of the social composition of the Governors, with the Iranis and Turanis the main group sharing the provincial posts throughout the country, though their respective strength varied. As for Princes, it appeared normal for the Emperor to appoint them in provinces as they came of age, so that towards the end of each reign the number of provinces under them tended to increase. Therefore, nothing unique about Shah Jahan's appointments of his sons to so many provinces in his later years.

Deputy Governor of Ataliq

As a rule only responsible persons of the highest qualifications and experience, worthy of that high office, were appointed governors. An exception, however, to this rule was sometimes made in the case of royal princes and sons of nobles of high rank. These were occasionally made governors of even the most important province. But in such cases a capable and experienced person was invariably sent as Ataliq (guide and preceptor) to the young governor, who was instructed always to follow the Ataliq's advice. Sometimes, because of de-facto governor. Besides the governor a committee of several high officers was also appointed to assist the viceroy.[26] There were several objects of the policy to appoint young princess to viceroyalties. On the people the presence of a prince among them had a great moral effect and opportunity of administrative experience and training in the art of government. It also developed in him a sense of responsibility and gratified his sense of dignity.

The administrative efficiency, however, was not suffered to deteriorate in the least in such provinces. The Ataliq who was held fully responsible for any maladministration or inefficiency. The moment he was found incapable or guilty of deliberates neglect of duty he was removed from office.

Tenures of Governors

The tenure of a provincial governor depended upon the will of the Emperor.[27] it is not possible to determine any uniform principle which governed these transfers but this mutch is clear, that an opportunity was given to every aspiring and capable man to enjoy the high-prized post.

The provincial governor exercised threefold functions civil, judicial and military.[28]As civilians, he was the executive head of the entire administration, as a judicial authority, he heard appeals from the decisions of the Qazis and Mir, Adls, as a military officer commanded the provincial quota and was responsible for its maintenance and upkeep. He could dismiss subordinate officers with the exception of those directly appointed by the Emperor.

He could not execute a death sentence without obtaining sanction from headquarters. He was the guardian of the civil rights of the people, and was expected to convene meetings of responsible officers under him to discuss administrative problems.

Officiating Viceroys Agents of Absentee Viceroys

In some cases it is noteworthy that the man who was appointed viceroy sent an agent of his own choice subject to the approval of the Emperor, to administer the province in his name, while he (the viceroy designate) himself remained behind either, in attendance, [29] in obedience to the emperor's order, or sometimes for personal reasons[30] through the indulgence the emperor, some time he also had to absent himself on public duty and a deputy was appointed to act in his place during his absence.[31]

Interim Viceroys

When a young viceroy was transferred to a very distant province, which required sometimes for him to assume charge or if he was delayed for certain other reasons[32], some able officer was dispatched to hold charge and carry on the administration till the arrival of the new incumbent[33]. In Agra and Delhi Governors were appointed only during the absence of the imperial court.

Governors of Sub Provinces

The governors of the Sub-Provinces, such as Orrisa and Sind, were appointed usually on the recommendation of the viceroy of the major provinces to which they were attached, or else the viceroy appointed his own man either by the express permission of the emperor or subject to his approval.[34]

Institution of Joint Governors

In the thirty 1st year of his reign, Akbar found it necessary to appoint two men to each province.

Appointment of the Viceroy and other High Officials

The viceroy of the province was appointed by the imperial order technically called the 'farman-i-sabati'[35], (فرما ن شبتى). The Diwan of the province was appointed by the 'hasbu-ul-hukm' (حسب أ لحكم) of the emperor and the sanad appointing him bore the seal of the Vazi-ul-Mulk' or the imperial Diwan.[36]

Diwan

The Diwan[37] was the chief financial officer in a Suba. In theory he was subordinate to the governor, but in practice was equal to him in a rank. He was directly appointed by the Emperor and was expected to keep an eye on the governor. In this reign the provincial Divan held many posts at once. Md. Waris[38] records the case of Sheikh Musa Gilani who in the 21st year was appointed Divan, Amin and Faujdar of Multan. Such instance may be multiplied.

The Provincial Diwan

In the provinces, the approval diwan was in charge of the financial administration while he was, under Akbar, subject to supervision by the governor, who was the vice-regent of the emperor in the province, he was directly responsible to the imperial diwan from whom he received his orders. There are indications in subsequent literature to show that the diwan became more and more independent of the governor under Jahangir and Shah Jahan.

Duties of the Provincial Diwan

"The Provincial Diwan is the second officer in the locality." The provincial Diwan was selected by the Imperial Diwan and acted directly under his orders and in constant correspondence with him. At the times of giving leave to a new Diwan. The High Diwan was to urge him to increase the cultivation and to select honest men only for the post of ***amin***. He was to report to the High Diwan twice every month the occurrences of the ***subah*** with a statement of the cash balance with him.

The diwan was specially urged to appoint as collectors (***kroris*** and ***tahsildars***) practical men who were likely to induce the ryots to pay the Government dues of their own accord, without the necessity of resorting to harshness or chastisement.

There is no compact account of the duties of the diwan available during the period under treatment, except for stray references. Abul Fazl in his introduction to the Ain-i-Akbari gives us some clue from which we may conclude the scope of that officer's functions. But the fullest account of the diwan's duties is to be founding two farmans (instruments of instructions) issued by the emperor Aurangzeb to his diwans, Mohammad Hashim and Rasikdas.[39] These farmans have been translated by Sarkar in his Mughal Administration (2nd edition pp. 197-223). These two framers can be boiled down to give the following main points:

> The emperor at first makes it clear that the aim of administration should be directed to the increase of cultivation and the welfare of the peasantry and people at large. Keeping this object in view the officers are instructed to assess and realize the revenue according to any of the methods which the riot may agree to, and strictly stop all sorts of prerequisites or illegal taxes which the officers might be extorting from the people. They should encourage the growth of cultivation and persuade the peasant to cultivate any lands lying fallow, by giving them every sort of help, by extending loans, constructing irrigation works and making the charges as easy as possible.

They are asked to realize arrears in easy installments and punish the officials who may have practiced oppression and conciliate the ryots. If any calamity befalls the cultivation in any place, they should make proportionate reduction in the revenue or even remit it according to circumstances. If any extra amount has been exacted by the collection officers they should be made to refund it.[40]

The government of the province was organized on the same lines as the government at the centre. Apart from the governor, every province had its own diwan, bakhshi, mir 'adl sadr (who was also the provincial qadi), kotwal, mir bahar and waqa'i nawis.[41] The diwan was the head of the department of finance in the province and his main duty was to see that the agrarian administration in his charge was kept upto the mark. For this purpose he was to be in constant communication with the revenue staff in the parganahs. It was in his office that all the returns of assessment and realization from the paraghanas were audited and then consolidated into abstract for transmission to the central ministry of finance. The original returns were transmited to the central ministry after a harvest for further auditing. He also kept a record of imah lands and the documents under which they had been issued.[42] Similarly all data necessary for the assessment of the state demand were kept in his office. He was especially instructed to ensure that the peasant were dealt with fairly and that every legitimate encouragement was given to cultivators.[43]

Bakshi

The provincial bakshi was responsible for issuing certificates to the mansabdars that the conditions of their mansab had been fulfilled. Only on the production of this certificate was the salary paid by the diwan. In case, the payment was made in the form of jagir, an account was maintained by the diwan of any deductions that had to be made because of his failure to fulfill any of the terms of the ***mansab.***

In case of the mansabdar's death, it was the provincial ***bakshi***'s duty to take over his jagir. A mansabdar could not leave the station where he was also responsible for the transmission of the reports of the waqa'i nawis to the Central government.[44]

The provincial ***sadr*** made recommendation of grants to the ***sadr-us-sudur.*** The provincial mir ***'adl*** performed the same functions in the province as the centre ***mir 'adl*** at the center. The ***kotwal's*** duty was limited to the provincial capital and he had no jurisdiction over the kotwals of other areas.

The provincial ***msir bahr*** was responsible for the maintenance of the river and seaports within his jurisdiction in good condition, to guard and supervise river communications and to keep the ***nawwarah*** in good order.[45] The waqa'i nawis kept the central government informed of the happenings in the province.[46] Later a ***sawanihnawis*** was added to send intelligence reports. He worked unknown to the officials and the public. He was, therefore, styled ***khufiyahnawis*** or the secret reporter.

The provincial officer worked under the general supervision of the governor, but they were really responsible to their counterparts at the centre.

Parganah

The Mughals did not have any assessment staff attached to the sarkar. The reason seems to be that there was little justification for duplicating the inspecting staff at the level of the sarkar.

The staff for the assessment and realization of the state demand on agricultural produce was centered in the parganah. The administrative machinery of the parganah did not undergo any remarkable change when the Mughals established their rule; the institutions developed by the sultans continued to function with minor changes in nomenclature and organization.[47]

The head of the parganah administration under the Mughals was the amil. It was the duty to see that all the procedures regarding the assessment and realization of the state dues were followed honestly and that the system ran smoothly and efficiently. He was particularly enjoined to expand the area under cultivation and it was realized that this could not achieved without ensuring the well-being of the peasant. The '***amil*** therefore, was to keep a strict watch over his staff to see that no injustice was committed and only the dues prescribed by the state were realized from the cultivator. All cultivators were to have direct access to him to ensure fair dealing.[48]

It was in the reign of Shah Jahan that his minister ***Islam Khan*** revived the tradition of the Sultanate and appointed an ***amin*** in every parganah. He was made responsible for assessment. The amil was left with police duties and the realization of the state demand.[49]

The Ain-i-Akbari mentioned the police duties of the amil and makes him responsible punishing contumacy and rebellion.[50] When a separate assessment officer called amin was appointed in the parganah, police duties gained more importance among the functions of the 'amil, and he came to be called a fawjdar as well. Thus there are number of documents in which a faujdar of parganahs have been mentioned.[51] It seems that some smaller parganahs the duties of the fawjdar and the amin were combined.[52]

It seems that there was not sufficient work in the parganah to keep both the amil and the amin busy. This is not unlikely because after the Ain-i-dahsalah had been promulgated and the Zapti system had worked for some time, the work of the assessment must have become lighter and Islam Khans experiment could not have had much justification from the very beginning. This must be the reason why in many parganahs the offices of the amil and amin were combined.

This seems to have been the reasons, which prompted Sadaullah Khan to correct new unit of chaklah. He withdrew the amin from each parganah and posted him in the chaklah, which consisted a number of parganahs. The duties of assessment the collection revenue were considered sufficient for him. It was then thought desirable to have another officer stationed at the headquarters of the chaklah as well for the punishment of rebels and keeping the roads safe for travellers. The chaklah, therefore, also name to have a fawjdar. The 'amil of the parganah was made subordinate to the fowjdar and the amin of the chaklah.[53]

Sarkar and the Parganah

Each subah was divided into a number of sarkars and each sarkar into parganahs of mahals. The parganah was the lowest official unit of administration and below the parganah was the village panchayat, which was popular in origin but recognized by the government. According to the Ain, in 1596 the empire comprised 105 sarkars and 2737 mahals of parganahs. But these figures were constantly changing owing to frequent re-arrangements and fresh annexations. The administrative head of the sarkar was called faujdar and that apart from sarkars, there were no other divisions of a subah, for the purposes of general administration, as suggested by Moreland.

It is recognized by Moreland that the two chief divisions of government, namely, the executive, called the 'Huzur' and the revenue called 'Mal', were definitely in existence. When it is proved that, the sarkar was the only division next to the subah, with the faujdar represented the executive half of the government.

Although there is no detailed record of the functions and powers of the faujadr in the sarkar and of the shiqdar in the parganah , we have enough evidence to enable us from an approximate estimate of the scope of their duties. The Ain-i-faujdar (in the Ain-i-Akbari) is a sort of summary of the instruction, which were issued by the government to him at the time of his appointment. The duties enjoined on him in this Ain were at least what he was expected to do.

They pertain broadly to three branches of administration revenue, police and army. On the revenue side, his part was only indirect and not direct. He was to assist the amalguzar in the realization of revenue if the cultivators turned contumacious. His main function was guarding the countryside or the rural areas of his sarkar. In the army he was regularly to inspect the local militia and keep it well-equipped and in good trim.

Many cases are on record in which even such high officials as the provincial viceroys were recalled as a result of the complaint of the people against their misrule.[54] We have ample and unmistakable evidence of the faujdars' duty in connection with the policing of the country. The Mirat-i-Ahmadi gives a detailed account of a network of thanas covering the parghanas, which were in charge of subordinate faujdars or thanedars under the control and authority of the faujdar-i-sarkar.[55] In another place we are incidentally told that when any important letters or documents were sent through official ***mace-bearers,*** they had letters requiring the local faujdars, zamindars and thanedars to escort them through their respective jurisdiction and safely handed them on the officers of the next district.[56] Foreign travellers also bear testimony to these duties of the faujdar. Thevenot tells us that 'the faujdar of Surat is obliged to secure the country about and to answer for the robberies that are committed there.[57] Finch refers to the faujdar of Delhi suppressing and destroying the thieves and robbers around the city.[58] We are also entitled that in virtue of his being the executive head of the sarkar, the faujdar was also empowered to exercise a general oversight of its administration, although he had no authority to interfere in the revenue or judicial affairs.[59] But he does not seem to have exercised the duties of a magistrate, which function in the sarkar was entrusted to the kotwal as will be shown later. Beside the faujdar and amalguzar there were two more officials in the sarkar who were in charge of justice and the religious department. These were the qazi and the kotwal. It is a noteworthy fact that the faujdar did not hold any magisterial powers and therefore he represented the governor in the sarkar only in one aspect of his duties, viz., maintenance of law and order. The magisterial side of the governor's functions was held by the Kotwal who was a magistrate not only for the headquarters' town but for the whole of the sarkar, viz., the faujdar, amalguzar, kotwal and qazi. The last two divided between them the entire judicial work of the sarkar.

The Amil of the parganah had the same duties as the amalguzar in the sarkar. But he had to deal directly with the peasantry in his work of assessment and realization of revenue. In addition to his proper work, he was also expected to assists the shiqdar together with the headman of the villages, in maintaining law and order and punishing the miscreants. In the revenue department, the shiqdar was to assist the amil in the collection of revenue from recalcitrant cultivators.

It seems quite certain that Akbar substituted the term faujdar for shiqdar-i-***shiqdaran***, perhaps because the latter was a rather cumbersome word, without effecting any change in his jurisdiction or functions. For similar reasons the term amalguzar was adopted in place of ***munsif-i-munsifan.***

Revenue Officers of the Sarkar and Parganah

The chief revenue officer in the sarkar was the amalguzar or amil. He was assisted by numerous staff of which bitikchi was the most important. The other notable subordinates of the amil were the karkuns, the fotadar or khazandar and the parganah officials. Of the three chief officials of the sarkar, namely, the kotwal, the faujdar and the amalguzar, the kotwal had no share in the revenue side of the administration, but the faujdar's duty was to render such assistance as might be required by the amalguzar in realizing revenue from recalcitrant and turbulent people. The main work of assessment and realization was carried on by the amil with the help of his ***karkuns*** and the rest of the staff and the semi-official functionaries, the ***qanungo***, the ***patwari*** and the ***headman***, the shiqdar also seems to have given him substantial assistance.

Other Political Divisions

In addition to the sarkar and parganah into which the greater bulk of the empire, including the states and principal of the autonomous vassal chiefs, was divided, administrative exigencies necessitated the creation of certain other political divisions or more correctly administrative centers were seaports, frontier outposts and forts, chaklas and thanas.

Sea Ports, an Independent Unit

Though nominally the ports formed a sub-division of a subah, for administrative purposes, the more important ports were constituted into separate units entirely independent of the provincial authorities. In the case of smaller and less important ports, either two or more were combined to make one unit,[60] or sometimes a minor port was placed under the jurisdiction of the chief officer of a major port in the neighbourhood.[61]

The Power and Function of Amalguzar

The powers and functions of the chief amil are fully described in ***Ain -i-Akbari by Abul Fazl***. These powers and duties would appear to be too wide and numerous for a single officer to perform. It is clear that he was the source of authority in which the various sub-branches of the revenue administration were centered and formed which they were controlled and conducted. But he was instructed not to adopt a policy of aloofness, but on the other hand to make himself easily accessible provision must have gone very far in minimizing the possibility of oppression and keeping in check the covetousness and rapacity of the lower officers. He was also authorized to punish robbers, murderers and other miscreants in order to protect the peasantry.

Amil

The alternative methods of assessment which the amil was to adopt were the three different forms of ***batai*** or sharing and ***kankut*** or estimation of ripened crops when ready to be harvested. He is then ordered with special stress not to entrust the ***kankut*** to be carried out by the headman lest it should encourage them to tyrannies, but to deal directly and civilly with the husbandmen. His next duty pertained to circumscribing and controlling the lower officials, such as surveyors, assessors and other officer of revenue, by taking securities from them, and fixing their daily rations when on active service. Through the headman and other village officials he would gather correct report of the cultivated lands and assess accordingly making due allowance for inferior crops, if any. On completion of the assessment of a village a copy of its abstract would be sent to the imperial secretariat within fifteen days. Should any calamity occur to any farm after the dispatch of draft estimates, the amil would immediately make an estimate the loss and dispatch a report to the court so that it might be approved or a commissioner might be deputed to investigate and ascertain the accuracy of the report.

In the matter of collection, the amil is advised to be amiable and courteous. This is followed by an indications as to the times of revenue collection. He is then asked to induce the cultivator to bring the revenue himself to the treasury so that the possible evils arising from the conduct of collectors might be avoided. Where the harvest was good he was to enforce punctual payment. Next are fixed the rates of taxation on those fields which are not sown but used as pasturage for cattle by the owner.

In regard to the amount deposited in the treasury the amil was solely responsible. He was to keep a written statement of the deposits and personally to see that it was correct. Here a very significant instruction is given to the amil. He is asked, after counting and putting the cash in sealed bags, to deposit it in a strong room and fasten the door thereof with several locks of different construction, the key of one of which he was to keep himself and leave the rest with the treasurer.

Then the amil was to send monthly reports of the daily receipts and expenditure to the court, and remit the money to the central treasury as soon as two lakhs of dams were collected. Then he is asked to inspects the work of the patwari and others subordinate officers, to examine suyurghals, to make rules for the guidance of servants and to accept no present from any government servant. He was also to provide the imperial government with detailed information regarding the condition of the rural people every month. Lastly he was to undertake the duties of the kotwal's office, should that office be vacant in the sarkar. It would seem that the amil was instructed to undertake the sub-urban police and judicial duties of the kotwal and not the municipal duties which that officer had to perform in the city under his charge. The amil was subject to supervision and inspection by the governor who could recommend his dismissal if he found him inefficient or dishonest.[62]

The Bitikchi and his Work

Next to the amil in the parganah administration came the bitikchi. Akbar kept only one bitikchi who kept the records in Persian.[63] From a perusal of the duties of the bitikchi set forth in Ain VI, it will become quite clear that the next to the amil, he was the most important revenue official in the sarkar and as Abul Fazl says, really indispensable to his chief, the amil.

Bitikchi is a word of Turkish origin, meaning a writer or recorder. He may best be characterized as the secretary of the revenue department in the sarkar, who did the entire work of preparing the necessary papers and records on the basis of which assessment and collection was carried out by the amil. In the preparation of these papers the following procedure was followed:

> First he took from the qanungos the yearly average of the revenue of each village on the basis of the average of the past ten years and acquainted himself with the customs (رسم آن سرزمین) of the locality (the sarkar in his charge), to the satisfaction of the amil. Next the bitikchi was to record the contracts made with the cultivators define the village boundaries, and estimate the amount of arable and waste land, and keep a note of the government servants employed in preparing the above records, such as the munsif, the zabit (ضا بط), the measurer (جویب کش) and the thanedar, and also the headman and the cultivator, and the kind of produce cultivated (by each person). After taking these individual records he was to prepare them for the whole village, noting down the village was to work out the assessment of each cultivator and make up the totals of each village. The collector (amil) was to realize the revenue on the basis of these records. But if these records were not ready by the time of collection, the bitikchi had instructions to proceed with his work on the basis of the patwaris's records of each village, and thus furnish the necessary papers to the collector. In the business of actual collection also the bitikchi had an important duty to fulfill. If the money was raised by the tahsildar, he was to keep his account, or if the peasant paid it to the treasury, he was to grant him a receipt signed by the treasurer. More important than this, he was carefully to scrutinize the rolls and records of the patwari, the muqadam and other assistants concerned, according to which the collections were made. Finally, the bitikchi was to keep daily and monthly accounts of income and expenditure and forward monthly abstracts and reports, as well as an annual abstract of the entire assessment at the end of the year under the amil's signature, to the imperial secretariat. If any balances were left he was to report them to the collector at the end of the year, as also about any thefts or loss of cattle in any village on which taxes were raised.

The Treasurer and his Duty

Potadar

This officer to whom Abul Fazl gives the name of khazandar (Ain VIII) was commonly known as potadar since ***Sher Shah's*** time. Ain VII, describing his duties opens with a remark on the advisability of the treasury being situated in a safe place and near the residence of the district officer (نزد حاکم).[64]

The duties of the treasurer were comparatively simple and far less onerous. These fall under three main categories; rules in regard to receive money; those regarding the manner of keeping the money and those regarding the disposal of the deposits. Concerning receipts, the khazandar was instructed to receive from the cultivator gold, silver or copper, any kind of coin which he might bring and not harass him. He was not to ask for any, of the coins. The coins of former reigns he was to accept as bullion, that is, as equivalent to the current value of their weight.

As regards depositing money in the treasury it can be seen that in conjunction with the amil the treasurer was to keep it in the treasury under several locks, one key being with the amil and the rest with the treasurer. The karkun and shiqdar also were to have a regular knowledge of the deposits in the treasury. In order to keep his accounts in agreement with those of the patwari's he was to take the patwari's signatures on the ***bahi*** or ledger.

The khazandar was not empowered to make any disbursements, without the sanction of the diwan (probably the provincial diwan is meant). In cases of emergency he could incur expenditure on the authority of the shiqdar and karkun, provided he represented the case to the government (without delay).

Qanungo

An important factor in the parganah administration was the qanungo who prepared statements showing in detail the area cultivated, the crops grown and the expected or actual yield, copies of which were sent after certification by the 'amil, the ***chaudhari*** and the qanungo to the provincial diwan. He gave to each assesee a document called a ***pattah*** which contained all data relating to the assessment of his holding. The assessment executed a deed confirming his acceptance of the assessment. This document called a ***qabuliyat,*** was retained by him and copies were sent to the office of the provincial diwan.[65] In case the crops were damaged by some unforeseen circumstances, he had to assess the extent of the damage and recommend appropriate reduction in the state demand.[66]

Each parganah had several qanungus,[67] who kept the records of the annual medium yield of the areas on the basis of which the decennial average was calculated in accordance with the A'in-i-dahshalah. Copies of these records were deposited in the office of the provincial as well as the central diwan.[68] In certain areas the duties of a qanungo were combined with those of the chaudhari, who was also associated with the parganah administration as a person cognizant of the condition in the parganah. The chaudhari was especially required to report to the 'amil's office all land brought under cultivation.[69] He was punished if he suppressed any information about cultivated areas.

In smaller parganah the duties of the amil and amin were sometimes combined.[70] It is interesting to note that the word mushrif was not completely discarded even under Mughal rule.[71] It was in common use under the Turkish sultans; later under the Afghans, it tended to be replaced by munsif and amin.[72]

The word munsif, literary a judge, is an index to the ideals of Indo-Muslim agrarian administration. Similarly an amin is a trustee who is expected to discharge his duties impartially. He was expected to act as an impartial judge in adjudicating the shares of the state and the cultivator.[73]

When an areas was assigned as a jagir, there were no change in its administrative organization. The usual records and registers were maintained and copies were submitted to the provincial and central diwans.[74] Persons coming from Iran or Central Asia and employed by the government were not assigned jagirs until they had gained experience and become familiar with local customs and the temperament of the people.[75] The collection of urban taxes was entrusted to another set of officials who were directly under the control of the diwan. In case such revenue was assigned to a jagirdar.

The maintenance of internal peace and order was an important function of the provincial governor. The duties of the heads of the administration in the sarkar and the parganah have already been discussed and it has been mentioned that they were responsible for the security of their respective charges. So far as the urban areas were concerned, every city of some proportions had a kotwal.[76] It was essential for an extensive empire to provide for the maintenance of law and order in rural areas. The governor and the fawjdars were entrusted with this duty.

Zamindar

The term Zamindar was applied to some tributaries. It was in use under the sultans and had gained some popularity by the time of the ***Lodis***,[77] but it came into more frequent use under the Mughals. They issued regular letters of appointment to the zamindars prescribing the amount of tribute they had to pay and assigning them their duties. These were "to treat the people well and to make all efforts to suppress refractory and rebellious trouble makers and bring them to the path of rectitude, especially to root out completely thieves and robbers, to increase cultivation and to guard the communications so that travellers could move without difficulty."

References

1. Lachhmi Narayan Shafiq f. 80b.
2. Dastur-u'l-amal, B.M. ms, or 2026, f. 34a.
3. Abu-l-Fadl, Ain-i-Akbari, iii A'in 3.
4. Abu-l-Fadl, Ain-i-Akbari, iii A'in 3, Sara'I, a caravansarain inn.
5. In a letter to Shahjahan's minister Sa'd-u-llah Khan. Aurangzeb writes," His Majesty has conferred upon me the ayalat of these four provinces (subahs) which from a large wilayat and because it is contiguous to the frontiers of rulers in possession of financial resources and armies, it cannot be compared with the province (subahs) of Bengal and Ahmedabad"; Qabil Khan and Muhammad Sadiq f.131b. Though Auraingzeb calls Bengal a subah, Bengal is called an ayalat by Abu-l-Fadl, Akbarnamah, iii, p. 266. in Ain-i-Akbari, however, the word subah is used.
6. The duties of a naib subahdar have been mentioned in kaifiyat-i-suba-jat-i-mumalik-i-mahrusah-i-HInduatan, f. 215b.
7. Mawardi, pp. 30, 31; Farra, p. 20.

8. A.H. Lahauri, Vol. II, pp. 710-711.
9. Islam Khan was appointed governor of Agra when Shahjahan went to the Deccan in November 1629. When Shahjahan went to Kashmir in 1638, Saif Khan was appointed Governor of Agra. The same procedure was adopted when the capital was transferred to Dilhi.
10. Auraingzeb was appointed governor of all four provinces which included Ahmadnagar, Berar, Khandesh and Telingana.
11. Avadh is not frequently mentioned during the reign.
12. ***Ain-i-Akbari***, pp, 280-281; ***Sarkar: Moghul Administration***, pp. 80-86.
13. A.H. Lahauri, Vol, II, p. 290: Salih, Vol. III, p.64. Mirat-i-Sikandari says that complaint against Azam Khan's tyranny was made by Sayyid Jalal, f. 87.
14. A.H. Lahauri, Vol. II, p. 282.
15. ***Ibid.***, Vol. II, p. 283; Shahjahan wrote of the arrears of one million rupees due to Zafar Khan, because the inhabitants of Kashmir were satisfied with his administration. Lahauri, Vol. II, p. 420.
16. Ibid., Vol. II, p. 158.
17. Mirat-i-Ahmadi, 163-170, tr. in ***Bird's History of Gujarat***, 389-400.
18. Provincial Governors under Shahajahan and analyses by Mohd. Athar Ali Center of Advance Study, Department of History, Aligarh.
19. ***Ibid.***
20. "Provincial Governor under Aurangzeb"; ***Mediaeval India, A Miscellany***, Vol. I, p. 97.
21. Irfan Habib, "The Family of Nur Jahan During Jahangir's Reign- A Political study"; ***Mediaeval India, A Miscellany***, pp. 74-95.
22. "Provincial Governor under Aurangzeb An Analysis", ***Mediaeval India A Miscellany***, pp. 96-133.
23. "Provincial Governors Under Auranzeb", ***Medieval India–A miscellany***, Vol. p. 98.
24. Based on the table in my article, "Provincial Governors Under Aurangzeb–An Analysis", ***Medieval India-A Miscellany***, Vol. I, pp. 107-123, the calculation of percentages for social composition in the text of that article was on the basis of persons serving as Governors and not as here, the years of office.
25. Irfan Habib, "The Family of Nur Jahan During Jahangir's Reign–A Political study"; ***Mediaeval India Miscellany***, pp. 74-95.
26. Mirza Abdur Rahim Khan Khana was appointed viceroy of Gujarat in 1575 and a committee of four nobles was sent to assist him,
27. A.H. Lahauri, Vol. II, p. 158.
28. Moreland classifies the tenure into two divisions, Kachcha and Pakka, India at the Death of Akbar, p. 31; Bernier remark that the tenure of governors was longer in India than in Turkey, p. 231, Beni Prasad, p. 104; Manrique says that the tenure was short, Vol. Vl. I, p. 53.
29. In the first year of Shahjahan reign when Mahabat Khan was appointed the

viceroy of Deccan he sent his own son Khan-i-Zaman as deputy to that province- Or. 174 fall 9A.

30. Peter Mundy, II, p. 235, Baqur Khan Sent his son to take charge of Gujarat of which he was appointed viceroy.
31. Or. 175, fal 124b Khan-i-Dauran of Malwa went to suppress rebels in Balaghat.
32. Provincial Governor of the Mughals by P. Sarkar published in 1941 by Kitabista Allahabad. p. 174.
33. Or. 175, -209.
34. On his succession Shahjahan appointed Yamin-ud-dualah Viceroy of both Lahore and Multan later on carried out through him deputy Amir Khan (Lahori, Vol. 1, pt. 1, pp. -125-126).
35. ***Ain-i-Akbari*** I, p. 194.
36. Mirat, (I.O.). III, fol. 72 ia. The letters of appointment of viceroys were called 'farmans', while those of other appointments were called 'sanads'.
37. Sarkar, ***Mughal Administration***, pp. 62-63; Peter Mundy, Vol. II, p. 12.
38. Waris, f. 7.
39. The former one is reproduced also in the Mirat-i-Ahmadi (see Baroda text, Pt. I, pp. 268-272).
40. Dr. Pant in his "Commercial Policy of the Mughals' however, quite soberly and dogmatically asserts (see p. 59) that "In assessing the cultivators the principle kept in view was: exact from the peasant the last dam that he can pay: leave for him just enough to exist but not to live", and again, "the land revenue was a tax levied on the theory of what the peasant can bear", A more factious and more sweeping statement is difficult to imagine. It is not easy to understand how a writer with any presumption to scientific research could make such utterly unscientific and purely imaginary generalizations.
41. Abu-i-Fadl, ***Akbarnama***, iii, p. 282 Waqa-i-nawis was also called Waqainawis.
42. Kaifiyat-i-subajat-i-murralik-i-mahrusah-i-hindistan, ff. 216, 217; Dastur-ul-amal, B.M. ms. Or. 2026, ff. 18-20 give an interesting list of the registers maintained at the office of the provincial diwan.
43. Kaifiyat-i-subajat-i-murralik-i-mahrusah-i-hindistan, ff. 216, 217.
44. Ali Muhammad Khan, Supplement, p. 175.
45. Nawwarah, from Hindi naw, a boat, was river navy.
46. Ali Muhammad Khan, Supplement, p. 175.
47. For the Administration of a Parganah under the Sultans see, ***History of Mughal Government and Administration***, H.K. Naqvi, 1990- Kanishka Publishing House, Delhi, printed at Sangita Printers, Delhi. ***Ibid.***, pp. 208, 209, 259, 260.
48. Abu-'l-Fadl, ***A'in-i-Akbari***, III, A'in, 7.
49. ***Ibid.***
50. ***Ibid.***
51. Kaifiyat-i-subajat-i-mumalik-i-maharusa-i-hindustan, ff. 217a, 227a.
52. Ashraf Khan, f. 7a. ***History of Mughal Government and Administration***, H.K. Naqvi,

p. 233.

53. ***Dastur-ul-amal***, B.M. Or, 2026, f. 34a.
54. R. and B. I 262-3.
55. Vide Supplement (Baroda text) p. 188 et. seq.
56. ***Mirat-e-Ahmadi*** (I.O.) III, fol. 73 2a.
57. Thevenot, Pt. III, p. 20.
58. In the face of these evidences the suggestions of writers like Sarkar and Moreland that the countryside was completely neglected and the village populations were left entirely uncared by the government, would appear to be groundless and unacceptable.
59. ***Provincial Government of the Mughal***, 1526-1658. Dr. P. Saran Ist published in 1941, printed by J.K. Sharmat at Allahabad Law Journal Press Published by Kitabista, Allahabad. p. 210.
60. The ports of Ghogha and Qandhar were put under one person Mirat, (Bar. Text) Supplement, p. 193.
61. ***Provincial Government of the Mughal*** 526-1658. Dr. P. Saran Ist published in 1941, printed by J.K. Sharmat at Allahabad Law Journal Press Published by Kitabista Allahabad, p. 214-215, see also Embasy, pp. 28-34.
62. ***Provincial Government of the Mughal***, pp. 286-287, Ain, I, 281-282.
63. Kewal Ram, f. 164 b. The non-technical word nawisindah is also used occasionally, e.g. Abul-Fadl, ***Akbarnamah***, iii, p. 117.
64. Here Abul Fazl is describing the functions of the parganah and sarkar treasurer, ***Provincial Government of the Mughal***, p. 289.
65. ***Ibid.***, f, 24b.
66. ***Dastur-ul-amal***, B.M. ms, or 2026, f. 22b.
67. ***Dastur-ul-amal***, B.M. ms, or 2026, f. 24b.
68. ***Kaifiyat-i-subajat-i-mumalik-i-maharusah-i-Hindustan***, f. 220b.
69. Shakir Khan, f. 154a.
70. ***Kaifiyat-i-subajat-i-mumalik-i-maharusah-i-Hindustan***, f. 227.
71. ***Ibid.***, f. 236b.
72. I.H. Qureshi, ***The Administration of the Sultanate of Delhi***, pp. 208-209.
73. ***Kaifiyat-i-subajat-i-mumalik-i-maharusah-i-Hindustan***, f. 232a.
74. ***Dastur-ul-amal***, B.M. ms. or. 2026, f. 21.
75. Khawafi Khan, ii, p. 187. This rule was laid down by Shah Jahan.
76. ***History of Mughal Government and Administration***, H.K. Naqvi, 1990, Kanishka Publishing House, Delhi, f. 224b. p 239.
77. e.g. Khusrav used the word Zamindar in Diwalrani Khidr Khan, p. 70; I.H. Qureshi, ***The Administration of the Sulatanate of Delhi***, p. 21.

5. Finance and Agrarian System

The best organized branch of the Mughal government was its Agrarian Administration. The Mughals devoted so much attention to Agrarian Matters because the state demand on agriculture produce was the mainstay of Mughal finance, which was natural in a land where the economy was mainly agricultural. Agrarian administration has received the closest attention of various governments established in the sub-continent throughout the history. The basis of the Mughal Agrarian System is if the recognition of the fact that the prosperity of the empire dependent upon the well-being of the peasant.[1] The level of agricultural production was to be not only maintained but also continuously increased.

The Hindus had developed in the course of time several methods of assessing the share of the state. The simplest of these was to divide the produce between the state and the peasant. When the crops were reaped they were stacked and then share of the state was taken out. This could be done before or after thrashing. Abul'Fazl calls the farmer, ***Betai*** or ***Bhaoli*** and the late long Betai. If the crops were divided while still starding by dividing the area of the field it was called Khet Betai.[2]

The difficulty in this process is that it is lengthy. The Muslim jurists divided agricultural land into three categories the first of these were "Ushri". These were the land belonging to the Muslims from the earliest times and those which were permitted by the state to become Ushri later these were lands which had been brought under cultivation,[3] with the permission of the state by Muslims. No Kharaj Land could become Ushri even if it was purchased by a Muslim or its owner turned a Muslim.

Kharaj–The second category was of the Kharaj Lands. All lands cultivated by non-Muslim subjects of the empire was Kharaj. Besides all land cultivated by the Muslims which was not Ushri and very little was Ushri was Kharaj.

Sulhi Lands–A third category was that of Sulhi Land as there lay outside the subcontinent, there is no need of discussion. So the two category of land during the Muslim rule in the subcontinent are the Ushri and Kharaji Lands. Later some Muslim states developed a category called and-i-mumlikat of the ownership vested in the state. There is no mention of this category in the historical a literature of the Muslim period. This category also may therefore be discussed. The only two categories found during the Muslim who are the Ushri and Kharaji Land.[4]

The Ushri Land paid either a 10th of the gross produce or a 20th depending upon the method of irrigation available. As there extent was limited the rest of the discussion will be devoted to Kharaj Land. The first category to come into existence was the Kharaj-i-Wazifa or a fixed demand irrespective of the actual yield either in kind or in cash or in both. Kharaj-i-Muqatiah, was in the form of fixed demand.[5]

It will be noticed that Kharaj-i-Muqasimah was not difficult in its basic concept from the Hindu method of sharing. The Mughal had found the main features of the Agrarian administration well established. The system of sharing, appraisement, and measurement were taken up by them in certain field the method of a fixed demand, which may be called contract was also in vogue, hence there is a continuity of tradition in the history of Agrarian Administration therein the Muslim Period. There were changes, but not of a fundamental nature.[6]

Measurement

A yard called a Gaz was adapted consisting of fortyone digits. An area such sixty yard square was called Bigah. The reform did not lie in adapting a new scale, but in standardizing the existing one. To bring greater uniformity the old practice of measuring length with a rope was given up, because it shrank well exposed to contact with moisture, instead bamboo rods joined together with iron chain were used which were less affected by the moisture.[7]

Classification of Land

The land was classified according to the length of its cultivation. Polaj was the land which was continuously under cultivation.

Parauti–land was left uncultivated only for a short time to cover its strength.

Chachar–was the land left uncultivated for three or four years.

Banjar–was the land which was not cultivated for the period longer than 7 or 8 years.[8] When banjar land was brought under cultivation only a nominal demand was laid upon in the shape of a ser or two of the yield per Bigah. This principle was maintained throughout this period.[9]

In every area where single schedule applied, sample willing were made of the best, the muddling and the poor crops, the figures were added and a third of the total was considered to be the medium produce, called 'hasil or mahsul' The method of assessment in the preceding paragraph was called the 'zabti' system and was encouraged by the government however, did not completely replace the older method of sharing appraisement also came in whenever, the extent of the damages to the crops by the natural or other calamities had to be assessed. Sharing was called by the Mughal Gallah Bakshi.[10] When the state and the cultivator came to an agreement whereby a fixed sum was paid and the area cultivated and the grown crops were not taken into consideration this was contract and was known as ***Nasaq***.[11] The Nasaq was not a group assessment because it was arrived at between the state and peasants.[12]

The Machinery of Revenue Under Shah Jahan

The administrative arrangements, under Jagir assignment system were geared mainly to cope with two problems. The first was that of imperial control: the assignee was entitled to assess and collect the revenue, but in both these matters he was required to conform to imperial regulations.

Todarmal began his recommendation of the 27th year (1682-83) by an article requiring all collection, whether by the jagirdar or the officials of the Khalisa to be in strict accordance with the authorized rates: everything started in excess of these was to be recovered together with such fines as might be imposed.[13] When in the late years of Shah

Jahan reform was undertaken in the revenue system of the Dakkin, the change over to crop-sharing was enforced not only in the Khalisa but also in the assignment of the jagirdars.[14]

Secondly, there would be the problem faced by the jagirdar who had to manage a new assignment after very short interval. A radical change in the organization of the Khalisa administration was brought about in 1574-75, when all but three provinces of the empire were placed under it. The whole land was divided into district, which was expected to yield 1 crore of ***tankas***. To each district was appointed an Amil or Amalguzar who came to be known as ***Karori***,[15] these revenue collectors seems to have been allowed the greatest latitude in action, for they are said to have guilty of much operation.[16]

The term Shiqdar probably continued to be used synonymously with ***amil*** but subsequently to have been used rather for its subordinate collector under the karori, the ***amin*** now appears merely as the head of the survey party send by the Karori to carry out measurement for the purpose of assessment the Karori also employed troopers known as sahbandi for enforcing revenue collection.[17]

The next important change came under Shah Jahan. His diwan Islam Khan (1639-40 to 1645-46) setup an amin in every mahal, transferring the work of assessment from Karori to his new colleague.[18] The Karori hence forward concerned himself chiefly with collecting the amount which the amin had assessed. Islam Khan successor Sada-ul-llah Khan (1646-7 to1655-56) is said to have further reduced the power of the Karori by putting an end to the practice of combining the offices of ***Karori*** and ***Faujdar*** (commandant) in the same person. An old territorial unit ***chakla***, comprising a group of mahal was received and an ami-i-faujdar was appointed over it, the Karori becoming really a subordinate of this official.[19]

The account of the actual collection of the amil and there agent were audited in many cases by the help of the village patwari's papers. This practice was recommended by Mir Fathullah Shirazi under Akbar, chiefly, with a view to prevent illegal exactions.[20] Shah Jahan's officials seems to have been concerned, on the other hand, rather with ensuring that all such collections (whether authorized or not) should be brought into the imperial treasury. In any case they are said to have this method of audit known as ***bar-amad,*** a part of the routine of administration.[21]

There were besides the Karori and amin, two other officials who were posted independently of them to each paraganah, namely, the Potedar or Khizanedar, the treasurer.[22] and Karkun or Bitikchi the accountant.[23] out of their assignment the princess sometime granted jagir to their own officials. There was nothing to prevent the jagirdar from sub-assigning a part of his jagir to any of his officials or troopers. In the reign of Jahangir, we find the Tarkhan the governor of Sind, who held a considerable part of that province in his own jagir, granting jagirs to his officials and resuming them at will.

A document of the reign of Shah Jahan, from Awadh, receipt that when a particular village had been in pay (***tankhwah***) to a noble, he in turn assigned into four of his troopers.[24] The local element was thereof largely excluded from the assignees administration. It was however, represented by two officials, who were independent of the assignee but were indispensable for him. These were the ***qanungo*** and ***chaudhary*** constituting the second layer of local revenue administration, of which we have spoken earlier. The ***qanungo*** (or, as he was known in the Dakkin, the ***desh-pandia***)[25] generally belonged to one of the "accountant castes" (Kayasth, Khatris, etc.).

The office usually ran in the family, but an imperial order was necessary for the recognition of the rights of any incumbent.[26] It seems to have been usual for the heir of the deceased ***qanungo*** to apply to the court for an order or sanad confirming him in succession. Once conferred the office was normally for life. Nevertheless, a qanungo could be remove by an imperial order. Under Shershah and Akbar there used to be only one qanungo for each parganah.[27]

The Qanungo–He provided the imperial administration with revenue and area figure that were used in determining the standard assessment for the purpose of jagir assignment.[28] His most important function however, was to place his records (specially the account of previous assessment ***muwazana-i-dah-sala***), etc. and personal knowledge at the disposal of the ***amin*** (or any other official acting as the assessors) sent by the assignee.[29]

The Chaudhary–called ***desai*** in Gujarat and ***deshmukh*** in Dakkhin[30] was perhaps an important functionary for revenue administration as the qanungo. But the general system of revenue administration in this region differs materially from the instituted and perfected by Akbar. The ***zabti*** [31] system aimed at the abolition of jagir system and the establishment of direct relation with the cultivators. Its chief features were measurement and calculation. All payment were made in cash and the state demand was fixed at one third of the gross produce. It should be noted, however, that the zabti system prevail only in the well established province of the empire.[32] Bengal, Sindh, Kabul, Khandesh and Kashmir were beyond the scope of its operation. There the revenue was collected either according to ***Gallabakshi***[33] or crop division system or ***Nasq***[34] i.e., the group assessment system. In the former direct relation with the cultivators were possible, but not so in the latter case.

Changes under Shah Jahan–In the reign of Shah Jahan the revival of the jagir system cut at the very root of the ***zabti*** system. About seven-tenths of the empire was framed out[35] and the extent of Khalsa lands (crown land) diminished considerably. Group assessment became the rule rather than the exception[36] and the state demand increased from one-third to about one-half. The burden of the peasant increased further, because he had to pay not only for the land under actual cultivation, but also for the land in his occupation.[37] In this way land revenue increased to 40 millions of rupees.[38]

Famines

The Deccan–In this reign, there occurred one sever famine in the Deccan, and some scarcity of food in the Punjab and Kashmir. The famine of 1630-31 had widespread repercussions it affected Golconda, Ahmadnagar, Gujarat and some parts of Malwa. Contemporary chronicles give heart-rendering accounts of the heavy mortality and of the intense suffering among the Deccan people. Life was offered for a loaf but none would by; rank was sold for a cake, but none cared for it.

For a long time dog's flesh was sold for goat's flesh and the pounded bones of the dead were mixed with flour and sold. Men began to devour each other and the flesh of a son was preferred to his love. The emperor established soup-kitchens and alms-houses for the benefit of the poor and destitute. Every Monday, 5,000 rupees were distributed among the poor of Burhanpur and remissions on a large scale were made in Ahmadabad.

Kashmir–in 1641, heavy rainfall caused serious damage to the ***kharif*** crops in Kashmir and consequently there occurred a great scarcity of food. About 50,000 people left the country, and migrated to Lahore where the Court was staying at that time. They appeared in a body before the jharokha window represent their misery to the Emperor Shah Jahan ordered that one hundred thousand rupees should be distributed among them, and cooked food worth 20 rupees should be daily provided to them. He sent 30,000 rupees to Tarbiyat Khan to be spent in famine relief work in Kashmir, and ordered him to establish five kitchens to distribute soup and bread. But Tarbiyat Khan failed to manage this situation and he was replaced by Zafar Khan. The Emperor gave the latter another 20,000 rupees for relief work in Kashmir.

Punjab–in 1646, scanty rainfall caused a famine in the Punjab, by order of the Emperor ten kitchens for the distribution of cooled food were established in the province and Sayyid Jalal was commissioned to distribute Rs. 10,000 among the poor and destitute. Sold children were ransomed by the government and restored to their parents. In February 1647 Shah Jahan sanctioned another thirty thousand rupees for relief measures in the Punjab.

There is no doubt in a country like India land revenue was by far the most important item in finance; but it was not by means the only one. Father Monserrate has the following interesting discourse on the subject: "The king he says", exacts enormous sums in tribute from the provinces of his empire, which is wonderfully rich and fertile both for cultivation and pasture and has a great trade both in exports and imports. He also derives much revenue from the horded fortunes of the great nobles, which by law and custom all come to the king on their owner's death.

Moreover, he allows no bankers or money-changers in his empire except the superintendents and tellers of the royal treasuries. This enormous banking business brings the King great profit; for at these royal treasuries alone may gold coin be changed for silver or copper and vice versa. The government officers are paid in gold, silver or copper according to their rank. Thus it comes about that those who are paid in one type coin need to change some of into another type.

In addition to this revenue obtained from grain, et. (cetra) mean land revenue, there are another considerable receipts. One is the tribute paid by the Hindus. There is second custom duty upon goods brought by Hindu merchants; it is five percent.

Hawkins statements that the yearly income of the Khalsa lands in this reign was 50 crores of rupees (Purchase, III, 30) is wild and unworthy of an author who is generally well informed. In Thomos Coryat's letters we are told that the Emperor's revenues are 40 millions crowns of six shillings value by the year (Purchase, IV, 474). At ten rupees to the pound this yield 12 crore of rupees.

We are on solid ground when we come to ***Badshahnama.*** According to that work the total land revenue of the Mughal empire at the time of Shah Jahan's accession was 700 crore ***dams*** which comes to 7½ crores of rupees, (II, 711).

Now Shah Jahan' reign, Mulla 'Abdul Hamid Lahouri, in the passage cited above, where he is summing up at the end of the twentieth regnal year, goes on to tell us that the total revenue of the other provinces had gone up by 100 crore ***dams,*** amounting to 800 crores; of rupees and that the revenue of the territory conquered since Shah Jahan' accession totaled 80 crore or 22 crore of rupees. Out of this 120 crore dams or 3 crores of rupees was the income from the crown lands or Khalisa. We are further told that the Khalisa income had never reached this figure before.[39] This is the revenue of 23 province.

Mandelso in a carelessly worded statement gives 17,45,00,000 rupees as the annual revenue for this reign (Voyages and Travels, p. 38). We noticed that the land revenue of the Mughal Empire rose steadily from the 40th year of Akbar's reign (1595-96) to 20th year of Shah Jahan's (1647), due partly of course to conquest, but also presumably, to stable conditions and settled administration.

In the last decade of Shah Jahan's reign, Balkh, Badakshan and Kandhar, which account for a revenue of 19 crore ***dams*** or nearly half a crore of the rupees, were lost to the Mughals.

Shah Jahan was, according to Bernier, "a great economist'. But we must remember that the expenditure has increased considerably in his reign (witness the heavy mansabdari list besides other evidence), and he had always been lavish his gift. Further that emperor has left more abiding monuments of architecture than any other king in ancient or modern times, in or outside India. According to the list in Badshahnama Shah Jahan must spent something like 3 crore on places and garden, mosque and mausoleum, castle and fortification.

Khafi Khan has the following statement about the treasure left by Shah Jahan. His ambitious language is placed before the reader as it is:

Rupees and ***asharfis*** 24 crore. Gold and Silver bullion, gold and silver vessels and jewels about 15 or 16 crore (M.L., I, 758.)

Life of Peasantry

The general approach of the state towards the peasants was benevolent.[40]

1. In case of difficulties or calamities the peasants were advanced loan called ***Taqwi,*** to enable him to cultivate his holding.[41]
2. The Mugals were extremely anxious to expand agriculture and special concessions in the demand were made if a cultivator brought new land under the cultivation.
3. The State also tried to improve the quality of the crops. Jahangir introduced the cultivation of pineapple and several new varieties of the grapes. Guava and custard apple were introduces by the Portuguese and their cultivation was encouraged by the Mughals. Muhammad Rida of Khurasan who raised the first crop was rewarded and honoured by Shah Jahan.[42]

Finance

The Mughals developed sound tradition and their sources of income were well defined and so were the channel of expenditure. The jurists of Islam have divided the legal sources of the income of the state into two broad categories. The first of these consist of those dues which a Muslim pays as a religious obligation and which state collects to expand in an organized and orderly manner. The second category includes the legitimate taxes which the state is entitled to collect for administrating affairs of the inhabitants of the area under its control. The farmer classification applies to ***Ushr*** and ***Zakat.*** The latter includes ***Jiziyah, Kharaj*** and such other taxes as the state can legitimately raise.

Zakat–the Zakat is prescribed by the Quran upon all Muslims who have a modest minimum of wealth which is technically called the *Hisab*. This was calculated as 1350 English grains of gold or 9450 English grains of silver or any other form of wealth of an equivalent value which the owner had in his possession for an entire year.

Zakat was a tax on the import and export of the commodities. Muslim traders trade two and a half percent on the value of the commodity imported, Christian and Jews paid three and a half percent, Hindus were required to pay five percent.

Jaziyah–the Jaziyah has been mentioned in the Quran in the general sense of a tax, the word has an ancient origin. It came to be used early in the History of Islam in the sense of a poll tax levied upon the non-Muslim resident of a Muslim State. In the other words the Jaziyah was a tax paid in lieu of service to the state which the assessee would have been called upon to defend if he were a Muslim in correct, Akbar abolished it and it was again reimposed during Aurangzebs reign.

Khams–Spoils of war was termed as Kham. According to Shariat 1/5th part of spoils belong to the state. The remaining 4/5th went to the soldier. The spoils were not divided on the above principle during Mughal period as pointed out by Quraishi, because soldiers were paid salary during Mughal Period and that's why the Mughal emperor kept the entire goods in their own treasury.

Taksal (Mint)–Had the most important place in the sources of revenue of state. People had freedom to get their gold and silver cast into coins in the mint during the Mughal period. The state charged some discount on account of change of worn-out coins. Thus government treasury was an exchange bank out of which state got a lot of income. Rs. Eleven Lakh were collected during the period of Aurangzeb from Surat province only. It shows that mint were spread at many places of the state from where state used to get a lot of income.

Nazrana–A considerable source of income was through the presents which will made to the emperor on various occasion. Sometime these presents were very rich, but every one who had audience of the emperor for the first time or after a long leave of absence made some presents to the monarch. Sometime it was as law as single gold coin.

This brought large sum of money and valuable commodities to the imperial treasurer but there was little net gains if any at all, because it was customary for the monarch to bestowed even more valuable presents upon the donor. Several times a year the emperor gave away robes of honour, which were invariably accompanied with some jewellry occasionally of very high value. The monarch was also made presents of elephant and of valuable horses. The mansabadars and others who made presents were generally the gainer in these exchanges of presents.

The legitimate revenue derived from the recognized demand of the state on agricultural produce was call mal, anything demanded from the cultivator in Wujuhat, if it comes to the state treasury the tax raised from many merchandise apart from the ***zakat*** were ***Jihat***, the local authority was called ***Sairi Jahat.***

Tamgha–a few assignments were given in perpetuity by Jahangir to some officers. These were called Al-***Tamgha*** assignments. This was a freak survival of an old Timurid tradition. These grants were so called because they were made out under the Al-Tamgha seal. Al-Tamgha assignment were also made for pious purpose, their extent also was not great on the whole. The Mughals during the days of the vigour of their empire were averse to creating hereditary element.

The Coinage

It must be regarded as a notable achievement for the time that the Mughals were able to establish currency of very high metallic standard and uniformity throughout their vast empire. They coined gold, silver and copper. The gold issues were almost cent percent pure, while in the silver proportion of the alloy never rose above 4 percent.[43]

The currency system, moreover was one of re-coinage, that is to say it was open to anyone to take bullion to the Mint and get it converted into pieces,[44] the result therefore was that the coins circulated at value practically correspond to their weight in the respective metals and the ratio at which one unit exchange for another of a different metal was a matter to be determined by the market and not the administration.

The Rupee

In so far as both the administration and the commercial world were concerned, the basic unit for all cash was the silver coin, ***rupya*** or, in its Anglicized form, the rupee.[45] Akbar inherited the unit for Sher Shah and throughout his reign it was maintained at the same uniform standard, stated in the A'in to be 11½ ***mashas*** or about 178 grains.

Jahangir, after his accession, raised the weight of the rupee by 20 percent, while he also instituted a new weight for the silver coins whereby by the new ***rupya-i-Jahangiri*** was supposed to weight exactly one ***tola.***[46] About, the beginning of his 4th regnal year, he ordered the issue of yet another rupee, known as the ***sawai*** which was 25 percent above that of Akbar's in weight. Shah Jahan does not seem to have made any change in the standard or weight of the rupee during his reign,[47] but Aurangzeb, after his assumption of the imperial title in 1569 introduced two minor alterations. As important feature of the Mughal currency was the depreciation in the value of the older rupees. From Abul Fazl statement it appears that in the case of the rupee the total charge amounted to about 5.6% of the net amount coined and there is evidence that it remain about the same during the rest of the period.[48] This was largely and often more than covered by the premium which the rupee enjoyed over silver bullion.[49]

The Anna

The Ain-i-Akbari lists a number of fractional pieces of the rupee down to the suki, which was 1/20th of it in value, the next higher unit being kala equal to 1/6th [50] the last named, therefore, bore the same ratio to the rupee as the Anna, or as it has been anglicized the anna this what does not occur in the Ain-i-Akbari but the hafi Iqlim, composed in 1593-94, contains a definite statement in regar to it. The Anna, it says, was then in use only in Bengal as part of a fixed scale under which 16 annas equal a rupee and 80 chitals (jital) made an anna. The ratio of this scale, it adds, were unaffected by the copper coin.[51] Already in 1620 we find it in commercial use at Patna.[52] It is however, during Shah Jahan's reign that it is indisputably established as the usual fractional unity in the official records of cash transaction all over the empire.[53] Akbar, as the

17th century Martial actually describe the anna as a "coyne and said down its weight, those he also found it was rare that is presumably minted in very small quantities[54]

Among the numerous gold coins listed by him, Abul Fazl specifies the round ***muhr*** as the only one in actual use for scale and purchases,[55] the others were either fancy pieces or reserved for imperial gifts. Even the muhr, knows also as the ***asharfi***, was not in general commercial use, but was mostly, employed especially by the aristocracy, for hoarding purposes.[56] It therefore never entered into financial records or accounts of the administration. The Ai says it weighted 11 ***mashas***[57] and the heaviest of Akbar's muhrs rise to 169 grains.[58] Jahangir made changes corresponding those in the rupee, by instituting the Nurjahani and, subsequently, the sawai, which were respectively 20 and 25 percent heavier than Akbar's muhr.[59] He also established a new weight for the gold coins whereby the Nurjahani was supposed to weight for the gold coins whereby he withdraw his new muhrs and re-establish that of Akbar[60] now regarded as increased it by about two grains troy[61] and probably unified the weights for the gold and silver coins as a result of each his muhr was officially assigned the weight of 9 ¼ [62]

The Dam and Other Copper Piece

The basic coin in the metal was the dam, which too, like the Mughal rupee, appears to have originated with Sher Shah.[63] It supposed the copper tanka of older mintage, of which it was recorded as being half in worth.[64]

The Ain-i-Akbari the weight was at 20 7/8 mashas[65] and the heaviest of Akbars extant dams rise to the weight of 323 grains troy[66] this weight was for the first time few years of his reign. But the growing scarcity of copper compelled him to order the issue of a new dam one third lighter than the old.

If Tavernier is to believed, time and weight depreciation affected the dam in the same way as the rupee.[67] Details of the discounts levied are, however, not available and we have to rest contain with the general reference from the means the half dam.[68]

Uncoined Currencies

Till the end of last century small sea shells, known as ***kauris or kudis*** (anglicized 'cowris') were still commonly used in Indian villages for prices which were too low to be expressed in copper money. Their use seems to have been universal in Mughal India and there can, be little doubt that for many of the daily transactions of the ordinary people the kauris would have sufficed. Their value generally increased with the distance from the coast[69] although it is possible that popular custom determined some of the local variations. In or about Agra 50 or 60 kauris use to be exchanged for a half dam in Gujarat on the other and about 80 shell were given for the same coin. But symptomatic of the very low prices prevailing in the two eastern provinces the use of kauris was most widespread in Bengal and Orissa.[70] A very large quantity of the shells was imported from the Maldives Island and there was an elaborate money-scale based upon the kauri. Generally speaking a rupee in the region seems to have fetched from above 2,500 to 3,200 kauris.[71]

Gold Value of the Rupees

The Mughal monetary system being one of an unrestricted coinage of great metallic purity, the rate at which muhr and dams exchange for the rupees must have closely correspondent to the market values of the three metals.[72] Hawkins (1608-12) took an asharfi of Akbar to be equal to 10 rupees[73] and Jahangirs statement in detail that the ratio stood at 10.7 rupees to the muhr in his 10th regnal year,[74] but was back at 10 in 1621.[75] In the next five years, however, a great rise must have taken place in the silver-price of gold, for in 1626, the muhr is stated to fetch 14 rupees[76] this is supported by the prices realized by foreign gold coin this year at Surat.[77] In 1633, muhr was sold for rupees 12 ½ each[78] in 1640 the price prevailing in Bengal was stated to be about rupees 13.[79] Value of muhr was back at Rs. 14 by 1641-42[80] and this weight is quoted again in 1644-45[81] and 1653.[82] in May 1961 the market rate for the ***aharfi*** was official recorded at the same town as Rs. 14 as 10, and approximately the same rate were reported from some other places in the Dakkin the same year.

In 1666, however, there was a sudden crash in the gold market and the muhr fell to 12 and 11 rupees. There was a very substantial rise in the silver price of gold during 17 century.[83]

Copper Value of the Rupee

The dams comment as much an index of the value of copper, as the rupee was of silver. It purchased 1.15 of its own weight in copper at the time of Akbar[84] and we may assume that this ratio remained about the safe for the rest of the period. It was greater importance in the case of this base metal than in that of gold or silver the price of copper seems to have been falling in the early years of Akbar's reign. First 35[85], then 38 dams went to a rupee. By the 27th Ilahi year 39 dams were regarded as equal to ordinary rupee but two years later the farmer were also declared to be worth 40 dams and when the Ain-i-Akbari was return the actual market rate still fluctuated around this figure.

Indeed copper remained stable till the close of the first decade of Jahangir's reign and the increase in the price of copper is noticed, however, 1619 in Gujarat. In 1626, the value of the rupee in terms of dams had fallen to 29 or 30 at Agra. The year 1628 and 1633 show that the rupee was down to 25 dams.[86] At Agra the dam rate for the rupee in the Dutch account rose steadily from 25 dams in January, 1637 to 29 in October, 1638.[87] In 1640 the rupees seems to have fetch 28 dams at Rajmahal, although copper must have been clearer there than at Agra.

In Shah Jahan's time the market was well organized. Hundees and insurance business were highly developed. Shah Jahan did not interfere much with the currency of the Empire for coins of other countries like Portugal, England, Holland, Spain circulated freely and there was the difficulty of stopping the operation of the 'Gresham law' if he tempered with his coins. The coins of the empire were full-value coins made of pure metal. The exchange rate of a rupee and a dam was constantly, fluctuating. Shah Jahan' reign is memorable for the mint reforms he introduced. He equalized conditions of minting money in Surat and in Ahmedabad. The following coins in free circulation.

Coined Gold

Mohur	Equivalent to	32 Shillings	
Rose Nobles	Equivalent to	6	and 8 pence
Old Jacobuse	Equivalent to	25	and 8 pence
Albertuses	Equivalent to	4	and 6 pence

Coined Silver

Rupee	Equivalent to	4 Shillings	and 6 pence
(½, ¼, [!, 1/16 of a rupee also)			
Rix dalers	Equivalent to	4 Shillings	and 7 pence
Spanish Reels	Equivalent to	4 Shillings	and 10 pence
Rial of Eight	Equivalent to	4 Shillings	and 6 pence
Ecu	Equivalent to	4 Shillings	and 6 pence
Mahmudi			

Coined Copper

Paisa, ½, 2 and 4 paisas. One paisa equivalent to 35 to 50 Badams (bitter Persian almonds) or equivalent to 80 cowris (shell) on the sea-side or 50 in Agra.

As the coins were full value coins, there was no danger of counterfeiting. Mints were also free and open mints, but it was not safe to give the metal for coinage direct to the mint as the officers of the mint knew art of exacting money. So it was always desirable to give the metal for coinage through a ***Shroff*** who used to charge a small commission.

In suggesting the desirability of shifting the factory from Surat to Ahmedabad, the factors laid stress on the mint advantages and also on the favourable exchange that Ahmedabad then enjoyed. The mint in Ahmedabad indeed used to charge two percent. More than the mint will be saved by the loss of exchange between (Surat) and this place (Ahmedabad), which is generally 1½, and 1¾ and 2 percent.[88]

The Surat mint was open "diverse months" if there was any competition. If the Portuguese and English wanted the bullion turned into coins, then days would be reserved for each nation. So there was a risk of having to wait for several days or even months. Even if there were no competition, the mint would not give more than six thousand rupees a day. This was not the case with the Ahmedabad Mint. This difference in the Mint conditions lasted till 1638 when by special command from the king (Shah Jahan) the mint of Surat is made equal to that of Ahmedabd and so the charge is increased seven per miles.[89]

Rials were much preferred as they appreciated a shilling and moreover there was no loss in melting and cutting rials as there was in case of bullion. The loss in the case of bullion used to come upto 1½ percent. Of course, gold was much the better of the two, viz., Rials and bullion silver.

Hundees were generally met at Surat at two months after date by paying a high rate of exchange.

> "At Lahore on Surat the Exchange goes up to 6 ¼ percent.
> "At Agra from 4 ¼ to 5 percent.
> "At Ahmedabad from 1 to 1 ½ percent.
> "At Sironj to 3 percent.
> "At Burhanpur from 2 ½ to 3 percent.
> "At Decca to 10 percent.
> "At Patna from 7 to 8 percent.
> "At Benaras to 6 percent.

At three last places (i.e. Dacca, Patna and Benaras) they give only letters of exchange on Agra and at Agra they give others on Surat, the whole only amounting to the sum I have stated.

> "At Golconda from 4-5 percent.
> And on Goa the same.
> "At Deccan to 3 percent.
> "At Bijapur to 3 percent.
> "At Daulatabad from 1 to 1 ½ pecent.[90]

Besides, it is not top be wondered at that the exchange is so high, for those who lend the money run, for their part, the risk that if the goods are stolen the money is lost to them.[91] For Mecca and Basra the exchange ranges from 22 to 24 percent and from 16 to 20 percent, for Homruz. The ***Jokham*** (risk), it must be admitted was very great and the rate consequently had to be forced up.

Jewel Treasury

Among the offerings made by prince Shah Jahan to Nurjahan at the time of the celebration of the prince's victory in the Dekkin there was, according to Abdul Hamid Lahuri, a ruby of good colour and very fine weighing 5 ½ tanks and valued at rupees 50 thousand (B.N., I, ii, 189). This stone is not mentioned in any other history the weight comes to 132 ratis.

A fortnight later on New Years Day, of R. Y. XIV (which fell on, Thursday, the 4th of Rubi II, 1028 A.H.= March 10, 1619 A.C.). Prince Shah Jahan offered to his royal father, among other things, a yaqut, weighing 22 surkhs of good colour water, and shape, valued by the jewellers at Rs. 40,000, and very fine qutbi,[92] ruby (lal-i-qutbi), three tanks kin weight also valued at 40,000 rupees (tuzuk, 256).

The account of some important ornaments in Shah Jahan's jewels treasury given by Mulla Abdul Hamid Lahuri is interesting the ser-pech turban (ornaments) which the emperors wears on high occasion consist, he says, of five large rubies and 24 large pearls, the central ruby weighing 12 tanks or 288 jewellers ratis. Although the price of this stone is only 2 lakhs of rupees on the royal registers, if a merchant were to obtain such a gem-stone, princes or nobles would pay even 4 lakhs 4 it and by it for presentation to the emperor money is so abundant and a such a present so rare. It is true that there are few rubies in the royal jewels treasury exceeding in weight for instance, the one which prince Shah Jahan bought for 2 lakhs and presented to his father on II, ***Shawwal***, 1026 A.H., when he waited for him after his first victory in the Dekkin. This is the heaviest ruby in the imperial collection.[93]

The best and the largest of the pearls in the sar-pech is of the shape of guava and weight 47 ratis and the price is Rs. 50,000 the total value of the ser-pech allowing only two lakhs of the large ruby, is estimated as 12 lakhs.

The historian tells us of ***tasbih*** (chaplet or necklace) which consisted of 5 rubies and 30 pearls, the total price of the ornament being 8 lakhs of Rs. The largest and the purest of the pearls are put on the ser-pech and ḷeft over are stung on this tasbih, besides these there are two tasbihs containing altogether 125 pearls between which are strung ortinately coloured ***yaquts*** these two tasbihs are valued at 20 lakhs. The central pearl of these tasbihs weight 32 ratis, and is worth Rs. 40,000.[94] Shah Jahan presented a famous stone to Jahangir shows that Shah Jahan knew more about precious stone than the jewellers and experts.

Tables[95] Rubies which Entered

No.	*Description*	*Weight of Cut Stone*
1	Ruby of 1 colour bestowed by Jahangir on Prince Shah Jahan. Akbar's Mother had presented it to Prince Salim at the laters birth	221 ratis
2.	Ruby on Nurjahan's necklace	72 ratis
3.	A Very fine qutbi ruby offered by Prince Shah Jahan to Jahangir	300 ratis
4.	An Engraved ruby of Timurid family sent by Shah Abbas of Persia to Jahangir, then bestowed by the latter on prince Shah Jahan. Later set in the middle slab of the rail of the Peacock Throne	312 ratis
5.	Central ruby of Shah Jahan's Ser-pech, superior in quality even to the much heavier stone of Jahangir	288 ratis

Shah Jahan's reign represent the hey day of material splendour and prosperity, and with his accession the art of collecting, valuing and classifying jewels entered on a new carrier. The leading spirit of the age, the emperor himself, was a greater lover of pearls and stone. Mulla Abdul Hamid Lahuri speaks of the ser-pech of Shah Jahan which consisted of five rubies 24 pearls and was valued at 12 lakhs and of the tasbih comprising five rubies and 30 pearls, valued at 8 lakh and 2 other tasbih[96] and yaquts (total price at 20 lakhs) most of these gems have come down from Akbar's time and continued during the reign of Jahangir and Shah Jahan.

We know that from Shah Jahan's coronation (8 Ijumaida, II, 1037) to the end of the first ***Nauroz*** (beginning of Sha'ban), in seven weeks odd-jewels, dressed and arms, and horses, elephant and cash to the value of 1,80,0,000 rupees worth distributed. This included 76 lakhs worth presented to Mumtaz-uz-Zamani, the Empress. Most of this wealth must have reverted to the treasury on her death. Deducting that amount from the total we have well over a crore of rupees left. So out of this total we may assume some sixty lakhs to stand for gems and jewels.

References

1. Abul'Fazl, ***Ain-i-Akbari*** III A in -7.
2. Muhammad Farman, p. 50-60.
3. ***The Administration of the Mughal Empire***, I. H. Quraishi- N.V. Publications.
4. Abul'Fazl, ***A'in-i-Akbari*** III Ap. 7-10.
5. ***Ain-i-Akbari***, pp. 11-13,
6. ***Ain-i-Akbari***, pp.12-13. ***Akbarnama***, IIIrd 381-82.
7. Abul'Fazl, ***Akbarnama***, IIIrd p. 45-49 and Dastu-ul-Amal, Badsha Nama, or 2026 f, 22b.
8. For a fuller discussion vide Indian Culture, Calcutta, January 1937, pp. 534-545.
9. Abul Fazl, ***Ain-i-Akbari*** III A'in 5 prohibits group assessment it was rare even in the days of anarchy following the decline of central authority.
10. A.N. III, 381 (Add. 27, 247, f. 331b).
11. This appears from Adab-i-Alamgiri, f. 118a.
12. ***Ain-i-Akbari*** III, p.117; Arif Qandhari, 197-8; ***Tabaqat-i-AKbari***, II, 300-301; Badauni, II, 189.
13. Badauni, II, p.189.
14. Agrarian System by Irfan Habib IInd Ed. O.U.P, p. 319.
15. Khulasatus-Siyaq, f. 79b Or. 2026, ff, 33a-34a.
16. Khulasatus-Siyaq, f. 79b Or. 2026, ff, 34a-b. C.f Lahori IInd 247.
17. ***Ain-i-Akbari*** III 4578.
18. Khulasatus-Siyaq, f. 79a, 91b, Or, 2026 ff. 34a 59a-b.
19. For his duties see, ***Ain-i-Akbari*** I, 289 Harkaran 54-56 Nigarnama-i-Munshi, ed, 137; Durr-ul-Ulum, f. 137b.
20. ***Tarikh-i-Tahiri***, Or, 1685 ff, 102b 103b. 18a-119b; ed. 222-23-352.
21. Allahabad, 789.
22. A'in, I, 476; Ma'lumatu-l-Afaq,f, 174a.
23. Agrararian System by Irfan Habib IInd Ed. O.U.P. p 331.
24. Abbas Khan, f, 106 A'in, I, 300.
25. A.N. II, 270 A'in I, 347; Nigarnama-i-Munshi, 91; Hidayat-ul-Qawayed, f. 18b.
26. Agrarian System by Irfan Habib, IInd Ed. O.U.P, p. 3330.
27. ***Ibid.***, p. 333.
28. Moreland's Article in the ***Journal of Royal Asiatic Society***, 1918.
29. ***Ibid.***
30. ***Ibid.***
31. ***Moreland Agrarian System***, pp. 234-37.
32. ***Ibid.***, p. 125.

33. ***Ibid.***, p. 124.
34. ***Ibid.***, p. 126.
35. A.H. Lahouri, Vol., I, pp. 362-64, Mira'y-i-Sikandari, f. 83b, Mandelso, p. 120
36. (***Badshahnama***. II 711-13)
37. Kewal Ram, F. 164 b, Kafiyat-i-Sabajat-i-Mumalik-i-Mahrusah-i-Hindustan, f. 219b.
38. Vide Supra, under Banjar and Chachar Lands.
39. Khafi Khan, p. 757.
40. Cf. Hodivala, Historical Studies in Mughal Numismatic, pp. 235-4.
41. Irfan Habib: ***The Currency System of the Mughal Empire***, Vol. IV, Nos, 1-2, p. 1.
42. ***Ain-i-Akbari*** I, 26, Sher Shah coin was very slightly heavier than Akbar's (Wright, coinage, & c. of the Sultans of Delhi), p. 383.
43. S. Lane-Poole, the Coins of the Mughal Period in Hindustan in the British Museum, p. IXXVI.
44. ***Ain-i-Akbari***, p. 32 Irfan habib ***The Currency System of Mughal Empire***, Vol, IV, Nos, 1-2, p. 3
45. Irfan Habib: ***The Currency System of The Mughal Empire***, Vol, IV Nos, 1-2, p. 3.
46. Irfab Habib: ***The Currency System of the Mughal Empire***, Vol, IV, Nos, 1-2, p. 4.
47. ***Ain-i-Akbari***, p. 26.
48. Ain Razi, Hafi Iqlim, Vol, I, ***Bibliography Indca***, pp., 94-95.
49. Factories, 1618-21, pp, 194, 204. For a letter English reference to the use of Anna in Bengal. Cf. also Moreland, Akbar to Aurangzeb, 331-32.
50. Selected Documents of Shah Jahan's reign, pp. 93-97, 98, 180, 914-5, 216-18, 220. The first of these documents is dated April, 30, 1642, Dast-ur-amal-i-Alamgiri. Ms. B. Madd. 6598, ff. 3a, 17b, written see point 1659, seems to be the first accountancy manual to set out the Anna-rupee scale.
51. Martial, 415, 418. He gives the weight as 11 grains troy, which is exactly 1/6 of the maximum weight of the extant rupees of Aurangzeb 180 troy.
52. ***A'in I***, 25; Or, 1840, f. 135a.
53. Cf. Lane Poole, ***The Coins of the Mughal Emperors in the British Museum***, p. IXXVI.
54. T.J., 96 is ordinary Muhr in British Museum and Indian Museum Collection rise, in the case of the heaviest specimens, to 269 grains.
55. This is the weight given in Or. 1840, f. 135 a.
56. The maximum weight of Aurangzeb's muhr in both the collection is 171 grains.
57. Or, 1840, f. 135a; f K, Ed, f, 6b; Master II, 304.
58. White Heads in ***JABS***, Ns, XXVIII, 96.
59. Irfan Habib: ***The Currency System of the Mughal Empire***, Vol, IV, Nos., 1-2, p. 12.
60. ***Ain-i-Akbari***, I, p. 26
61. Hodiwala Mughal Numismaic, pp. 226.
62. ***Ain-i-Akbari***, I, p. 26
63. Hodiwala Mughal Numismatic, pp. 226.
64. Tavernier, I., 25.

65. ***Ibid.***
66. Tavernier, 1, pp. 15-26, Van Twist, JIH, XVI, 72, 73, 74 for a similar interpretation of English references see Hodiwala, Mughal Numismatics, 140N, and Moreland Akbar to Aurangzeb, p. 331.
67. Mundy, II, 311, Tavernier, 24, says 50-55, but pleasart, p. 29 equates the paisa with as many as 80.
68. Van Twist, tr, by Moreland, ***JIH***, XVI, 72.
69. Irfan Habib Currency System of the Mughal. Vol. IV, p. 13.
70. ***A'in-i-Akbari***, p. 392.
71. Factoris 1665-67, pp. 255, 327-29, Tavernier's 1, 71,
72. ***A'in-i-Akbari***, pp. 25.
73. Irfan Habib the ***Currency System of the Mughal***, Vol IV, No, 1-2, p. 1.
74. British Factories 1618-21, p. 320.
75. Pelsaert, he described the muhr as weighing tola or 12 masha which would suggest that it was Muhr-i-Nurjahani.
76. ***Surat Factories***, 1925-29, pp. 155-56.
77. Peter Mundy, II, p. 290.
78. Manrique Travels, tr. Luard II, p. 129.
79. A.H. Lahuri, ***Padshahnama***, bibliography, Vol. II, p. 259.
80. ***Ibid.***, Vol., II, 396.
81. Tavernier Vol., I, p. 246.
82. ***JRAS***, 1925, pp, 314-16 (W, Foaster Communication) Factories NS, p. 267-8.
83. ***Ain-i-Akbari***, Vol.1, p. 33.
84. ***Ibid.***, p 176.
85. Irfan Habib, ***The Currency System of the Mughal***, Vol. IV, Nos, 1-2, p. 18.
86. Moreland Akbar to Aurangzeb, p. 148.
87. "The English Factories in India (1634-1636)" by William Foster, p. 218.
88. ***Ibid.***, p. 84.
89. ***Travels in India by Tavernier***, Edited by Ball, Vol, I, p. 36.
90. ***Ibid.***, p. 37.
91. The editor preferred the reading Qibti (Egyptian) to Qutbi, p. 267.
92. The Imperial Treasury of the Indian Mughals by Abdul Aziz, p. 285.
93. Imperial Treasury of the Mughal Abdul Aziz, p. 392.
94. ***Ibid.***, p. 94.
95. Ms Mandelso's Travels in Western India, (A.D 1638-39), pp. XV-XVI.
96. ***Ibid.***, p. 281-282

6. Army and Mansabdari System

Mansab

The word mansab is literally "the place where anything is put or erected" (***nasb kardan*** to place fix appoint); and then as a secondary meaning, the state or condition of holding a place, dignity or office. It seems to have been in use in Central Asia before the Mughals descended into Hindustan; and Ross translates it by the vaguer term "privileges". This word mansab is represented by the word rank, as its object was to settle precedence and fix gradation of pay; it did not necessarily employ the exercise of any particular office and meant nothing beyond the fact that the holder was in the employment of the State and bound in return to yield certain services when called upon.

Mansab, was not a term confined solely to the military service; every man in State employ above the position of a common soldier or messanger, whatever the nature of his duties, civil or military, obtained a mansab. In fact, they were for all grades, except the very lowest, only two modes of obtaining support from State funds, a man must either enter its active service as the holder of a mansab or he must petition for a ***madad-i-mua'sh*** (literally, "help to live"), attended on a mosque (***mutawalli*** or ***khadim***), a man of learning and religious life (***darvesh***), a local judge (***qazi***), or an expounder of the Mohammedan law (***mufti***).

The highest ***mansab*** that could be held by a subject, not of the royal house, was that of commander of 7000 men, though in the later and more degenerate times we find a few instances of promotion to 8000 or even 9000. The ***mansab*** of a prince ranged from 7000 upto 50,000 and even higher. In the ***Ain-i-Akbari*** (Blochmann, 248, 249) sixty-six grades are stated, beginning at commanders of 10,000 and ending at those set over ten men.[1]

All the later authorities agree in holding that the lowest officer's mansab was that of twenty men; and these writers record, that there was not more than twenty-seven grades, and beginning with that of 7,000 and ending with that of twenty. In the earlier days of the dynasty, rank was granted with a niggard hand. In Akbar's time the highest rank was that of 5,000 and it was only towards the end of his reign that a few men were promoted to 7,000, while many officers exercised important commands although holding a comparatively low ***mansab***. The great accession of territory in the Dakhin and the incessant wars connected with these acquisitions may account in part for the increase in the number and amount of ***mansabs*** granted by Shah Jahan and Aurangzeb.

The steps of promotion altered as the officer rose in grade. The usual gradation was as follows (***Dastur-ul-Aml***)

From	20	to	100	each rise was by	20
From	100	to	400	each rise was by	50
From	400	to	1000	each rise was by	100
From	1000	to	4000	each rise was by	500
From	4000	to	7000	each rise was by	1000

There is a slight discrepancy between this table and the facts as we find them in practice.

From	20	to	60	a man rose by 10 each time
From	60	to	100	a man rose by 20 each time

It ought to be amended thus to distinguish between the two kinds of rank, the original ***mansab,*** which governed the personal allowances, was known as the ***zat*** rank (zat = body, person, self), and the additional men were the military obligation of a mansabdari was designated by the word sawar (=horseman). Thus a man would be styled "***2500 zat,*** 1000 ***sawar.*** It is said that men below 500 never had ***sawar*** added to their rank.[2]

The entire military organization of the state dependent on what is known as the Mansabdari system. Akbar introduced the Mansabdari system to prevent fraud and embezzlement by his military officers, and to secure the stability of the military organization. During his reign the strict observance of the ***Dagh-o-Tashish*** (branding) regulation[3] ensured conformity between the rank of a ***mansabdar*** and the actual quota of troops maintained by him. But under his successors the institution of some new military distinctions created a wide breach between theory and practice. The institution of the Army and the ***Mansabdari*** System interpenetrated each other, so that the one is unintelligible without the other. These two, again have a far reaching effect on the texture of Mughal Indian society, since the only aristocracy in land was the military peerage graded according to the ***mansab*** and more than half the population in a court town or a camp was composed of soldiers, their dependents and the camp followers–i.e., the 'army'. This will show the great importance of the army from the political as well as the social standpoint.

So we find that the Mansabdari system is the army, the peerage and the civil administration all rolled into one. The mansab, although primarily a military rank, really constituted the term in which official hierarchy and independently social status expressed. A mansab did not by itself imply any particular office. Sometime the enforcement of a mansab was equivalent to mere grant of a source of income to a person by way of recognition it may be, of purely professional services or skill (as those of physician or a poet).

In Akbar's time the highest mansab that could be held by a subject not of the royal house, was that of commander of 1000 men, though in the later and more degenerate times we find a few instances of promotion to 8000 or even 9000.

In Shah Jahan's time, for instance, the usual practice was that where a ***mansabdar*** held ***jagir*** in the ***dagh*** horsemen equivalent in the number to one-third of his horse rank; e.g., an officer with the rank 3000/3000 had in such a case to brand 1000 horse. If however, he was told of to serve in a province of the Empire other than that in which his ***jagir*** was situated, he had to present only one-fourth of his horse rank so that a 4000/4000 officer branded in this case only 1000 horse. At the time of the dispatch of an expedition to Balkh and Badakshan (Rabi II, 1056

A,H.), in view of the difficulties and of the distance of the seat of operations a further concession was made and, it was decided that during that campaign officers need only brand one-fifth : an ***amir*** with 5000/5000 branded on that occasion only 1000 horse[4] (B.N., II, 506).

In its most highly developed form–for instance, in the reign of Shah Jahan- a full ***mansab*** is expressed thus: ***Chahar hazari zat wa si hazar sawar,*** or more briefly, ***Chahar hazari si hazar sawar,*** which means 4000 personal and 3000 horse rank. We will denote it thus: 4000/3000. Or if the ***zat*** and ***sawar*** ranks were equal: (1) ***Chahar hazari zat wa chahar hazar sawar,*** (2) ***Chahar hazari zat wa sawar, or*** (3) ***Chahar hazari chahar hazar sawar***; i.e., 4000 personal and 4000 horse, or 4000/4000 according to our notion. A few peculiarities may be noticed first: (1) The ***zat,*** i.e. personal rank is always whether equal to, or higher than, the ***sawar,*** i.e., horse rank.[5] (2) The order in the lists and consequently the order of precedence follows the zat and not the sawar rank; the former being presumably more important, so that 4000/2000 was considered higher than 3000/3000.

The ***mansab*** is called ***zat,*** i.e. self, because it regulates the allowance for himself (and his household) as distinguished from that for the cavalry enlisted by him.

Zat Rank

The main frame-work of the whole system took shape in the latter half of Akbar's reign. Much of the development took place behind the scenes, as it were; so that we only see glimpse of it wherever, there is an odd mention or a casual notice. But all the time a cast-iron system was being moulded by successive efforts. We get a complete view of it in the A'in, as it stood in XL R.Y. (1003-4 A.H.), when Book II of A'in was completed.[6]

Sawar Rank

The grant of ***sawar*** in addition to ***zat*** rank was an honour. Dr. Paul Horn, 15, suppose, however, that these horsemen were paid out of the ***zat*** allowances. In that case a man who had no ***sawar*** would be better paid than another who was honoured with the addition of ***sawar*** to his ***zat*** rank.

Significance the *zat* and *sawar* "Blochmann"

There is a great divergence of opinion on the significance of the terms ***zat*** and ***sawar***. Blochmann holds that the ***zat*** indicated the number of soldiers a ***mansabdar*** was expected to keep, and the ***sawar*** the actual number maintained by him, and that he drew his salary for the former.[7] But this view is inadmissible for two reasons. First, it defeats the very object of the institution of the ***sawar*** rank; and secondary, there were certain officers who held ***zat*** rank only; and if we accept Blochmann's view they would have to maintain more men than those who held both ***zat*** and the ***sawar*** rank, and thus lower their status.

"Irvine"

"Irvine" thinks that the grant of the ***sawar*** rank was an additional honour, and indicated the actual number of horsemen over and above those of the ***zat***[8] this view is untenable for three reasons. First, if we accept it the total number of the Mughal troops would mount to an incredible figure; secondly, if the honoured officer was expected to maintain an extra number the honour would be more a source of burden to him than real distinction; and thirdly, in some cases the total number of horsemen maintained by a ***mansabdar*** would be greater than that of a prince, which is incredible

Dr. Tripathi

Dr. R. P. Tripathi discusses this question thoroughly and comes to the conclusion that the ***sawar*** rank was an honour for which an officer was paid an extra allowance, without maintaining the number of horsemen indicated by it.[9] In other words the ***sawar*** rank had nothing to do with the actual number, which was regulated by the ***zat*** only. What amount of allowance per head was paid to an officer for his ***sawar*** rank is still a disputed question.

U.N. De

U.N. De rightly maintains that the ***zat*** was the personal rank of the mansabdar and the ***sawar*** rank indicated his military obligation:

Do Aspa Sih Aspa

A further distinction, over and above the ***sawar*** rank, came into existence in the reign of Jahangir. It was to make some proportion or the entire quota proportion of the quota of a ***mansabdar, Do Aspa Sih Aspa.*** It is distinctly mentioned in the ***Padshahnama***[10] that a ***Do Aspa Sih Aspa*** officer had to maintain twice the number of horsemen maintained by a similar officer of the sawar rank.

Thus a commander of 5000 ***zat*** and 5000 ***sawar*** was expected to maintain 300 ***Sih Aspa*** troopers, 600 ***Do Aspa*** troopers and 100 ***Ek Aspa*** troopers. But if his rank was increased to 5000 ***zat*** and 5000 ***sawar*** all ***Do Aspa Sih Aspa,*** he was expected to maintain 600 ***Sih Aspa,*** 1200 ***Do Aspa*** and 200 ***Ek Aspa.*** It should however, be born in mind that there were very few cases in which the entire quota was made ***Do Aspa Sih Aspa.***

Classification

On the basis of the ***zat*** and ***sawar*** rank the ***mansabdars*** (except officers above 5000, who were exempted from this classification) were further classified into three classes. Below 5000, if the ***zat*** and ***sawar*** ranks were equal, an officer belonged to the first class; if the ***sawar*** rank was half or more than half, he belonged to the second class; but if the ***sawar*** rank was less than half, he belonged to the third.[11]

Zat was the personal rank of the ***mansabdar,*** by which his position and status was determined in the imperial service. He received a fixed salary as per his mansab. ***Sawar*** was the ***mansabdars*** military obligation.

Dah-Bist Principle

20 mansabadar were required to maintain 10 tabinan and 20 horses of different descriptions:-

Contingent

3 Sih Aspa	3 × 3=9
4 Doh Aspa	4 × 2=8
3 Yok Aspa	3 × 1=3

10 Tabinan	**20 Horses**
Salary	
Sih Aspa	1000 Dams per month
Do Aspa	800 Dams per month
Yok Aspa	600 Dams per month
	96000 Dams per month

Gradation Ranks

From 3000 ***zat*** to 7000 ***zat*** the grade of ranks varied by 1000. There was only one officer who held the rank of 3500. From one thousand to two thousand five hundred, the scale varied by 500 and below one thousand to 500 it varied by 100. It appears that 500 was the lowest distinction. It was very widespread and in this reign the largest number of ***mansabdars*** held this rank. [12]

Distinctions

Besides the ***zat*** and ***sawar*** ranks there were other distinctions also, which were conferred on deserving officers. The ***tuma-o-tugh,*** which was ordinarily reserved for the princes, could also be conferred on a ***mansabdar*** of not less than 7000 ***zat, sawar.***[13] Standard and drums were also meant for higher officers.[14]

Reviews

Mansabdar's had to bring their contingents for review at those who held a ***jagir*** brought them once a year and were allowed six months as a period of grace. But the ***Naqdi*** or those who received their salary in cash, brought their contingents every six months and were allowed only two months as a period of grace.[15]

Mansab and Imperial Policy under Shah Jahan

It is now a by word in studies of the Mughal nobility, that at least, from 1575 to 1707, the ***mansabs*** granted and held are the most reliable index of the size and composition of the ruling class of the Mughal Empire. The position not only of individuals but whole sections has been measured by ***mansab*** statistics, whether it is Beni Prasad speaking of the promotions of the ***Noor Jahan Junta*** or S.R. Sharma attempting a measurement of the Hindu Nobility.

In these respect, Shah Jahan's reigns offer much sounder evidence. The entire (or almost the entire) reign is covered by three detailed official chronicles, the Badshahnamas of Qazwini (the first decade)[16] of Lahauri (the first and second decade)[17] and of waris (the third decade)[18] these chronicles enter almost every important mansab promotion or reduction, as well as the deaths or dismissals. Lahauri and Waris provide us with lists of all mansab holders of 500 ***zat*** and above, with their sawar ranks, and deaths or dismissals of such nobles as took place within the respective decades, with years thereof. This decennial information enables us, as we shall see, to cross-check the information in the main narratives of the chronicles.

The fact that such wealth of information has existed in the chronicles of Shah Jahan's reign has already attracted the attention of individual historians. Irfan Habib has tried to calculate the actual increase in total ***mansabs*** between Akbar's death and the 10th year of Shah Jahan's reign.[19] A.J. Qaisar has similarly attempted a calculation of the distribution of revenue-resources of the Mughal Empire among the various ranks of the nobility.[20] Their purposes were well served by the lists of the 10th mansab information, scattered in the pages of these chronicles can be used to answer (or at any rate, attempt to answer) a number of other questions. To answer these and similar other questions, we must prepare a full annual records of mansab grants.

1. For the first ten years, we have two separate official accounts of Qazwini and Lahauri, they sometimes diverge but Athar Ali preferred Lahauri, since he is as a rule more detailed. However, Qazwini supplies some promotions, which Lahauri omits.

He records some grants of mansab to the 'Deccani' nobles, which Lahauri omits because the nobles lately defected. Qazwini is also more elaborate in respect of deaths and demotions. In all such cases Athar Ali has of course supplemented Lahauri's information with Qazwini's.

2. Lahauri has a habit of often giving not the actual mansab promotion (***as asl-o izafa***). This leads us into difficulty, when there is no reference in previous pages to the mansab held by the officer earlier. This is especially so, where the officer concerned

> was obviously holding a rank of less than 500 zat since it is not the unusual practice of these official chronicles to refer to mansabs of officials of lower ranks.

In all such cases Athar Ali has restored to a simple device for the second decade of Shah Jahan's reign, however, there is a reference to the promotion on the basis of ***asl-o-izafa***, and checked the list of the 10th year. If his name is on that list, he deducted the old rank from the new rank and so calculated the promotion. If the name is missing from that list, which is confined to ***mansabdars*** of 500 zat and above only, Athar Ali assumed that in the 10th year the officer was either not in service, or, if in service, his rank was below 500 ***zat***, 500 ***sawar*** (since sawar rank does not normally exceed the zat rank). He accordingly assumed that the promotion was larger than the differences between the mansab held as ***asl-o-izafa*** (after promotion) and 500 ***zat***/500 ***sawar***. A promotion of this magnitude has been credited to the officer separately from the annual figures.

Since Waris invariably gives the precise promotion, this problem does not trouble us in the third decade. On the other hand during the first decade the problem is insoluble because, we do not have a list of mansabdars at the beginning of Shah Jahan's reign, to which we could refer in the same way as we can to the list of 10th year. Athar Ali has therefore, no option but only to total up the mansab promotion which are either specified or deducible from two separate statements about the mansabs of individual persons and to ignore all the other ***asl-o-izafa*** references. This means that our information for the first decade is much less complete than for the second and third decade and is not also equally reliable index.

Since all the three chronicles confined there references as a rule to ***mansabdars*** of 500 zat and above any statistics based on their information will be incomplete. Howfar, incomplete is another question? In the 28th century, Lahauri calculated the strength of cavalry of the mansab holders at 1,85000 hypothetically basis of the one-forth value. That is the total of sawar mansabs at that time must have been 7,40,000 [21] his list of the same year shows that those holding the ranks of 500 zat and above held in the aggregate, 5, 21,000 sawars. [22] In other words, the listed category held 70.4% of all ***sawar mansabs***. Therefore, we can be surely said that our mansab information at least covers 70%

of the mansabs held and we may be allowed to assume that the trends noticeable in this sector were probably true for mansabs in general. Athar Ali adopted the ***Hijary Years Moharram to Moharram*** for convenience and calculated all the mansab promotions recorded, arranged year-wise. The column for mansab reduction includes succession of mansabs by deaths, dismissals or retirements.

Mansab Grants/Promotions & Reductions

A. FIRST DECADE

Year	*Promotion*		*Reduction*		*Net*	*Promotions/ Reductions*
1037	48,500/	55,050	15,000/	14,500	33,500/	40,550
1038	13,900/	10,400	7,500/	4,750	6,400/	5,650
1039	56,500/	50,050	34,300/	21,700	21,700/	28,350
1040	45,800/	34,220	61,600/	48,000	–15,800/	–13,780
1041	26,000/	35,100	62,400/	44,600	–36,400/	–9,500
1042	11,500/	20,300	47,800/	40,255	–36,300/	9,955
1043	7,000/	4,7002	4,100/	16,920	–17,100/	–12,220
1044	53,600/	74,000	28,100/	28,880	25,500/	45,120
1045	13,700/	30,450	30,700/	22,650	–17,000/	+7,800
1046	19,000/	23,650	23,400/	27,500	–4,400/	–3,850
	2,95,500/	3,37,920	3,35,400/	2,69,755	-39,900/	+68,165

B. SECOND DECADE

Year	*Promotion*		*Reduction*		*Net*	*Promotions/ Reductions*
1047	28,200/	46,150	23,600/	13,650	4,600/	27,500
1048	43,700/	25,900	19,700/	17,900	24,000/	8,000
1049	9,200/	45,700	36,200/	26,915	-27,000/	18,785
1050	13,200/	26,650	27,600/	20,100	-14,400/	6,550
1051	17,800/	33,900	26,500/	27,350	-8,700/	6,550
1052	19,300/	27,000	21,400/	18,320	-2, 00/	8,680
1053	14,100/	19,600	10,400/	8,700	3,700/	12,900
1054	2,300/	29,130	50,200/	34,550	-27,900/	-5,420
1055	32,800/	40,050	33,400/	39,600	-600/	450
1056	45,100/	50,100	19,100/	14,000	35,000/	36,100
	2,54,700/	3,44,180	2,68,100/	2,24,085	-13,400/	1,20,095

C. THIRD DECADE

Year	*Promotion*		*Reduction*		*Net*	*Promotions/ Reductions*
1057	26,900/	21,750	51,200/	37,570	-24,300/	-15,820
1058	37,700/	36,950	34,900/	25,000	2,800/	11,950
1059	29,100/	54,770	20,500/	17,350	8,600/	37,420
1060	14,400/	9,700	31,700/	29,050	-17,300/	-19,350
1061	20,000/	18,160	20,700/	19,300	-00,700/	- 1,140
1062	44,500/	27,300	42,700/	46,500	+1,800/	-19,200
1063	29,100/	21,470	18,500/	12650	10,600/	8,820
1064	33,200/	23,750	16,100/	15,950	17,100/	7,800
1065	24,000/	17,100	13,800/	11,550	10,200/	5,550
1066	64,500/	47,380	11,800/	7,830	52,700/	39,55
	3,23,400/	2,78,330	2,61,900/	2,22,750	61,500/	55,580

Before set out to offer any interpretation of these figures, it can be checked how accurate they are likely to be. This can be done by checking the decennial results of annual tables, with the changes in the total mansab in the 2nd and 3rd decades as deducted from comparison of the decennial list in Lahauri and Waris.

When the mansab evidence taken from the narrative of the first decade, what strikes us is the moderate scales of promotions granted by Shah Jahan zat promotion in the first two years of his reign inspite of his considerable political difficulties in the beginning. Whereas, Aurangzeb had granted a net enhancement of 89,000 ***zat*** in his first two regional year. Shah Jahan granted only 39,900 in the net increase in ***sawar*** mansab (46,200) in Shah Jahan's first two years did not fall much beyond the net increase of ***sawar*** granted by Aurangzeb in his first two years.[23] Does it mean that Shah Jahan was inclined to enhance the sawar mansab (requiring maintenance of larger military contingents), while not willing to increase the ***zat*** mansab, which involved only an increase in the personal pay of the ***mansabdars.*** In fact, over the entire first decade the mansab statistics show great discrepancy between the trend in the ***zat*** and ***sawar*** ranks.

Another interesting feature of the first decade is that military ventures are immediately reflected in the mansab promotions. In 1039

(1629-30), ***Khan-i-Jahan*** rebelled; and in 1044 (1634-35) Jhujar Singh. These are besides the first a regnal year, the peak years for net grant of ***zat*** and ***sawar*** mansabs.

Passing on to the second decade, we find from the comparison of the list of the 10th and 20th years that zat mansabs increased by 40,000 while the sawars went up by 86,000. The primacy of sawar enhancements over zat was thus still being maintained. Indeed the figures calculated from Lahauri's narrative; show this still more sharply; a net enhancement of 2,100 in zat as against 1,22,595 in sawar. As for the political events, the Balkh campaign (1646-47 A.D.) found its reflection in the highest figures for net zat and sawar enhancements in 1056 A.H. (1646-47 A.D.) during the entire decade.

The pattern changes radically in the 3rd decade zat enhancement now dramatically take primacy. The comparison of the lists of 20th and 30th years shows that there were net zat enhancements of 1,33,350 as against 53,625 sawars. It is difficult to explain why Shah Jahan's mansab policy changed in the third decade. It is possible, however, to see in it a symptom of the crisis, which ultimately came with the war of succession mansabs were now being given not to increase or maintain military strength but to win support for functional purposes (principally, perhaps, for strengthening Dara Shikoh's position).

ALLOWANCES, SALARIES, AND IN'ÁMS

The princes had daily allowances before they were old enough to receive a ***mansab***. At the time of Shah Jahan's coronation the daily allowances of his sons were fixed as follows:

Dara Shikoh	Rs. 1,000
Shah Shuja	Rs. 750
Aurangzeb	Rs. 500.
Murad Baksh	Rs. 250. [24]

In the ensuring tables we give some mansabs and their corresponding salaries and as some of the rank-holders had different ranks and salaries at different times, the period or year has also been indicated.

PRINCES

Rank-holder	*Time*	*Rank*	*Salary p,a.*
Dara Shikoh	II Decade	20,000/20,000 (10,0002-3h)	40 crore dams=1 crore Rs
Dara Shikoh	1067 A.H.	20,000/20,000 (10,0002-3h)	60 crore dams=1½crore Rs.
Dara Shikoh	1068 A.H.	20,000/20,000 (10,0002-3h)	83 crore dams=2,07, 50,000 Rs.[2]
Shah Shikoh	II Decade	15,000/10,000 (8,000 2-3h)	24 crore dams=60 lakh Rs.
Aurangzeb	II Decade	15,000/10,000 (8,000 2-3h)	24 crore dams=60 lakh Rs.
Murad Baksh	II Decade	12,000/9,000 (8,000 2-3h)	12 crore dams=30 lakh Rs.
Murad Baksh	1064 A.H.	15,000/10,000 (500 2-3h)	16 crore dams=40 lakh Rs.

These emoluments include not only the zat and sawar rank salaries but also in many cases ***in'am*** or gratuity, which is often distinctly stated as such. It came upto a tidy amount in many cases: in case of Prince Dara Shikoh, for instance, it went up, towards the end, to 20 crore ***dams.***[25]

NOBLES

No.	*Rank-holder*	*Time*	*Rank*	*Salary p.a.*
1	Yaminud-Daula & II, 258 Asaf Khan	I & II Decade	9,000/9,000(2-3h)	16.20 crore dams= 40,5000 Rs.
2	Khan Dauran Bahadur Nusrat Jang	I Decade	6,000/6,000(2-3h)	10.80 crore dams = 27 lakh of Rs
		II Decade (2-3h)	7,000,/7000(5,000)	12 crore dams = 30 lakh Rs.
3	Ali Mardan Khan Amirul-Umara	II & III Decade (2-3h)	7,000,/7000(5,000)	12 crore dams = 30 lakh Rs.
4	Allami Sa'dullah Khan	III Decade	7,000,/7000	12 crore dams = 30 lakh Rs.
	"	1060 A.H.	7,000,/7000 (2-3h)	12 crore dams = 30 lakh Rs.
		or	7,000,/7000 (5,000 2-3h)	lakh Rs.

In the case of the Princes, the salaries even without the ***in'ams***, are far in excess of what we can calculate for their ***mansabs***. But then this was a privileged class and considerable latitude seems to have been allowed. As regard the nobles, the pay corresponds fairly accurately to the ***mansab***. We need only examine one case by way of illustration. The pay of the rank 7,000/7000 (5,000 2-3h.), which was enjoyed by several nobles of the highest rank in the third decade, may be calculated as follows:-

Zat Rank Salary 1.40 crore ***dams***

Sawar Rank Salary (10,000 +2,000, i.e. 12,000 troopers at 8,000 ***dams*** each). 9.60 crore "

11 crore ***dams***

these ***amirs*** drew 1 crore ***dams*** as ***in'am*** in addition, their total emoluments becoming 12 crore s. For this purpose zat rank enhancements were not only sufficient but requisite. The following are the tables of the zat and sawar under Shah Jahan.

1628-36

	Iranis	*Turanis*	*Afghans*	*Indian Muslims*	*Other Muslims*	*Rajput*	*Marathas*	*Other Hindus*	*Total*
Zat	43,900	26,300	7000	11,500	3000	15,500	2500		1,09,700
Sawar	63,400	35,150	14,400	17,750	41,00	13,150	1550		1,49,500

1637-41

	Iranis	*Turanis*	*Afghans*	*Indian Muslims*	*Other Muslims*	*Rajput*	*Marathas*	*Other Hindus*	*Total*
Zat	15,200	10,500	3700	700	2500	5100		100	37,800
Sawar	20,750	19,050	7,000	76,000	2800	7900		-	65,100

1642-58

	Iranis	*Turanis*	*Afghans*	*Indian Muslims*	*Other Muslims*	*Rajput*	*Marathas*	*Other Hindus*	*Total*
Zat	88,500	56,300	13,300	25,000	5100	42,800	1000	500	2,32,500
Sawar	95,280	57,000	16,500	30,800	4330	51,600	500	1200	2,57,210

Irani's

It emerges that the share of Iranis in the total award of the mansab remained unsurpassed from the beginning till the end. The foremost reason for the favourable attitude towards this group was its commendable role in the brief succession. The Irani's sincerity, devotion and submission. Alongwith their efficiency both in the battlefield and the administrative offices, have also been pointed out earlier to be the cause of their larger share in mansab figures. In this regard, one should also keep the fact in mind that the Iranis formed a single largest group among the Jahangir nobles. [26]

In view of this fact and their attitude towards the crown, Shah Jahan had practically no ground to change the policy of favour to this group. It may also be pointed out that the Iranis usually held a larger share in sawar mansab, except the last phase where their proportion becomes the same in both *zat* and sawar mansabs, 33 percent of the total sawar mansab. Since the Iranis had powered a higher degree of dependability from the days of Akbar, Shah Jahan too confirmed his faith in them. That is probably why they held almost 33 percent of the total sawar mansab under their control. However, the total sawar mansab declined in the third phase.

A. Proportion of Iranis Among the Mansabdars of Shah Jahan

Mansab	*Total*	*Iranis*
1628-36		
5000 zat and above	38	14
3000 to 4500 zat	79	21
1000 to 2700 zat	225	58
Grand Total	342	93
1637-41		
5000 zat and above	27	12
3000 to 4500 zat	54	18
1000 to 2700 zat	174	45
Grand Total	255	75
1642-58		
5000 zat and above	38	15
3000 to 4500 zat	81	23
1000 to 2700 zat	329	94
Grand Total	448	132

Turanis

Turanis got lesser opportunities in military expeditions[27] as well as administrative offices.[28] That is probably why they shared a lesser proportion in the total mansab award,[29] as is evident from the figures in table. It was less than half the share of the Iranis. But a notable rise in the proportion of the Turanis may be seen in the second phase. Inspite of the decline in the total award of mansabs, they improved in both zat and sawar rank and emerged as the second-largest group in the nobility after the Iranis.

B. Proportion of Turanis Among the Mansabdars of Shah Jahan

Mansab	*Total*	*Turanis*
1628-36		
5000 zat and above	38	6
3000 to 4500 zat	79	12
1000to 2700 zat	225	35
Grand Total	342	53
1637-41		
5000 zat and above	27	7
3000 to 4500 zat	54	10
1000 to 2700 zat	174	33
Grand Total	255	50
1642-58		
5000 zat and above	38	10
3000 to 4500 zat	81	17
1000 to 2700 zat	329	69
Grand Total	448	96

Afghans

The Afghan enjoyed almost 9 percent of the total zat and the 10 percent of the total sawar mansab. These figures suggest the continuation of Jhahangir's favourable policy inspite of the rebellion of ***Khane-e-Jahan***[30] from table, it emerges that their share in the total zat falls from 9 percent (of the proceeding phase) to almost 7 percent. Their decline in the total sawar mansab is still more sharp. From 10 percent they fall to almost 6.5 percent of the total award of sawar mansabs. This confirms the doubt that Shah Jahan had become suspicious. Therefore, he tried to curtail their power, which rested mainly in sawar mansab. Hence the greater reduction in their share of sawars.[31] However, the crown and the Afghan nobility, being interdependent upon each other, tried to improve the condition Shah Jahan by giving them opportunities, and the Afghans by proving their loyalty. As said earlier, in the ***Balkh-Badakshan*** expeditions and later on in Qandhar, they were given adequate representation,[32] and served the crown with all sincerity. This rise of the Afghans in the last phase highlights the feature of the interdependence between the crown and the nobility, simultaneously; it confirms that the rebellion of ***Khan-e-Jahan*** Lodhi did not cause any permanent breach between Shah Jahan and the Afgahns.

C. Proportion of Afhgans Among the Mansabdars of Shah Jahan

Mansab	*Total*	*Afghans*
1628-36		
5000 zat and above	38	2
3000 to 4500 zat	79	9
1000 to 2700 zat	225	26
Grand Total	342	37
1637-41		
5000 zat and above	27	1
3000 to 4500 zat	54	2
1000 to 2700 zat	174	21
Grand Total	255	24
1642-58		
5000 zat and above	38	1
3000 to 4500 zat	81	8
1000 to 2700 zat	329	29
Grand Total	448	38

Indian Muslims

Indian Muslim's share in mansab awards simply confirms their enviable position. The figures in table suggest a constant rise in their proportion in both zat and sawar ranks. More important is the fact that their share in the sawar mansab was never less than their share in the zat mansab. In 1637-41, which was the period of universal decline, Indian Muslims in fact gained in sawar mansab. So it may said to be that after the Turanis, Indian Muslims were the recipients of special imperial favours. This favourable attitude towards Indian Muslim was the result of their sincerity and devotion to the Mughal crown at all critical moments. From the battlefield to administrative jobs in almost all capacities, they proved their worth and were marked with special favour.[33] Hence their rising proportion in mansab awards was the reflection of their services, which confirmed them as confident and reliable servants of the crown.

D. Proportion of Indian Muslims Among the Mansabdars of Shah Jahan

Mansab	*Total*	*Indian Muslims*
1628-36		
5000 zat and above	38	2
3000 to 4500 zat	79	6
1000 to 2700 zat	225	24
Grand Total	342	32
1637-41		
5000 zat and above	27	2
3000 to 4500 zat	54	5
1000 to 2700 zat	174	21
Grand Total	255	28
1642-58		
5000 zat and above	38	5
3000 to 4500 zat	81	5
1000 to 2700 zat	329	49
Grand Total	448	59

Rajputs

As a keynote of state policy, the Rajputs were always kept in good proportion throughout Shahjahan's reign. Their share in the total mansab grant remains almost the same, inspite of some notable fluctuation in the total mansab figures in table E. the gradual rise in their proportion in these promotion figures from the first to the last phase again confirms Shah Jahan's faith in this group. This position of confidence, which the Rajputs enjoyed throughout this period, was mainly due to their excellence military services and due to the goodwill they earned by serving the Mughal crown rising above racial and religious considerations. Their active co-operation and solid support to the state, not only against the Persians.[34] Uzbeks[35] and others,[36] but also against their own racial members,[37] who rebelled against the crown, are enough to justify their high proportion in the total mansab figures of various phases of Shah Jahan's reign.

E. Proportion of Rajputs Among the Mansabdars of Shah Jahan

Mansab	*Total*	*Rajputs*
1628-36		
5000 zat and above	38	6
3000 to 4500 zat	79	12
1000 to 2700 zat	225	35
Grand Total	342	53
1637-41		
5000 zat and above	27	4
3000 to 4500 zat	54	8
1000 to 2700 zat	174	29
Grand Total	255	41
1642-58		
5000 zat and above	38	6
3000 to 4500 zat	81	15
1000 to 2700 zat	329	53
Grand Total	448	74

Marathas

During the first phase, therefore, almost 12 percent of the total zat and 11 percent of the total sawar mansab was held by them. The extraordinary favour shown to this group however, started fading away with the settlement of Deccan affairs.

The rise or decline in the share of the nobles in total mansab awards was closely linked with the changing political conditions and with their political and military utility for the state. Racial and religious factors, generally, did not occupy a pivotal place in regulating the proportion of the noble in the total mansab figures. It was basically the quality and period of service which determined the fortunes of mansabdars.

F. Proportion of Marathas Among the Mansabdars of Shah Jahan

Mansab	*1628-36*		*1637-41*		*1642-58*	
	Total	*Marathas*	*Total*	*Marathas*	*Total*	*Marathas*
5000 zat and above	38	6	27	1	38	1
3000 to 4500 zat	79	9	54	6	81	6
1000 to 2700 zat	225	17	174	12	329	9
Grand Total	342	32	255	19	448	16

Zamindar

Shah Jahan's favourable policy towards the Rajput zamindar is further confirmed from a constant rise in their share in both zat and sawar mansab from the beginning till the end of his reign. In the first phase they held more than one-half of the total zat and sawar award given to the zamindars. In the succeeding phase, inspite of decline in the mansab figures, the share of Rajput zamindars in the sawar mansab rose to more than 66 percent of the total sawar mansab of zamindars. The last phase shows an even more favourable trend. In which their share in the total zat and sawar mansab of zamindars rose to more than 67 percent, it should also be noted that the Rajput zamindars held a higher proportion in sawar mansab than in zat. This confirms their position vis-à-vis the crown; this faith was never shaken even though there was some problem raised by them in every phase.

This favourable attitude was obviously because of the maintenance of the good traditions of the past both by the Rajput zamindars and the Mughal crown. The figures given earlier also highlighted Shah Jahan's favourable inclination towards the Indian Muslim zamindars. Although there can be no comparison between them and the Rajputs, the fact remains that from just a marginal position in the first phase, they made notable progress in the second and third phases. Both in zat and sawar mansabs, their share almost doubled what they held in the first phase.

G. Share of Zamindars in the Total Mansab

Rajput	*Marathas*	*Indian*	*Muslims*	*Afghans*	*Total*
		1628-36			
Zat	1,12,500	92,500	3500	2000	2,10,500
Sawar	81,500	72,400	2200	1000	1,56,700
		1637-41			
Zat	75,000	35,000	4000	2000	1,16,000
Sawar	61,700	21,300	2900	1000	86,900
		1642-58			
Zat	1,38,000	29,500	7500	2000	1,77,000
Sawar	1,20,900	16,900	5900	1000	1,44,700

It may be said that Shah Jahan's policy towards the zamindars was based mainly upon the attitude of various groups within his faction. In the case of those who had given the impression of loyalty and devotion, he reaffirmed his faith and favoured the individuals and their descendents like the Rajputs. However, in the case of defaults like the Marathas, he kept trying new people. The nominal share of Afghans remained the privilege of non-khanazads. The higher proportion of khanazad zamindars in the total award of zamindars is due to the high figures of Rajputs. In other words, khanazad Rajputs occupied the bulk of the share of zamindars in both zat and sawar mansabs during all the three phases of Shah Jahan's period, zat and mansab, which confirms the higher degree of trust and confidence, reposed in Rajput khanazads among the zamindars.

The zat and sawar ranks still continued but it is positively certain that the figures of the rank did not imply that a particular manslaughter kept the number prescribed by his mansab. To check fraudulent practices Shah Jahan revised the branding (dagh) regulations. An officer in the subah to which he was appointed was required to have 1/3rd of his horses branded, and if he was deputed on state duty in another province in Hindustan ¼, i.e. in the first case a mansabdar holding a rank of 3000 zat and 3000 sawar was required to get 1000 horses branded and in the second case only 750. The number to be branded in the case of officers who were sent to Balkh-Badakshan in time of war fixed at 1/5 owing to the difficulties of the journey and the rigours of the climate.

According to the Abdul Hamid Lahauri the imperial army in 1648 consisted of 200,000 cavalry, 8000 mansabdars, 7,000 Ahdis or gentleman troopers, 40,000 foot musketeers and artillery men and 185,000 cavalry men under the princes and noble, making a total of 4,40,000. Besides these there were troops in the parganah under the command of the faujdars, kroris and amils and therefore the strength of the royal army must have been considerably greater than the figure stated above. The various branches of the army continued to work as before, and there was no dearth of fighting material and during the Qandhar campaign special effort were made to secure it by the government. Dara carried with him to Qandhar a large army consisting of 4 heavy guns, 30,000 iron shots, great and small, 1500 mans of gunpowder, 5000 pakhalis, 3000 ahadis, 60 war elephants and a great number of banjaras for transport. Though numerically the army of Shah Jahan, was very large its efficiency was by no means proportionate to its numbers is shown by its repeated failures against Qandhar and the disaster that followed the Balkh campaign.[38]

Mnasab Salary Scales under Jahangir and Shah Jahan

In an important article, W.H. Moreland argued that the salaries sanctioned for mansabs or ranks were radically scaled down by Shah Jahan immediately after his accession in 1628. Besides two general statements in the English East India Company's records, from which this could be inferred, he appealed to the pay-scales established by him from a ***farman*** of Shahjahan, issued in 1630, where the salaries of the ranks "were substantially" reduced and scale was enforced in Aurangzeb's reign.[39] Here the ***dhat*** rank salaries are in accordance with the scale enforced at Jahangir's accession 1605 which in turned was a slightly revised version of the scale of that salary 1595 set out in A-in-i-Akbari[40] where after this collection gives us the new schedule of Shah Jahan issued in the 14th regnal year (1641).[41] Of these the crucial document is a long one belonging to the 8th regnal year (1635), which furnishes full details of fixation of pay including direct statements of dhat-ranks.[42]

Dhat Salary

Rupees Per Month
1605Schedule Moreland's "1630"

Dhat Rank	*Class*	*A'in*	*(Class 1 Only)*	*1634-38*	*Corrected*
200	II	950	900	—	950
200	III	900	900	—	850
150	III	800	800	—	770
100	II	600	600	—	600
80	III	350	410(?)	370	370
50	III	230	250	—	227.2

That Moreland should yet have found his erroneous results based on net pay in 1630 to be close enough to the later standard scale is a matter of some interest; what it must lead us to ask is whether in respect of the Dhat-ranks even the 1641 schedule and all later schedules essentially repeating its scales represent a substantial reduction of pay at all. But before we take up this question, let us marshall our evidence on the sawar rank pay as well.

During Akbar's reign sawar-payments appear to have been in two stages, ***bar'awurdi***, a standard initial payment, and ***daghi***, the final payment fixed on contingent actually brought to be branded.[43] Later on, the ***bar'awardi*** rate alone remained as the standard rate for the sawar-rank. The Ain-i-Akbari records the ***bar'awardi*** rates as Rs. 25/-

per sawar for Turani and Irani commanders and Rs. 20/- for Indian commanders.[44] But in the 40th regnal year these ("monthly ***bar'awardi*** rates") were decree cased to be as follows: Mughal, Afghan and Indian: ***Sih-Aspah,*** 1000 ***dams; Do-Aspah,*** 800 ***dams;*** and ***Yak-aspah,*** 600 ***dams.*** The Rajput to draw 800 dams under the first and 600 dams under the second,"[45] If we interpret this by the formula used in the standard schedule of 1641, then the rate for the ***yak-aspah*** alone determined the ***bar'awardi*** rate for ordinary ***sawar-rank,*** while the other categories involved a calculation of a higher rate for special contingents later made into the ***do-aspah sih-aspah*** rank.[46]

The latter calculation was made on the basis of a standard contingent of a 3 ***sih-aspah,*** 4 ***do-aspah,*** and 3 ***yak-aspah*** given in the Ain-i-Akbari and repeated in the 1641 schedule.[47] If so, the rate per unit or ordinary ***sawar-rank*** for all noble was just 600 ***dams*** (Rs. 15/-) per month; but for the higher rank it was 800 ***dams*** (Rs. 20/-) for all nobles, except the Rajput for whom it was 660 ***dams*** (Rs. 16.50) only.[48]

Moreland's 1630 ***farman*** again shows the rate to be in conformity with the 1605 schedule, because it yields 8,800 ***dams*** per unit of ***sawar-rank*** per annum.[49] The pay statements in the SDSR continue to give the same rate: the monthly rate is at 800 ***dams*** per month and all calculations of monthly pay made accordingly. The conversion into the annual claimed is achieved by multiplying the monthly sum by 11 to allow for irmas (***siwa-i-hissah-i-irmas***). So that in effect the annual pay per unit of ***sawar-rank*** was 8,800 ***dams.***[50]

The last documents where the annual rate of 8,800 dams is followed belong to 1638.[51] The second of these documents, of December 1638-January 1639, enables us to date in the schedule (***bina bar tafawut-i-dastur al-amal***) involved a reduction in the total pay claim of a mansabdar of 100 ***dhat,*** 20 ***sawar,*** of the sum of 14,200 ***dams.*** This would have happened only if (a) the ***dhat*** salary was now changed to 1,80,000 ***dams*** given in the 1641 schedule as the dhat until then in force for 100 ***dhat*** Class III, and (b) the ***sawar*** pay was reduced from 8,000 ***dams,*** the new rate confirmed in the 1641 schedule.[52] The sole reduction in the rate of the sawar-rank after Akbar would then appear to have been decreased in 1638, and this was a reduction by one-eleventh only.

As for the ***do-aspah sih-aspah*** rank the payment of it by the 1641 schedule was double than that of sawar-rank, being 16,000 ***dams***; the rate was exactly double that of the ***sawar-rank*** ordinary (***bar-awardi***).[53] the difference between the two rates was thus larger than under Jahangir; but unless a document giving the rate of ***sih-aspah do-aspah*** rank before 1638 turns up, it would be difficult to say what rate Shah Jahan had followed for that rank before the new sawar-rate came into force in 1638. Lahauri, indeed, says under the 1st regnal year (1628), while describing the award of a ***do-aspah, sih-aspah*** rank, that "the pay for such rank is double than that of the ordinary ***yak-aspah.***" But this cannot be construed to mean necessarily an earlier rate of 17,600 ***dams*** (8,800×2) for ***do-aspah, sih-aspah***, since Lahauri may simply have in mind what the rate was when he himself was writing, which was so rare the rates assigned to it possessed relatively minor financial significance.

In a pay statement of December 1638-January 1639,[54] the crucial evidence of the shift from the 1605 schedule to the new one; for here the hold ***dhat*** pay of Rs. 540/- per month for 100 ***dhat***, III, is replaced by 1,80,000 ***dams*** per annum, assigned to the first version of the new scales; in the 1611 schedule. If we find also calculates at the new ***sawar-rate*** of 8,000 ***dams*** per annum instead of 800 ***dams*** per month. The basic change must then have been decreased by the latter half of 1638.

For the sawar pay, the 1641 schedule lays down the annual rate of 8,000 ***dams*** (***bar'awardi***) while for the ***do-aspah, Sih-aspah*** rank it lays out an elaborate formula, giving for 10 sawars the composition 3 ***sih-aspahs*** (24,000 ***dams*** each), 4 ***do-aspahs*** (16,000 ***dams*** each) and 3 ***yak-aspahs*** (8,000 ***dams*** each), giving 160,000 ***dams*** for 10 sawars and so by inference 16,000 ***dams*** per unit of ***sawar-rank*** converted into ***do-aspah, sih-aspah.***[55] The rate of 8,000 ***dams*** for each unit of sawar rank is applied rigorously in all pay-statements after 1641, including those from SDSR already cited for establishing ***dhat*** salaries. We have also seen from a pay-statement of 1638-39 that the rate must have come into effect before the end of 1638. As for the ***do-aspah, sih-aspah*** rank the rate of 16,000 ***dams*** is applied in a pay-statement of 1645, but in a special conventional form. The *sawar*-rank in this case was "1,000 sawar of which 200 sawar ***do-aspah, sih-aspah.***" The rate of 8,000 ***dams*** is then applied to the entire 1,000 treated as to 200 ***do-aspah, sih-aspah.***[56] The result is the same if the bar'awardi rate had been applied to 800 sawar, and the double rate (16,000 ***dams***) to the 200 ***do-aspah sih-aspah.***

The conclusion may be summed up as follows:

1. The ***dhat*** pay scales of 1595 (the Ain-i-Akbari) and 1605 continued in effect until 1638.
2. The sawar pay, at 800 ***dams*** per month for each unit of sawar rank, in force in 1605 also remained in effect until 1638.
3. The dhat and sawar pay before 1638 was made out for only 11 months, the twelfth month being continued as ***irmas.*** Under Akbar some mounts were given to mansab-holders in lieu of ***irmans***; but there is yet no evidence that this was done under Jahangir and Shah Jahan.
4. A further deduction ***chawatha-i-khasah,*** was made from the annual ***dhat*** pay (less ***irmans***).
5. The deduction known as ***rasad-i-khurak-ifilan*** probably originated well before 1615 and continued after 1638/1641 under the name of ***khurak-i-khasah*** deduction were done away with and the ***dhat*** pay-scales were re-scheduled.
6. Under the new schedules of 1638/1641 there was a net reduction of less than 10% on ***dhat*** pay and of 9% on the sawar pay.
7. Under the new schedule of 1638/1641 there was a net reduction less than 10 percent of dhat pay and of 9 percent on the sawar pay.

Abul Fazl has been generous enough to give us full information about the salary of a mansabdar of 100 zat. The monthly salary of an officer with 100/100 rank he says is Rs. 700, while that of a rank-holder of 100/0 (who is generally counted as a ***dakhili***)[57] is Rs. 500. For every increase of 10 in the horse rank, the officer gets an addition of Rs.20 to his monthly salary. So it can be constructed the following scale.

Mansab	*Monthly Pay in Rs.*	*Class*
100/100	700	I
100/90	280	II
100/80	660	II
100/70	640	II
100/60	620	II
100/50	600	II
100/40	580	III
100/30	560	III
100/20	540	III
100/10	520	III
100/0	500	III

A *farman* of Shah Jahan dated 1630 contains a schedule of emoluments and assignments for eleven different ranks and classes. It gives totals of the zat rank salary of the officer and the pay of his troopers from which Moreland has correctly deduced the two items separately. We are here concerned with the zat rank salary only. The following comparative table taken from Moreland[58] gives in ***dams*** the zat rank salary of the mansabdars in Akbar's time (Col.1), in 1630 (Col.2), and in Aurangzeb's time (Col.3).

Comparative Table of Zat rank Salaries per Annum (In Thousand of Dams)

Rank	*Class*	*Akbar's Reign*	*1630*	*Aurangzeb's Reign*
600	II	1320	8625	900
400	II	840	478.5	480
40	III	720	462	460
300	II	600	379.5	380
300	III	576	363	360
200	II	456	313.5	280
200	III	432	280.5	260
150	III	384	254.1	210
100	II	288	198	180
80	III	168	122.1	120
50	III	110.4	75	75

From another set of three assignment orders of Shah Jahan in favour of Raja Jai Singh (dated 1048 A.H., Rajab, 1060, and Ramazan, 1026, respectively) the zat salary for the rank 5,000 (I class) on those dates was 2,50,000, which conforms exactly to Aurangzeb's schedule.

This is abundant proof that the new scale of salaries which is found both in ***Ma'lumatul-Afaq*** and the directories consulted by Irvine[59] which refer to the period round about Aurangzeb's death was in force throughout the reigns of Shah Jahan and Aurangzeb and was introduced as early as 1630 or even a year or two earlier.

On comparing the zat rank salaries of Akbar's with those of Shah Jahan's or Aurangzeb's time, the first idea that strikes is that Akbar's mansabdars drew a much higher pay. As it is seen in Shah Jahan's reign, the salary of sawar rank was paid for from 12 to 5 months in the year. But that has no application to the zat rank. The reason was abvious: the pay varied with the number of horses kept. It may be noted that the mansabdars had to maintain not only the transport indicated against each rank in the list, but also the emperor's elephants as well as various other animals kept for amusement and curiosity. Abul-Fazl tells that the emperor 'put several ***halqas*** in charge of every grandee (***amir***) and required him to look after them.

On the subject of Shah Jahan's reforms the historians, official and non-official, are silent. In these it is nothing but reckless awards of mansabs, which point to a continuation of his father's policy it is true that the stream of awards flowed even more profusely in this than in Jahangir's reign and gathered momentum as it went. But Shah Jahan seems fully to have realized the gravity of the situation and adopted some important restrictive measures by way of remedy. He knew he could not start a second time with confiscation of existing ***mansabs*** and ***jagirs***. But with a sure hand he managed to introduce the following reforms:

It has already been noted that there was a drastic reductions in the zat rank salaries, which were in force in 1630. Secondly, it will be noted under Troopers' pay[60] the salary of an ordinary trooper was reduced to 8,800 ***dams*** a year in or before 1630 and to 8,000 ***dams*** a year in or before 1048 A.H.[61]

To insist on the maintenance of a full contingent corresponding to the ***sawar*** rank of an officer was beyond his power. Towards the end of Jahangir's reign, the strength of an average contingent must have fallen considerably below 25% of the sawar rank, while full sawar rank salary was drawn by the officer.[62] Shah Jahan could only save the situation by fixing a percentage and insisting on it, as the irreducible minimum. He issued orders that when the mansabdar served in the province where his jagir was situated he must maintain a contingent corresponding to one-third of his sawar rank; and if he was posted elsewhere the strength of his regiment must not be less than one-quarter of his sawar rank. This rule incidentally from the passage in Badshahnama, where the author is speaking of the expedition to Balkh and Badakshan (XIX R.Y.), and says that although those are the rules, owing to the distance of those regions, the ***mansabdars*** appointed to this expedition were given the special privilege of brand only one-fifth of their horse rank.

Shah Jahan, on the occasion of his coronation (1037), bestowed the rank 8,000/8,000 (2-3h.) on ***Yamiu'd-Daula*** Asaf Khan in ***obsentia***. In the following month, on the first ***Nauroz*** of the reign, he brought to the muster 5,000 well-mounted and well-equipped cavalry, and received in consequence an increase of 1,000/1,000 (2-3h.), his total rank now becoming 9,000/9,000 (2.3h.).[63]

Under the previous rank his nominal regiment would be 16,000 strong, the 5,000 which he passed for muster, is thus just under 1/3 of his sawar rank. 9,000 (2-3h.), i.e. for 18,000 horse. It is meant that a mansabdar who produced 25 or 33 troopers got the pay for 100 troopers, and coolly pocketed the emoluments of the remaining 75 or 67, which was over and above his zat rank salary; whereas Akbar had insisted on full strength of the contingents and got 100 troopers when he paid for 100 troopers, allowing only 5 % on the pay for odd expenses.[64]

On the face of it was not a favourable arrangements from the point of view of state finance; but it proves that Shah Jahan boldly faced a desperate posture of affairs, brushed away all delusions and resolved impossible theories into solid facts. Next Shah Jahan introduced a rule by which the salary varied with the amount. A little preliminary explanation is necessary before this rule can be stated in an intelligible form.

The term ***yak-aspa*** is used either ambiguously or technically by the authorities; so that if we are not careful we are likely to get confused. The ordinary sawar rank with which we have so far dealt[65] was called ***yak-aspa*** (i.e. with one horse), as distinguished from, ***do-aspa, si-aspa***(with two or three horses). This does not mean that each soldier had one horse in the former, and two or three horses in the latter, case.

Shah Jahan introduced the following rule:[66] The salary of ***yak-aspa*** sawar rank was to be paid not always for 12 months in the year, but for 12, 11, 10, 9, 8, 7, 6 or 5 months, according to the number of contingent. In other words, while the number of horseman remained constant, the number of horses maintained by them varied with the number of months for which the salary was drawn. From the detail given by 'Abdu'l-Hamid Lahuri (B.N., II, 507) the following table can be constructed **(a).**

Table (a)

Number of months for which salary drawn	*Si-aspa*	*Du-aspa*	*Total number of horse-men*	*Total number of horses*
12	300	600	1,000	2,200
11	250	500	1,000	2,200
10	—	800	1,000	1,800
9	—	600	1,000	1,600
8	—	450	1,000	1,450
7	—	250	1,000	1,250
6	—	100	1,000	1,100
5	—	—	1,000	1,000

A mansabdar with 4,000 or 3,000 sawar rank who had to maintain, say, 1,000 horsemen, had to keep. Now about ***Du-aspa Si-aspa***: the 2-3 horse rank, made its appearance towards the end of Jahangir's reign. It grew more common under Shah Jahan. 'Abdu'l-Hamid tells us, in continuation of the passage already referred to, that if the sawar rank was ***do-aspa,*** the number both of horses and horseman was doubled. Thus an officer with the horse rank 4,000 (2-3h.), who drew salary for 12 months, had to maintain under the 1/4 rule and so on with 11,10, etc., months.

600 ***si-aspa***
1,200 — ***du-aspa i.e.*** 2,000 horsemen with 4,400 horses
200 ***yak-aspa***

So the salary of the ***tabinan*** in ***du-aspa si-aspa*** rank was exactly double the salary in the corresponding yak–aspa rank–a fact incidentally verified by a statement. The Nominal share of Afghan remained the privilege of the non-Khanzada. The higher proportion of khanzad zamindars in the total award of zamindar is due to the high figures of Rajputs. In other words khanzad Rajputs occupied the bulk of the share of zamindars in both zat and sawar mansab during all the three phases of Shah Jahan's period, zat and mansab, which confirm the higher degree of trust and confidence reimposed in Rajput Khanzad among the zamindars.

The zat and sawar rank still continued but it is positively ascertained that the figure of the rank did not imply that a particular manslaughter kept the number prescribed by his mansab. To check fraudulent practices. An officer in the subah to which he was appointed was required to have one third of his horses branded and if he was deputed on state duty in any other province in Hindustan, ¼ in the first case a mansabdar holding a rank of 3000 zat and 3000 thousand sawar was required to get 1000 horses branded, in the second case only 750. The number to be branded in the case of officers who were sent to ***bulk badakshan*** in time of war fixed at 1/5 owing to the difficulties of the journey and rigours of the climate.

Army

According to Abdul Hamid Lahauri, the imperial army in 1648 consisted of 200,000 cavalry, 8000 mansabdars, 7000 ahadis or gentleman troopers, 40,000 foot soldiers and artillery men and 185,000 cavalrymen under the princes and noble, making a total of 4,40,000. Besides these there were troops in the pargagnah under the command of the faujdars, kroris and amils and therefore the strength the royal army must have been considerably greater than the figure stated above the various branches of the army continued to work as before and there was no dearth of fighting material and during the Khandar campaign special effort were made to secure by the government. Dara carried with him to Qundhar a large army consisting of four heavy guns, 30,000 iron shots, great and small, 1500 man of gunpowder, 5000 pakhalis, 3000 ahaids, 60 war elephants and a great number of banjaras for transport.

Classification of Mansabdars

From this cumulative evidence the conclusion is irresistible that ***amarat*** ranged from 1,000 upwards, at least during the reigns of Shah Jahan and Aurangzeb.

Ahadis

The mansabdari system was essentially based on an indirect method of recruitment. The Emperor fixed the rank of an officer and it was his duty to recruit men conformably to his rank. But soldiers were also directly recruited to the State army. Such recruits were known as Ahadis [67] or gentlemen troopers and were grouped under the general designation of Household Cavalry. They received a better salary than ordinary soldiers.

Irregulars

Another branch of the army which may be styled as irregulars [68] consisted of the troops raised by tributary chiefs of ***Rajputana*** and other ***Zamindars.*** But those who entered the regular mansab had to maintain besides their racial leaves, the number of troopers required by their rank. This huge military organization consisted of four branches of service, Infantry, Cavalry, Artillery and Navy.

Infantry

The infantry as a fighting arm had lost it s significance.[69] It was now a composite body consisting of some combatants and a large number of non-combatants or camp followers. The latter included the ***Khidmatiyas,*** the ***Durbans,*** or porters, the ***Kahars*** or ***Palki*** bearers, the ***Pahalwans*** or wrestlers and the ***Mewras*** or spies. The combatants included ***Shamshirbaz*** or gladiators and ***Barqandaz*** or musketeers.[70]

Cavalry

But the most important branch of service was the Cavalry, which was the main property of the mansabdari system. Great care was taken that the troopers should maintain the right type and full quota of horses.[71] On an average every soldier had to maintain two horses, one for actual service and the other as reserve. Thus the cavalry, on the whole, was efficient and well-organized and Bernier pays a deserving tribute to it.[72]

Artillery

The artillery in the reign of Shah Jahan was manned mainly by Europeans,[73] the Dutch, the English, the Portuguese and the French. It was of two kinds, heavy artillery and light artillery. The latter according to Bernier was extremely well appointed.[74] But the heavy artillery was ineffective and was inferior to the contemporary Persian Artillery.

Navy

There was no navy worth the name,[75] but the flotilla of boats for transport purposes was called ***Navarah***. On two occasions, however, this ***Navarah*** was used as a fighting arm, once against the Portuguese of Hugli,[76] and again during the war in Assam.[77]

References

1. William Irvine, ***The Army of the Indian Mughals***, published by Eurasia Publishing House Pvt. Ltd, pp. 3,4
2. Mirat Ahmadi by Ali Mohammad Khan composed 1174 (Hithograph) Bombay 1307h 1889.
3. ***The History of Shah Jahan*** (Ain-i-Akbari pp. 144-145).
4. Abdul Aziz, ***The Mansabdari System and the Mughal Army***, Idara-i-Adabiyat, Delhi, pp, 1,2,3,11,12.
5. Hasan Qulij 300/500 (A.N., III, 826.).
6. Ain-i-Akbari, I, 231: Blochmann, 594. There are however, anomalies. Some of the items in it were only true in 933 A.H. as Blochmann (256, n. 1) points out.
7. See, Blochmann, pp. 238-47.
8. Irvine, ***The Army of the Indian Mughals***, Euresia Publishing House, 1962, p.9
9. Indian Historical Records Commission Vol. V. 1923, pp. 60-2.
10. A.H. Lahauri, Vol, II, pp. 505-508.

11. Dastu-ul-Amal, , British Museum no 1641 c (1118 H) Insha by Yar Muhammad (1170H) Calcutta 1270(H) 1853
12. See the List of Mansabdars in Waris. B.M. Or. 1937.
13. Dastur-ul-Amal, B.M. Or. 1937.
14. ***Ibid.***, and Chapter III of Irvine: Army of the Indian Mughals.
15. Beni Prasad, ***History of Jahangir***, Allahabad, 1962, pp. 177-180; S.R. Sharma, ***The Religious Policy of the Mughal Emperors***, Asia Publishing House, 1962, pp, 83-84, 124-127.
16. B.M. MS. No. Or. 173.
17. A.H. Lahauri Badshah Nama, Bib. Ind. 1867-68.
18. I.O. 329 (I have also consulted Rampur Ms which is defective.).
19. "The Mansab System", ***Proc. Ind. Hist. Cong.*** 1966.
20. "Distribution of the Revenue-Resources of the Mughal Empire Among the Nobility", ***Proc. Ind. Hist. Cong.***, 1965, pp. 237-42.
21. A.H. Lahauri, ***Badshah Nama***, II, 715.
22. Do Aspa Sih Aspa, has been counted as Double.
23. M. Athar Ali, ***The Mughal Nobility under Aurangzeb***, p. 10.
24. ***Badshah Nama.*** I, i, 96-97.
25. ***The Mansabdari System and the Mughal Army***, By Abdul Aziz Idarah-i-Adabiyat, Delhi, pp. 132-135
26. Abdul Aziz, ***The Mansabdari System and the Mughal Army***, pp, 136-137.
27. Athar Ali, List of Jahangiri Nobles (Apparatus of Empire Delhi, 1985, pp. 41-90) suggest the number of Iranis (1000 zat and above) as 82 out of 271.
28. A.H. Lahauri, p. 241-242.
29. ***Ibid.***, pp. 293-96.
30. Such a gap between the share of the Iranis and Turanis also existed during the Jahangir's period. Athar Ali, ***op. cit.***, n. 22, pp. 41-90.
31. On the basis of Athar Ali's Table (***op. cit.***, n 22, pp 41-90), it may be said that in spite of the many favours of Jahangir, the Afghans enjoyed almost 6 percent of the total zat and 35 percent of the total sawar mansab distributed during his reign.
32. The rise or decline in the share of various ethnic group in the mansab is shown in table.
33. A.H. Lahauri-211, pp-415, 416, 462, 463..
34. For their role in political and military affairs, see Chapter 3 and its appendices.
35. For the actual figures of Rajputs who participated in such expeditions, salih- III (L) pp, 70-2.
36. Lahauri, II. Pp- 415-16.
37. ***Ibid.***, II. Pp. 483, 491, 503.
38. ***Ibid.***, II. Pp. 632-640
39. India Under Shah Jahan by Rajkumar, Ansar Publication Pvt. Ltd. 4374/4B, Ansari Road. Ist edition 2000.
40. W.H. Moreland, "Rank (mansab) in the Moghul State Service," ***Journal of the***

Royal Asiatic Society, 1936, pp. 641-65.

41. A'in-i-Akbari Blochman Bibliography Indica Vol. I, p. 1785 the scale of 1605 is gien in a ms of the Iqbalnama of Mutammad Khan, British Library, 1834.
42. ***Ibid.***, pp. 4-19.
43. I. Habib, ***PIHC***, pp. 232-34. This has been confirmed by Shireen Moosvi's reading of the evidence in ***JRAS***, 1981, pp. 1798-82.
44. ***Ain-i-Akbari***, Vol., p. 175.
45. ***Akbarnama***, p. 672. ***Sih-Aspa*** means a horseman with three horses; ***so-aspah***, with two; and ***yal-aspah***, with one.
46. SDSR. 79 (under Tahinaman). The formula employed there is discussed in Section IV of this paper.
47. ***Ain-i-Akbari***, Vol. I, p. 188.
48. But e.f. Moreland, ***JRAS***, p. 658, and S. Moosvi, ***IESHR***, pp. 336-37.
49. Moreland, JRAS, p. 656.
50. As already stated, the best document where this can be repeatedly checked from statements of pay of various individuals is a ***parwanchah*** of the 8th regnal year, i.e. 1635 (SDSR, pp. 4-19).
51. ***Ibid.***, pp. 83-84, for the relevant portion of the schedule.
52. ***Ibid.***, pp. 83-84, for the relevant portion of the schedule.
53. ***Ibid.***, p. 84. Moreland, ***JRAS***, p. 646.
54. ***SDSR***, p. 73 The evidence of this document has already benn examined in Section II above.
55. SDSR, p. 84. The figure 2,40,00,00 ***dams*** given for 1000 sawars under the heading sih-aspah, do-aspah, yak-aspah must be a misprint.
56. Blochmann's translation of this passage (p. 248) is defective and has misled Horn (p.15).
57. Article by ***JRAS***, for October 19, 26, p. 657.
58. P.M. MSS. Or. 1690 and Or. 1641.
59. ***Ain-i-Akbari*** in Blochmann, 275.
60. The Mansabdari System and the Mughal Army, By Abdul Aziz, Idarah-i-Adabiyat, I Delhi 1972 Printed in India 2009 Qasim Jan Street, Delhi (India). Sect, iv, pp. 79-80
61. The Mansabdari System and the Mughal Army, By Abdul Aziz Idarah-i-Adabiyat, Delhi, pp. 80-81.
62. ***Ibid.***, p. 80,
63. ***Badshah Nama***. I, 113 and 193.
64. So we can understand that the sawar rank was a much more profitable business under Shah Jahan than under Akbar.
65. The Mansabdari System and the Mughal Army, By Abdul Aziz Idarah-i-Adabiyat, Delhi, pp.82-83 Excepting a couple of item in Jahangir's reign (p.77 above).
66. ***Ibid.***, pp. 83-84.
67. The Army of the Indian Mughals By William Irvine, p. 43; and A'in p. 187.

68. V.Smith's , Akbar, p. 360: Bernier, pp. 209-210.
69. Irvine, quoting Dr. Horn says that the Mughal army consisted of cavalry, infantry, and artillery, but the second and third branches held a very subordinate position towards the first, p. 57; ef. Bernier's remark on camp followers, p. 43.
70. ***Ain-i-Akbari***, pp. 188-190; Mandelslo says that the infantry manage the musket tolerably well, p. 118; Bernier says that musketeers cut a sorry figure, p. 217.
71. Manrique says that the horses were mostly 'Arab, Persian and Turkish, Vol. II,p. 277; Manucci says that every horsemen in the King's service must have a Turkish Horse, Vol. II, p. 376.
72. Bernier, p. 48-9.
73. ***Ibid.***, p. 217; Mandelslo notices that the Moghuls have a great train of artillery but essentially inferior, p. 118; Manucci, Vol. I, p. 95.
74. Bernier, p. 218.
75. Manrique attributes the want of efficient navy to the timidity of Moghuls, Vol. II, p. 278; Vol II, p. 168.
76. See the account of the reduction of Hugli.
77. See the account of the Assam Campaign.

7. Law and Justice

The Judicial System and Its Branches

The judicial system of Mughal Empire was of a curious structure, to understand it clearly one must banish our minds all modern ideas of:

1. A duty graded centrally controlled department of state action.
2. One law Code for all the people.
3. A High Court Supreme over all the judicial agencies in the state.
4. A chief justice or a full branch of High Court judges whose interpretation of the law overrides that of advocate general.
5. A sovereign person as the fountain of justice more of these was in operation in the Muslim State.[1]

It is true that the prophet and the early caliphs or Khalifas often decided disputes in person. But this primitive arrangement was soon afterwards discarded with the growth of the Islamic empire and the change in the character of its head. The prophet and the pious Caliphs i.e. Hazrat Abu Bakr, Hazrat Usman and Hazrat Ali (his four successors) had been Pope an Emperor in one, the authority in law making and executive administration alike.

Islamic Jurisprudence is known by the name of ***figh***, literally "wisdom" and the jurisprudential of the Romans. The development was resulted from the necessities of governance arising from the expansion and the organization of the khilafat as a political institution. In theory the fiqh is believed to be derived from the Quranic law (the Sharia) and is thereof regarded immutable by any human institution. In actual practice the faith has more often not drawn upon foreign law, mainly Romano-Bywanitine Law, but thanks to the fiction of Hadis, all such material borrowed from other sources was ascribed to the Prophet and his great companions and became a part of the revelation.

The ***fiqh*** is mainly drawn from two sources, the Quran and the Sunna which consists of the traditions revealed to explain the 'Quran'. Practical needs however compelled the recognition of other sources. It was found that the fiqh did not cover all cases. Hence the ***Faqihs*** were compelled to apply analogous cases on such occasions. This was the origin of the third source called qiyas (analogy). Different elements of the fiqh.

Another source which received recognition was ijma or universal consent.

The various schools of law or jurisprudence grew up in later times accordingly as they attacked importance to the for some time there was a struggle for predominance among them, out of which eventually four schools emerged successfully and were recognized by the jurists of Islam.[2] These four schools are:

i. Abu Hanifa (699 AD- 766 AD)- The Hanafi School
ii. Malik Ibn Anas (715 AD- 795 AD) -The Maliki School
iii. The Shafi (767 AD- 820 AD) -The Shafi School
iv. Ahmad Bin Hambali (780 AD-855 AD)- The Hambali School

The theory of Islamic jurisprudence does not recognize the non-Muslims as a citizen of the state for the simple reason that the existence of a non-Muslim was not contemplated as a member of the Islamic state. In its view the state is an organization or instrument to sub-serve the ends of the creed of Islam and consequently non-Muslims can have any place in it.

The expansion of the rule of caliphs; however over non-Muslims countries brought them face to face with the practical problem of dealing with their non-Muslim subjects, who could neither be converted wholesale nor exterminated. The jurists, therefore gave to these non Muslim subjects a qualified position by imposing on them certain disabilities, restriction together with a certain amount of special fine by way of price for the privilege of being suffered to exist in an Islamic state.[3]

The Scope of King's Judiciary

In this field again there was a great divergence between theory and practice. In theory, the sovereign was the fountainhead of justice possessing unlimited scope and authority over all sorts of causes and disputed wherever and in whichever community they might occur. But in actual practice the jurisdiction of the state system of justice was very much restricted. It is clear that in religious and commercial matters the parties were allowed full freedom to have their cause tried by religious and commercial courts.

In addition to these the village panchayats were allowed to continue in full enjoyment of their ancient powers of deciding all disputes occurring in the village, except in cases of very serious crime, such as murder or organized robbery. If the village jury failed to give satisfaction to other party (which rarely happened) the latter could prefer an appeal in the government court. The Qazi and other officers of the judicial and religious department were appointed even in the smallest town the disputants were allowed to have recourse to their communal bodies or trade guides to justice.[4]

Under the Mughal emperors of India there were three separate judicial agencies all working at the same time independent to each other. These were the courts of Religious law, Common law and Political cases respectively, the Qazi, for the first the governors and all grades of subordinate local authorities, as well as tribal heads and the caste Panchayat for the second and the Emperor or his government for the third.

The sacred law (*shara*) was administered by the Qazi, the theory in the infancy of the Islamic state that the Qazi has to decide all civil and criminal cases, had been long ago abandoned in practice. "Only such questions as are popularly fit to be closely connected with religion e.g., disputes on points of family law or inheritance, legal questions concerning pious foundations and are brought to be decided in the conformity to Canon Law, before the Qazi all other questions come within the province of the secular authorities. The Qazi is not considered qualified to give his own interpretations of the law, he is tied down to the decisions of earlier authorities' scholars as laid down before him by the Mufti.[5]

The Mufti was originally called ***Mujtahid*** and formally ***Wakil-e-Shara*** or champion of the Quranic law, and can be referred as Advocate General. The Qazis had not only to decide cases, but they had also to administer pious foundations (***waqfs***) and the states of orphans imbeciles and other persons. They had also to draw up contracts of marriages for women without male relatives. The evidence of a ***Zimmi*** or other non-Muslims was not valid in a Qazi's court.[6]

Judges of secular cases. These were either the sovereign agents, such as local governors and subordinate authorities down to the ***faujdar*** and the ***kotwal*** or the ***Brahman Pandits*** and the caste elders (***panchayat***) for the Hindus and the villagers, none of them was subordinate to the Qazi or connected with his court. They administered the unwritten customs (common law) or codes of tribal traditions and had no concern with the Shara or established Quranic Law, but were expected to posses the customary love of their tribe or caste.

In Turkey, the customary law called ***Ada***, and civil law as ***Qanun***. In medieval Islam, customary law was called ***urf***, but this term came to be narrowed down for the summary justice which may be called political cases. Zimmis could dispose in these courts.

Urf–frequently ***urf*** is simply the decision made in various cases by the sovereign or his agent, such as a provincial governor not the Qazi-act according to the requirements of the state demand or as prejudices dictate. Mainly it was offence against the state and against the law and order e.g. rebellion and disloyal conduct, deposing the coinage rioting, theft, highways robbery and murder- which came before it.[7] This point is made clear in Timir's Institutions.[8]

Justice of Mughal Emperors in Person

The Prophet and the early Caliphs often decided disputes in person as judges, as did their governors and prefects in the various provinces. Justice was always administrated in Muslim lands to a great extent by local authorities. This was sometimes called ***Nazar Fil-Mazalim'*** or as Aurangzeb called his own Wednesday session of justice, ***Diwan-i-Mazalim.***[9]

According to the ancient political ideal, which both the Hindus and the Muhammadan accepted the sovereign in the fountain of justice, and it is his duty to try cases personally in open court. The Mughal Emperor acted upto this ideal, and we possess contemporary accounts written by court historians and Europeans travellers alike, as to the manner in which they dispensed justice.

Shah Jahan and Aurangzeb both held no public Darbar on Wednesday, but reserved that day for holding a court of law. The emperor came direct from the Darshan window to the ***Diwan-i-Khas*** (or hall of Private Audience) at about 8:00 A.M and sat on the throne of justice till mid-day.[10]

This rows was filled with the law officers of the crown. The judges cannon law (QAZI), judges of the common law (ADILS) MUFTIS, theologians (ULEMA), jurists learned in precedents (FATWA), the Superintendent of the law court (DAROGHA-I-ADALAT), and the KOTWAL or prefect of the city police. None among the courtiers was admitted unless his presence was especially necessary.

The officer of justice presented the plaintiffs one by one, and reported their grievances. His majesty very gently ascertained the facts by inquiry, took the law from the ***ulema*** and pronounced judgment accordingly. Many persons had came from far off provinces to get justice from the highest power in the land. Their plaints could not be investigated except locally, and so the Emperor wrote orders to the governors of those places, urging them to find out the truth and either do them justice or send the parties back to the capital with their reports.[11]

The Emperor was the highest court of appeal and sometime acted as a court of first instances, law. But from the nature of things, only a few plaintiff could reach his throne and he could spare time for adjudicating only a small portion of the appeals that were handed to him, though some of the Mughal Emperor, made a parade of their devotion to duty, notably Jahangir, who hang a gold coin from his palaces balcony to the ground outside Agra fort, to which the people in the sheats could the their petitions for royal justice in order to be drawn up to the Emperor, without their having to grease the palms of the palace porters and underlings, courtiers and other middlemen.[12]

The main defect of the department of law and justice was that there was no system, no organization of the law courts in a regular gradation from the highest to the lowest, nor any proper distribution of courts in proportion to the area to be served by them.

The division of the judicial work is noticed by the early European traveller WILLIAM FINCH- wrote in 1611.

"The castle of Agra has four gates, once to the west, towards the Bazar, (is) called the KACHAHRI or court of Rolls, where the kings ***wazir*** sits or every morning some three hours, by whose hands pass all matters, rents, grants, lands, farmans, debts etc. Tuesday is the day of blood, both of fighting beasts and justice, the king judging seeing execution" (carried) out in the plain on the river bank below the Darshan Balcony.[13]

Five Years Later Terry Observed

"The Emperors were doing himself moderation in all matters of consequences which happen near his court, for the most part judging SECUNDUM allegata and PROBATE trials are quick. The government in cities and provinces proceeded in like form of justice.

MANUCHI describes the scene of the royal dispensation of justice:

> "The king holds public audience in the AMKHAS (meaning the ***Diwan-i-Am***), and there it is usual for the aggrieved persons to appear and make complaint. Some men demand punishment for murderers, other complains of injustice and violence or other such like wrongful acts. The king ordains with arrogance, and in few words, that the thieves be beheaded, that the governors and ***Faujdars*** compensate the plundered travellers. In same cases he announces that there is no pardon for the transgressor, in others he orders the facts to be investigated and a report should be sent to him" [14]

In India, the Mughal period beings with the victory of Babar in 1526 over the last Lodi Sultan of Delhi. His son, Humayun, though he lost his kingdom to Sher Shah in 1540 regained it after defeating the descendants of Sher Shah in July 1555. The Mughal Empire continued from 1555 to 1750.

The Mughal Empire (***Sultanat-e-Mughalia***) was administered on the basis of the same political divisions as existed during the reign of Sher Shah. For the purposes of civil administration the whole empire was divided into the Imperial Capital, of Delhi, the Mughal Emperors were also absolute monarchs. The Mughal Emperor was the supreme authority and in him the entire executive, legislative, judicial and military power resided.

The Administration of Justice: Constitution of Courts

During the Mughal period, the Emperor was considered the "Fountain of Justice". The Emperor created a separate department of Justice (***Mahukma-e-Adalat***) to regulate and see that justice was administered properly. On the basis of the administrative divisions, at the official headquarters in each province, district parganah and village separate courts were established to decide civil, criminal, revenue cases.[15] At the Delhi Imperial Court of India, highest courts of the Empire empowered with original and appellate jurisdiction were established. A systematic gradation of courts, with well-defined powers of the presiding judges, existed all over the empire. At Delhi, which was the capital (***Daral Sultanat***) of the Mughal emperors in India, three important courts were established.

The Emperor's Court, presided over by the Emperor, was the highest court of the empire. The court had jurisdiction to hear original civil and criminal cases. As a court of the first instance generally the Emperor was assisted by a ***Darogha***-e-***Adalat***, a ***Mufti*** and a ***Mir Adl,***[2] In criminal cases the ***Mohtasib-e-Mumalik*** or the chief Mohtasib, like the Attorney-General of India today, also assisted the Emperor. In order to appeals, the Emperors presided over a Bench consisting of the Chief Justice (***Qazi-ul-Wazat***) and ***Qazis*** of the chief justice's court. The Bench decided questions both of fact and law. Where the Emperor considered it necessary to obtain authoritative interpretation of law on a particular point, the same was referred to the Bench of the Chief Justice's Court for opinion. The Public was allowed to make representations and appeals to the Emperors court in order to obtain his impartial judgment.

The ***Chief Court of the Empire was the second important court*** at Delhi, the seat of the Capital. It was presided over by the Chief Justice (***Qazi-ul-Quzat***). The court had the power to try original, civil and criminal cases, to hear appeals from the provincial courts. It was also required to supervise the working of the provincial courts. In administering justice, the Chief Justice was assisted by one or two *Qazis* of great eminence, who were-***Darogha-e-Adalat, Mufti, Mohtasib, Mir Adl,*** The ***Mufti*** attached to the Chief Justice's court was known as ***Mufti-e-Azam.***

The Chief Justice was appointed by the Emperor. He was considered the next important person, after the Emperor, holding the highest office in the judiciary. Referring to the qualifications of a Chief Justice, Sir J. Sarkar has observed, "Men of high scholarship and reputed sanctity of character wherever available were chosen.[16] Sometimes a Chief Provincial ***Qazi*** was promoted to the post of the Chief Justice.

The ***Chief Revenue Court*** was the third important court established at Delhi. It was the highest Court of Appeal to decide revenue cases. The court was presided over by the ***Diwan-e-Ala.***

Apart from the above-stated three important courts there were also two lower courts at Delhi to decide local cases. The court of ***Qazi*** of Delhi, who enjoyed the status of ***Chief Qazi*** of a province, decided local civil and criminal cases. An appeal was allowed to the court of Chief Justice. The Court of ***Qazi-e-Aksar*** was specially constituted to decide case of the military area in the capital. The court moved from place to place with troops. In each court as stated above, the four officer attached were–***Darogha-e-Adalat,*** a ***Mufti,*** a ***Mohtasib, Mir Adl.***

Provinces–In each province (***Subah***) there were three courts, namely, the Governor's own court and the bench, and the Chief Appellate Court, the Chief Revenue Court. The Governor's Own Court (***Adalat-e-Nazim-e-Subah***) had original jurisdiction in all cases arising in the provincial capital. It was presided over by the Governor (***Nazim-e-Subah***)

The Provincial Chief Appellate Court was presided over by ***Qazi-e-Subah.*** The court had original civil and criminal jurisdiction. Provincial Chief Revenue Court was over by ***Diwan-e-Subah.*** The Court was granted original and appellate jurisdiction in revenue cases.

District (Sarkars)–In each District (***Sarkar***) there were four courts, namely, the Chief Civil and Criminal Court of the District, ***Faujdari Adalat, Kotwali and Amalguzari Kachahri.***

The Chief Civil and Criminal Court of the District was presided over by the ***Qazi-e-Sarkar.*** The Court had original and appellate jurisdiction in all civil and criminal cases and in religious matters Qazi-e-Sarkar was the principal judicial officer in a district. He was officially known as "***Shariyat Panah***". Six officers attached to his court were–***Darogha-e-Adalat, Mir Adl, Mufti, Pandit*** or ***Shahstri, Mohtasib*** and ***Vakil-e-Sharayat.*** Appeals from this court lay to ***Qazi-e-Subah.***[17]

Faujdari Adalat dealt with criminal cases concerning riots and state security. It was presided by the ***Faujdar.*** Appeals lay to the Governor's Court. Kotwali Court decided cases similar to those under modern Police Acts and had appellate jurisdiction. It was presided by *Kotwal-e-Sahar.* Appeals lay to the District ***Qazi.***[18]

The ***Amalguzari Kachehri*** decided all revenue cases. ***Amalguzar*** presided over this court. An appeal was allowed to the Provincial ***Diwan.***

Parganah–In each ***Parganah*** there were three courts, namely, ***Adalat-e-Parganah, Kotwali*** and ***Kachehri.***

Adalat-e-Parganah was presided over by ***Qaqzi-e-Parganah.*** The Court had jurisdiction over all civil and criminal cases arising within its original jurisdiction. It included all those villages which were under the ***Parganah*** court's jurisdiction. Four officers attached to ***Adalat-e-Parganah*** were ***Mufti, Mohtasib-e-Parganah, Darogha-e-Adalat*** and ***Vakil-e-Shara.***

Court of kotwal was presided by ***Kachehri*** which decided such cases as are found in the modern Police Act. Appeals were made to the court of district Qazi. Amin was the presiding officer in Kachehri which decided revenues cases. An appeal lay to the District ***Amalguzar.***

Villages–The village was the smallest administrative unit. From ancient times the village council (Panchayat) were authorized to administer justice in all petty civil and criminal matters.[19] Generally, the panchayat meetings were held in public places. It was presided by five ***panchs*** elected by the villagers who were expected to give a patient hearing to both the parties and deliver their judgment in the ***Panchayat*** meeting. ***Sarpanch*** or Village-Headman was generally President of the Panchayat. No appeal was allowed from the decision of a ***Panchayat.*** Village ***Panchayats*** were mostly governed by their customary law.

Institution of Lawyers–Litigants were represented before the Courts by professional legal experts. They were popularly known as ***Vakil Ibn Batuta,*** who was working as a judge during the reign of

Mohammad Tughlaq, mentions ***Vakils*** in his book.[20] Mawardi[21] referring to the legal profession, states that specialized knowledge of law was necessary both for acting as a Qazi and for the legal practice. Moreland[22] appears to be mis-informed, where he expresses the view that the legal profession did not exist during the Muslim period in India. On the basis of other contemporary material[23] available in India, it is clear that the legal profession existed at any rate in the Mughal period.

Government advocates were for the first time appointed in the reign of Shahjahan to defend civil suits against the State. During Aurangzeb's reign whole time lawyers were appointed in every district, who were known as ***Vakil-e-Sarkar*** or ***Vakil-e-Shara.*** They were appointed either by the Chief Qazi of the Provinces or sometimes by the Chief Justice (***Qazi-ul-Quzat***). Sometimes they were appointed to assist the poor litigants by giving them free legal advice. ***Vakils*** had a right of audience in the court. It was expected that the ***Vakils*** should maintain a high standard of legal learning and behaviour.

Judicial Procedure–A systematic judicial procedure was followed by the courts during the Muslim period.[24] It was mainly regulated by two Muslim Codes, namely, ***Figh-e-Firoz Shahi*** and ***Fatwa-i-Alamgiri.*** The status of the Court was determined by the political divisions of the kingdom.

In civil cases, the plaintiff or his duly authorized agent was required to file a plaint for his claim before a court of law having appropriate jurisdiction in the matter. The defendant, as stated in the plaint, was called upon by the court to accept or deny the claim.[25] Where the claim was denied by the defendant, the court formed the issues and the plaintiff was required to produce evidence supporting his claim. The defendant was also given an opportunity to prove his case with the assistance of his witness. Witnesses were cross-examined. After weighing all the evidences, the presiding authority delivered judgment in open court.

In criminal cases a complaint was presented before the court either personally or through representative. In every criminal court there was attachment of a public prosecutor known as ***Mohtasib,***[26] he instituted prosecution against the accused before the court. The court was empowered to call the accused at once and to begin hearing of the case. Sometimes the Court insisted on hearing the complainant's evidence before calling the accused person. Ordinarily, the judgment was given in open court. In exceptional cases, where either the public trial was against the interest of the State or the accused was dangerously influential, the judgment was not pronounced in the open court.

Evidence was classified by the ***Hanafi*** law into three categories: (a) ***Tawatur*** i.e., full corroboration; (b) ***Ehad*** i.e. testimony of a single individual; (c) ***Iqrar*** i.e. admission including confession. The court always preferred Tawatur to other kind of evidence.

All those who believed in God were competent witnesses but at least two women witnesses were required to prove a fact for which the evidence of one man was sufficient, the testimony of one woman was recognized only in those cases where women alone were expected to have special knowledge. The principles of ***Estoppels*** and ***Res-judicata*** were also recognized by the Muslim law.

Trial by Ordeal–The Muslim law prohibited the use of trial by ordeal to determine the guilt of a person. It was not favoured either by the Sultans or by the Mughal Rulers in India. As stated earlier,[27] the trial by ordeal was mostly used during the ancient Hindu period. In the non-Muslim States, which were under the protection of the sultans and Mughals, however, the old system of trial by ordeal somehow continued. The Muslim Rulers neither adopted it nor interfered in the non-Muslim States to stop it.

Sultan Jalal-Ud-din Khilji (1290-1296) made the earliest attempt during the Muslim period, to adopt the system of trial by ordeal in the case of Sidi Maula when the court declined to convict him for sedition. The Sadre Jahan and other judges refused to allow Sultan Jalal-ud-Din to test the truthfulness of Sidi Maula, by Ordeal of Fire.[28] Emperor Akbar also tried to encourage the system of trial by Ordeal most probably in order to please the Rajputs.[29] The Muslim law experts strongly opposed this move to introduce the trial by ordeal and therefore, Akbar gave up the idea. In his records, Hamilton[30] who came to India during the reign of Aurangzeb, has mentioned a trial in South India where the accused person was required to put his hand in a pan of boiling oil.

It may, therefore, be concluded that though at the times even the Muslim rulers tried to encourage the trial, the system on the whole fell into disuse due to the impact of Muslim law in India.

Qazis and Their Works

Every provincial capital had its qazi appointed by the Supreme Qazi of the Empire (the Qazi-ul-Qauzat). A qazi was also posted to every town and to the most of the villages with a Muhammadan population and large enough to be classed as qasbas. The other villages had no qazi of their own, but could carry their suit to the qazi of the neighbouring town in whose jurisdiction they lay. As the provincial qazi jurisdiction was very vast and he had no assistant or deputy legally competent to share his burden, only a small part of the dispute in the provinces could be tried by him.

The Qazi, His Position and Powers

The qazi's business, in strict theory was to play the part of a jury he was to take the law from others and pronounce a verdict in the particular case on the basis of the evidence adduced. This expenditure of the law was the ***mufti***, whom we may rather loosely call the Advocate general. The ***mufti*** is the officer who expounds and applies the law to cases, and the qazi, according to all the schools of Muslim law except that of Shafi, because, "A qazi's business may be pass to decrees merely on the opinions of others.[31]

Though many of the qazi's were very learned lawyers, yet the primary and indispensable qualifications of a qazi were, in theory at least honesty impartiality virtuousness and pure detachment from the society of the place.[32] (***Hedaya, also Hed, Q.***).

The qazis or judges are not invested with sufficient power to redress the wrongs of these unhappy people (viz., the pleasant artisan or tradesman oppressed by the jagirdars, governors and farmers of the revenue). This abuse of authority may not be felt in the same degree near capital cities, or in the vicinity of large towns and seaports, because in those places acts of gross injustice cannot easily be concealed from the court.

The qazi should be perfectly sound physically and mentally. He should be a free citizen. No slave was entitled to hold the post. Faith in Islam was an essential condition. No unbeliever could be a judge over Muslims. He should be a man of irreproachable integrity and honesty, and should have a knowledge of law both theoretical and practical.[33]

Duties of Qazi

A qazi on his appointment, is enjoined to take possession of all the records, etc., pertaining to his office and to demand the 'divan' (the bag containing the records and other papers) of the former qazi. He should take over charge of all these papers through his Amins and the latter should ask the retiring qazi for separate files of different subjects, such as property, orphans, marriage and inheritance.

The most typical and definite opinion in this respect is that of Sir Jadunath Sarkar, viz., that "The main defect of the department of law and justice was that there was no system, no organization of the law courts in a regular gradation from the highest to the lowest, nor any proper distribution of courts in proportion to the area to be served by them".[34] But it is curious that the above statement is by the following remark "Every provincial capital had its qazi, appointed by the supreme Qazi of the empire the (***qazi-ul-quzat***); but there were no lower or primary court under him and therefore no provincial courts of appeal. A qazi was also posted to every large town and seat of a faujdar, the smaller towns and all the villages had no qazi of their own, but any plaintiff living in them, could carry his suit to the qazi of the neighbouring town in whose jurisdiction they lay."

There was a qazi also in every parganah headquarter and also in other towns wherever it was found necessary to post. It is also admitted by Sir Jadunath that the jurisdiction of the qazi of the sarkar extended over the whole of its area and the people living in the towns of a sarkar could carry their suits for decision to the sarkar court.

According to Muslim jurisprudence, the qazi must discharge his duty in a mosque or some other public place, the Jama Masjid of the town being specially recommended. As a concession, however, he was permitted to hold court in his house occasionally, but in that case the public were to have free access there, and the two parties were to be placed by Qazi on an absolutely equal footing as regards seats, conveniences and general treatment. (***Hedaya,* 337**).

Muslim Law, Its Character and Sources

The crudeness and insufficiency of the judicial system were aggravated by the fact that the only law recognized by the Emperor and his judges was the Quranic law, which had originated and grown to the maturity from outside India. It was supposed to have been defined once for all within the pages of the Quran as revealed to the Arabian Prophet and his Traditional sayings (***Hadis***).

No Indian Emperor or Qazi decision was ever considered authoritative enough to lay down a legal principle, elucidate any obscurity in the Quran, or supplement the Quranic law by following the line of its obvious intention in respect of cases not explicitly provided. Hence, it becomes necessary for Indian qazis to have at their elbow a digest of Islamic law and precedent compiled from the accepted Arabic writers.

Description of Punishments allowed by Muhammadan Law

The punishment for crimes were of four classes:-

(a) Hadd,-means a punishment prescribed by Canon law and considered as the right of 'God which therefore, no human judge can after the original design in the institution of ***hadd*** is determined, it warns people from the commission of certain offence'. (b) tazir, (c) qisas and (d), tashhir. To these we may ad detention in prison without trial, somewhat like our ***hajat*** (lock up) but more severe.

Hadd must take certain prescribes forms of punishment, viz.,

i. Stoning to death for adultery; scourging for fornication (100 stripes).
ii. Scourging for falsely accusing a married woman of adultery (80 stripes).
iii. Scourging for drinking wine and other intoxicating liquors. For a free man was 80 stripes for wine drinking.
iv. Cutting off the right hand for theft.
v. For simple robbery on the highway, the loss of hands and feet; for robbery with murder, death either by the sword or by crucifixion.[35]
vi. For apostasy, (***kufr***) death.

Tazir–Tazir is punishment intended to reform the culprit. According to ***fiqh*** tazir is inflicted for such transgressions as have no ***hadd*** punishment and no expiation prescribed for them. The kind and amount of tazir is left entirely to the discretion of the judges... The judge can completely remit ***tazir***. The process of trial is simple in contrast to that for ***hadd.*** Hence attempt was often made to escape tazir by bribery. It was not the 'right of God'. It could take one of these four forms:

i. Public reprimand.
ii. Jirr, or dragging the offender to the door (of the court house) and exposing him to public scorn; somewhat like putting a man in the pillory.
iii. Imprisonment or exile.
iv. Boxing on ear; scourging.[36] The strips must not be less than 3 nor more than 39 (or 75 acc to the Hanafi school, as in Abu Yusuf and if he continue to offend, he shall be scourged at the distraction of the judge,")

Private Vengence, Public degradation, and C

Qisas-Qisas or retaliation: This was the personal right of the victim or his next of kin, in the case of certain crimes, notably murder. If he demanded the legal punishment, the qazi was bound to inflict it, and neither he nor the king could exercise the royal clemency by modification or abrogation of the sentence. If, on the other hand, the next kin of the deceased was satisfied with the money damages, called 'price of blood' (***Arabic diya***) offered by the murderer, or pardoned him unconditionally, it was his look-out, and neither the qazi nor the king was to take any further notice of the crime.

For minor offences the retaliation was, as laid down by the mosaic law, "a tooth for a tooth and an eye for an eye," with certain exceptions.[37]

Tashhir–Tash-hir or public degradation was a popularly devised punishment of universal currency throughout the Muslim world and even Hindu India and Medieval Europe. The judge may blacken the face of the culprit cut his hair or led him through the streets."[38] This is the Arabian practice.

Theft (***sarqa***) is punishable with the cutting off of one hand, one foot. But if the offender has robbed and killed, he is to be put to death... and his body publicly exposed for three days on a cross or in some other way. Here the punishment of death is considered a ***haqq Allah*** and blood-money is out of the question. All accomplices are punished in the same way. The judge can inflict the above punishments, as ***hadd,*** only when all the legal conditions are fulfilled.[39]

The capital sentence (***qatl***) is inflicted, after the offence has been legally proved, in the following cases:

i. Demands the life of the murderers (***qisas)*** and refuses to accept the alternative of money compensation (***diya*** or 'price of blood');
ii. In certain cases of immorality; the woman sinner is stoned to death by the public,[40]
iii. On highway robbers.**(Quran, v. 37 et seq)**;
iv. On apostates (***murtadd***) from Islam (**Quran, iv. 91 et seq**)

"The conversion of a Muslim to another non-Muslim religion is punishable with death. A *zindiq,* i.e., any one who professing to be a Muslim is really liable to death sentence. "Every unbeliever who does not pay the ***jizya*** ... may at any time be killed by any Muslim without the latter being liable to any kind of punishment or (money) damages." The killing of an apostate is an obligatory duty.

Murtadd.- In the hadis we have the death penalty for apostate.. "In the ***fiqh*** there is unanimity that the male apostate must be put to death. A woman apostate is to be imprisoned according to the Hanafi School, but must be put to death according to all other three Schools of Law.[41]

Zindia–"is defined as a heretic whose teaching becomes dangerous to the state, this crime is liable to the capital punishment,[42] (Quran, V. 37 XXVI. 49) and to damnation. The only crime systematically punished by the Prophet himself by death had been Sabb Al-Rasul (institute to the Prophet).

The Muslim jurist made ***Zindiqism*** (i.e. heresy or free thinking) an intellectual rebellion instituting the prophets honour (and therefore punishable with death)" for e.g., the execution of all Mallaj.[43] (Ency. Ist IV 1228). In addition to the above the Hanafi school of law declares killing as lawful in the following three cases:-

i. When the Ghazi kills unbelieving prisoner of war, in the case when the reason for killing, him exactly balance those for granting his life.
ii. When the Imam kills his unbelieving prisoner of war, in the case

when the reason for killing him exactly balance those for granting his life.

iii. Killing in self-defense in defending one, own life person or property, or a helper. Any one who puts to death a murtadd (apostate) of whatever kind without powers granted by the authority, is generally liable not Qisas but only to Tazir. So also is any one who kills unbelieving prison of war without authority (of the Imam).[44]

Law of Civil Imprisonment

When a creditor establishes his claim before the Qazi and demands the imprisonment of his debtor, the Qazi must not precipitately comply, but should first order the debtor to render the right. But if he neglects to comply with the decree and his capacity to discharge the debt is proved, then he must be imprisoned.

When the two parties voluntarily resort to an arbitrator (SALIS), his award is legally valid, and it is the Qazi's duty on a reference to him to give effect to the award if, he approved of it (Hedaya, 338, 343).

Development of the Mughal Police System

The Mughal police organization like most other branches of administration was shaped out of the vestiges of the Police System of Sher Shah which had survived the disorders following his death. The wonderful security was so effectively established that it became proverbial and was remembered long after his death. Sher Shah built his Police System on the basis principle of local responsibility the leading men of a locality, the headman and muqaddams, for instance of village were held responsible for the safety of the area within their village. In maintaining their security and guarding their jurisdictions the headman were assisted by the Amils and the ***Shiqdars***.

If the headman were unable to trace the thief or the robber they were thrown into prison and made to compensate for the stolen property. If the murder went untraced the headmen were to be hanged.

Sher Shah's justification for this sovereignty was that the headman of particular locality must be aware about the habitual miscreants, their identity as well as their place, therefore theft, murder or robbery cannot be taken place without the knowledge of the headman.[45]

It is not easy to determine that upto what extent the principle of local responsibility was kept up by Akbar on the basis of rural police and his successors. But it was maintained in as much as the local police officers is that the ***Faujdar*** and ***Kotwal*** were held responsible for thefts and robberies committed within their jurisdictions.

It can be concluded that the government organization of Police was made more elaborate and thorough. In the first place it should be noticed that under the Mughals functions of Police were no more confined to the maintenance of peace and protection of the supervision had always been a semi-police and semi-judicial function and although it does not seem to have been maintained under Akbar but it is soon reverted under his successors.[46] In the organization very important modifications were brought. The entire responsibility and authority of the Police department in the sarkar was directed between the ***Faujdar*** and the ***Kotwal,*** the former being in-charge of the rural area and the latter in-change of the chief town and its subaas.

These two officials were assisted by the ***Shiqdar*** and ***Amil*** in the Parganah. Wherever necessary the ***Parganah*** was limited into several smaller jurisdictions each consisting of a few villages under a ***Thanadar.***

Place which were very dangerous and infested with thieves and robbers were entrusted to the care of special ***Faujdars*** provided with adequate forces and a suitable subordinate staff. The road between Agra and Delhi required a special guard. Daud Khan Quraishi who was Faujdar of Mathura Mahaban and Jalesar was also put in charge of that record with a contingent of 2000 horse under his command.

The Muhatasib

The Muhtasib was an important police officer in the Muslim Khalifas. Under the Abbasids, the muhtasib was an overseer of markets and morals, or prefect of police. The Muhtasib's duties were very wide. He was to maintaine good morals and prevents unlawful acts. He had to uphold institutions and make regulations conducive to public prosperity and general security. It was his duty to make municipal regulations and to enforce them. In the interest of morality it was also his duty to find husbands for widows and to see that no divorced woman remarried before the expiration of the legal period,[47] to investigate complaints regarding paternity: to protect slaves and servants from the cruelty of their masters; to punish owners of beasts of burden for ill-feeding or overloading them; to see that foundlings committed to his care were properly looked after, etc. He had also to forbid visits to questionable quarters of the town and the public sale of wine and drugs.

He was, however, forbidden to meddle with the secrets of families.

Among municipal laws his duty was to enforce laws governing trade for forbidden transactions, e.g. usury, unlawful sales, counterfeiting of goods, extortionate charges, and so forth. He was to inspect weights and measures in sales. He could also compel debtors to pay debts but only on the applications of the creditor. The rule generally obtained that when the accused denied his guilt or his liability the jurisdiction of the Muhtasib ended and that of the Qazi began as to be needed evidence and legal procedure. The Muhtasib could interfere on his own initiative but the Qazi can initiate the same only on complaint.

Fraud in weights and measures was especially penal and the Muhtasib's duty was to provide standard weights and prevent use of unstamped weights and measures. It was also his duty to protect people from molestation by neighbours and to punish Muslims slandering and ill-treating person's of other faiths. The Muhtasib was expected to perform a number of humanitarian duties. He was not to permit maltreatment of slaves and servants.[48] He was to prevent cruelty to animals so that they were not overloaded and made to work beyond their capacity or otherwise ill-used.[49] He was to arrange for the care of foundlings and orphans.[50] Schoolmasters were not to be immoderate in inflicting punishment upon children.[51] He was responsible for the proper maintenance of the public utilities. He was to see that the water supply, the city walls, the public thoroughfares, the markets, hospices and inns were all maintained properly.

The amenities existing for travellers were in his care. Areas earmarked for the encampment of carvans were not only to be maintained but if too many carvans arrived at the same time, priorities for the use of these areas were to be fixed by him.[52] He was to see that river and seaports were kept in good condition and that boats were sea worthy and not overloaded.[53] In the city itself it was his duty to prevent encroachments on public thoroughfares and squares,[54] to order the demolition of structures which were likely to collapse and endanger life.[55] He was to forbid the use of high buildings, if the Muhtasib has sometimes been called the censor of public morals. This little is justified only to the extent that it was his duty not to permit any public violation of the law or decencies.[56] He was also expected to see that the public prayers were organized.[57]

The state of security and protection in the country during the reign of Sher Shah have been very highly admired by all contemporary and later writers. His policy was to give deterrent punishments and to use a drastic remedy against every source of trabble or evil. This policy, though looks very harsh, achieved its purpose admirable throughout the kingdom, no such uniform and summary answer can be given in respect of the efficiency or otherwise of the extent of general peace and security achieved by the police under the Mughals.

In times of stable government and under strong rulers the general state of security in the country was quite satisfactory maintained.[58] The contemporary European travellers on this subject testify to the peace and prosperity of the people and the abundance of all sorts of commodities both of necessities and luxuries. The roads and highways enjoyed a degree of safety which was quite enough for trade and commerce to go on unobstructed. Trade and commerce were carried on between the most distant parts of the country both by rivers and roads, there were Sarais and halting places provided with every comfort for travellers at short distances on road sides. These provisions made travelling in normal times quite easy and safe and encouraged commerce.

Manrique

These roads were linked on either side with shady trees and at fixed shags had comfortable carvans Sarais which offer refuge and shelter for travellers in sickness or fatigue or from rain. They were exacted at the expense of neighbouring villages or at the cast of Princes or rich and powerful men who wished to keep their memory green.[59]

The government took proper steps to keep these roads safe for travellers and merchants.[60] It was the duty of the Faujdar to guard against day light robbery. Other local official were also expected to assists in the maintenance of security on the roads. Nevertheless cases of blackmail or robbery were of frequent occurrence but when local officials failed to trace the criminals they were compelled to make good the losses incurred in their jurisdiction or they were dismissed.[61]

Regarding the security of the country as part from the large towns, is entirely wrong to say that there was no officer for law and order in the ***Mufusil.*** It has been shown already that country had a suitable staff of ***Thanadars*** and soldiers under him, according to the need of each place. THENOVOT- says that the faujdar was responsible for the security of the country just as the ***kotwal*** was responsible for in town.

Prison

The forts of Gwalior Ranthambore and probably, Rohtas served as state Prison for Political offenders; but for common felons there were local Prison known as BANDIKHANA. Bedsteads were allowed to prisoners, but they were allowed to have private medical attendance.[62]

References

1. Mughal Administration by J.N. Sarkar Ist Ed. Published in Calcutta 1921, Administration in Law and Justice in Medieval India by Raj Kumar Anmol Publications, p. 205.
2. Mughal Administration by J.N. Sarkar Ist Ed. Published in Calcutta 1921.
3. Administration, Law & Justice, Medieval India by Raj Kumar in Anmol Publications, p. 206.
4. Administration, Law and Justice in Medieval India by Raj Kumar Anmol Publications, p. 207.
5. (Islamic Ency- Ist II 606).
6. ***Ibid.***, p. 207
7. (***Ibid*.**, vol. IV 1031).
8. Mughal Administration by Jadunath Sarkar, 1952, Calcutta, Publishing House.
9. Ency. Ist II 606-7. Amedroz, Paper on the Mazalim Jurisdiction in the Akram Sullaniyya of Mawardi in ***J.R.A.S.***, 1911, pp. 635.
10. Mughal Administration by Jadunath Sarkar, 1952- Calcutta, Publishing House.
11. Studies in Aurangzeb Reign- Chapter II.
12. History of Mughal Government and Administration, H.K. Naqvi- 1990 Kanishka Publishing House.
13. Purchas IV 72, 73.
14. Steria 11-462.
15. B. Ahmad, ***The Administration of Justice in Medieval India***, pp. 143-166.

16. ***Alamgir Namah,*** p. 1077.
17. ***Henry*** Elliot and Dawson, ***History of India,*** Vol. III, pp. 172-173.
18. Alexander Dow. ***History of Hindustan,*** Vol III, p. 752.
19. Sir Charles Metcalf in the Report of the Select Committee of the House of Commons, Vol. III, App. 84, p. 331. The village communities are little republics having nearly everything they want within themselves and almost independent of any foreign relations. They seem to last where nothing lasts. Dynasty after dynasty tumbles revolution succeeds revolution."
20. Ibn Batuta, ***Travel,***s p. 194.
21. Mawardi Al, Akhamus Sultanyah (J.R.A.S. 1910), p. 764.
22. W.H. Moreland, ***India at the Death of Akbar,*** p. 35.
23. For details see, Kalematut Tayyebat K.C.C., "Lawyers Who Were Employed by Litigants". (Br. Mus. M. S. Add. 26238).
24. M.B. Ahmad, ***The Administration of Justice in Medieval India***, pp. 176-188.
25. ***Fatwa-e-Alamgiri,*** Calcutta, Vol. I, p. 1, 84-87.
26. Badaoni, ***Muntakhab-ut-Tawarikh,*** Bib, Indica, Vol. I, p. 187.
27. See. Trial by Ordeal.
28. Zia-ud-Din Barni, ***Tarikhi-e-Firoz Shahi,*** p. 21.
29. Vincent A. Smith, ***The Oxford History of India,*** p. 345.
30. Captain Hamilton, ***A New Account of East Indies,*** Vol. I, p. 315.
31. ***Mughal Administration*** by Sir Jadunath Sarkar, IVth Edition, Published by M.C. Sarkar and Sons, Ltd., Calcutta, 1952, p. 96-97..
32. ***Ibid.,*** p. 97-98.
33. Von Kremer, p. 284.
34. ***Mughal Administration*** (2nd ed.), p. 107.
35. If a man or women steal, cut off their hands... Quran, V. (37-38). To this Jalaluddin Al Bedari adds the commentary, " For the first offence the criminal is to loose his right hand which is to be cut off at the wrist, for the second offence, his left foot at its ankle for the third, his left hand for, the fourth his right foot.
36. ***Mughal Administration*** by Sir Jadunath Sarkar, IVth Edition, Pub by M.C. Sarkar and Sons, Ltd., Cal, 1952, p.103-104.
37. Hughes, 481. ***Encyc.,*** Isl. Ii. 1038
38. ***Encyclo, Islam,*** I, 132.
39. ***Ency. Isl.,*** IV- 173-74
40. ***Encyclo, Isl.,*** s.v. zina, iv. 1227.
41. ***Encyclo, Isl.,*** iii. 737.
42. ***Quran,*** V. 37 XXVI. 49.
43. ***Ency. Ist.,*** IV 1228.
44. ***Ency. Islam*** (ii) 824-828.
45. ***Administration Law and Justice in Medieval India***by Rajkumar, Anmol Publication Pvt. Ltd., New Delhi Ist Ed. 2000, p. 250.
46. ***Administration Law and Justice in Medieval India***by Rajkumar, Anmol Publication

Pvt. Ltd. New Delhi, Ist Ed. 2000, p. 251.

47. Mawardi- p. 234, 243, 244.
48. Mawardi, p. 229.
49. Mawardi, pp. 234. 243, 244.
50. Von Kraemer, pp. 292, 296.
51. Mawardi, pp. 233, 234, 240, 241; Ibn Khaldun, I, p. 406.
52. Mawardi, p. 178.
53. Ibn Khaldun, I, p. 406; Mawardi, p. 244.
54. ***Ibid.***
55. Ibn Khaldun, I, p. 406.
56. Mawardi, p. 238, 239.
57. Mawardi, p. 230-233
58. ***Administration Law and Justice in Medieval India*** by Rajkumar Anmol Publication Pvt. Ltd. New Delhi, Ist Ed. 2000, p. 254-255.
59. Manrique praised India Carvans Vol., II, p. 97-99
60. Tavernier,Vol, I, p. 292, Mandelso says that the governor of Ahmedabad had to look to the safety of roads, p. 114. Manrique also refer in general terms to the security of the roads, Manucci, pp. 450-51.
61. ***Ain-i-Akbari,*** p. 234, Peter Mundy Vol, II, p. 47, Manucci Vol, Ii, p. 204.
62. Manrique, Vol. I, p. 430.

8. Trade and Commerce

India's commercial organization during the sixteenth and seventeenth centuries may be studied broadly under two aspects, internal and foreign trade. Internal or domestic trade implies distribution of goods produced within the country and comprises both inland and coastal trade, includes trade with Asiatic (and Indonesia), African and European countries. Smooth working of this vast internal and foreign trade of India required not only a fairly adequate system of communications but also an organized land and water traffic as well as a complex mechanism of the marketing organizations with banking and credit facilities and mercantile establishment in her industrial centers, inland emporiums and ports.

Shah Jahan promoted peace but he did not encourage trade. The disastrous famines and the greed of the officials also crippled trade to a great extent. The Dutch, however, carried on their trade in the East in Persia, in Sumatra, Macao's Japan. The brightest period of the Dutch prosperity was Shah Jahan's reign.

Relation with Asiatic Powers

Turkey- the relations of the Indian Mughals with the Sultan of Turkey and the Sharif of Meccas. Communications between Turkey's the Mughal government opened in very peculiar circumstances. Zarif, a dealer in horses obtained permission from the emperor in 1637 to visit Albania to secure fine horses for the royal stud. The emperor gave to zarif a letter and some presents including a sword for Sultan Murad. Murad sent Arsalan Aqa as envoy to the Mughal court and zarif accompanied him. Arsalan Aqa stayed in India for above 8 months.

For the next ten years there was no exchange of embassies between

Turkey and India. In 1650, the Surat officers reported the arrival of the Turkish envoy Sayyed Muhddin. Thereafter till the end of his reign there is no record of any future exchange of envoys between Turkey and India.

Mecca

During the reign of Shah Jahan large sums were constantly remitted for the benefit of the Sharif and people of Mecca and Madina. Md. Waris remarks that from his accession till 1651 Shah Jahan remitted to Mecca about one million of rupees. The curious method of sending the money was that whenever any leading officer started on the holy pilgrimage he was entrusted with merchandise, which when sold in Mecca, brought cent percent profits. This profit together with the capital was divided among the sharif and the poor and destitute of the Mecca and Medina.

The period of Shah Jahan is marked by a rapid decline of the Portuguese power and the rise of the Dutch and the English. With the exception of a brief period in the reign of Akbar, we do not find the Portuguese to have maintained amicable relations with the Mughals. In fact they always extracted concessions from the later by seizing their trading vessels, or intercepting the passage of pilgrim ships to Mecca. No Indian boat could venture out into the open sea without a Portuguese passport for which the officers at Daman Dieu charged heavily. Thus Portuguese were regarded by the Mughal as the necessary evil, which they tolerated because they could not get rid of it. In both the maritime and commercial supremacy, the Portuguese were supplanted by the Dutch.

Dutch

The first factory of Dutch was established at Surat by Pieter Van Den Brocke and two years later Pieter Qillesz Van secured a satisfactory grant of trading privileged from Prince Shah Jahan who was governor of Gujarat. They continued to trade peacefully till the end of Jahangir's reign and when Sah Jahan was going from Junnar to Agra for his coronation, the Dutch offered him presents and it was favourably received by him. But in March 1628 their merchants at Agra were imprisoned for purchasing saltpeter without the Emperor sanctions. However, they secured their release by a little judicious bribery.

In 1635 a relation between the Dutch and the English, which had been amicable so far become strained though the leviers concluding peace with the Portuguese. In the end of the Dutch concluded a settlement with the Mughal authorities according to which the Dutch were allowed a free trade in Indigo.

In this favourable circumstances, the Dutch trade increased considerably, and they outdistanced both the English and the Portuguese. The Dutch attempted to monopoly the tin trade, which involved the Gujarat Merchants who complain against them to the court. On Shah Jahan's return to Delhi, the Dutch messenger one over some of the member principles of the court especially Jahan Ara Begum because Surat belonged to her. Their demand for exemption from custom duty was rejected. A ***farman*** granting them exemption from road duties in Bengal was promised to them, and they were permitted to repair and build boats at Surat and to erect a house in Swally. In return the Dutch agreed to grant free passes to Indian vessels going to China and other part in Dutch control.

The English

The most vigorous competitors of the Dutch both in commerce and navel supremacy were the English. They have arrived earlier in India and were solely but steadily expanding their trade. In December 1627, when Shahjahan arrived in Gujarat on his way to Agra, the President of the Surat factory, went to Broach to offer him presents. In 1630 Rastell saved a Mughal junk from the hand of the Portuguese during the famine of 1630-1631 hit the English trade hard and they had to close all their factories in the Deccan except Surat. Shah Jahan removed the embargo on the indigo trade but forbade the ships visiting Surat to anchor anywhere else except swelly and also the building of frigates in India.

In Shah Jhan's reign the saltpeter and opium trade developed very greatly. The exportation of cloths was checked and in its place arose a great demand for yarns. The manufacturers in England demanded yarns and not the manufactured cotton goods. Trade in indigo was very slack.

The shawl industry of Kashmir and the Punjab, the carpet industry of Agra and Amritsar, the ***Kimkhwab*** (cotton and silk cloth interlaced with gold and silver threads) and other embroidery works of Ahmedabad, the cotton goods of Bengal and the manufacture of porcelains, the carving in ivory and inlaid metal vessels reached their zenith in the reign of Shah Jahan.

Indigo–The trade in indigo suffered from three of the following causes:

a. Accident of season. The disastrous Gujarat famine of 1630; the excessive Biana rains of 1621 and 1640 which turned indigo fields into floating ponds; and the complete destruction of the crops in 1625 and 1646 by locusts.
b. In 1633 Shah Jahan made it a royal monopoly just as the Shah of Persia had the royal monopoly of silk in Persia. In the autumn of 1633 " A royal edict confining the sale of indigo throughout the Moghul dominions for the three years to a Hindu Named Manohar Das, who was to be assisted by a loan from the royal treasury, which was to share in any profit that might result." The Dutch and English protested strongly, but without result, because behind the Hindu Merchant stood an influential noble, Mir Jumla.[1]

To break this monopoly a solemn agreement was entered into at Surat on 19th November, 1633 by the Dutch and the English, with the effect that no party should purchase indigo for one year at the same prices and any purchase of indigo should be a sort of a joint venture. And, further the Dutch and the English solemnly pledge, themselves not to accept indigo as fright. This combination between the Dutch and English compelled Shah Jahan to dissolve his partnership Manchar Das and Mir Jumla on 14th April, 1635.[2]

The English made an attempt to develop the indigo trade in Thatta (Sind) and were successful in securing a ***nishan*** in 1644 from Dara Shikoh who was then the Governor-in-charge of Thatta.

Saltpeter

Saltpeter was in great demand. It was required by the foreigners for the manufacture of gunpowder. Shergarb near Agra, Thatta, Patna and

Ahmadabad were important saltpeter producing centers. Up to 1650 the trade was moderate but the establishment of the Dutch and the English factories at Patna gave this trade a great impetus. Patna became the most important center. Here the same capacity of the Mughal official can be seen and the same greed of the king to force the trade in saltpeter into channels which would flow towards the Imperial Treasury, as it is obvious in the case of indigo. "This commodity (saltpeter) hath this year cost as much trouble, being prohibited transportation by order from the King, upon false information from the Governor against ours and the Dutches proceeds in Masulipatam but especially theirs. Both hath suffered equal discontents; though its lycense (as are all other garunts) first given to us. Some bribes and extraordinary expense, it hath cost to work its release and no doubtedly it will require to regain our former freedom for buying that commodity."[3]

Yarn

The factors during Shah Jahan's reign received letters from the company to decrease investments in cloth and to increase the purchase of yarn. The quality of yarn produced in India had much deterioted and they (Company Director) wanted to encourage weaving in their own country. So the demand of yarn went up. The price of finer qualities of yarn was 12 to 14 pence per lb, one hundred bales being exported by Surat on 29th November 1641.

Opium

Opium was much in demand, both in India and for export purposes. In India, the Rajputs and the Mughals used to eat it, and it was also required for medicinal purposes. Foreigners also exported it to their countries, for it was much used in the manufacture of medicines.

Cotton Goods

Peter Mundy points out that there were various restrictions imposed on the manufacture and sale of cotton goods. The actual cost of bleaching is stated to have been Rs. 2½ to Rs. 3½ per score of pieces, beside the cost of cleaning materials, which means that it was 2 annas to 3 annas the piece (equal 14½ yards long). There was an allowance of 25 percent to the vendor; that is, the score meant 16 not 20 or to put it in another way, Rs. 20 counted as Rs. 25. Thirdly there was the ***raza***, or a fragment of 10 percent of the total length of a piece cut off by the owner before putting it out to bleach. Next, there was a fluctuating, unsettled brokerage on the unbleached goods, while on the bleached ¾ percent to 1 percent was chargeable as brokerage, together with a duty of ¾ percent to 1 percent more reckoned at 5 piece the piece. Of this duty 2 pieces went to the governor, 2 to the broker, and 1 to the merchant.[4]

Mandelso mentions a kind of embargo put by Shah Jahan on the use of ***Kimkhwabs*** manufactured in Ahmedabad. As he himself used to wear it, so his subjects had no right to wear the cloth.

Silk

The sale of skein silk seems to have been a monopoly of the Governor, and it had to be bought through his agent, the Town Magistrate (***Kotwal***) in Patna.[5] It appears that during Shah Jahan's reign official's interference in trade had reached its maximum. The King was busy in building his Palaces and Mausoleums and his officials were busy killing trade by extortion.[6]

Kasimbazar in Bengal was an important mart for the purchase of raw-silk. Patna, on account of its central position, became the most important silk mart in India. The following information about the cocoons and the production of silk, being of general importance, is given below.

From 250 to 400 cocoons go to the pound. To compose an ounce of eggs of the largest breed of silkworms of 4-casts, it would require 37,440 if each of these eggs produced a worm, and they all lived, from one ounce of eggs 373 lbs. of cocoons would be obtained.

"One ounce of worm consume in the

Ist age	....	....	6 of leaves.
2nd age	....	....	18 of leaves.
3rd "	....	....	60 of leaves.
4th "	....	....	180 of leaves.
5th "	....	....	1098 of leaves.

Total 1,362 lbs of leaves from the hatching to the formation of the cocoon.

"During the life of the silk worm there has been excrement to the amount of 745 lbs. 8 ozs., and uneaten leaves or fragments, 155 lbs. odd. 458 feet 4 inches of spun silk extracted from a common cocoon of 4 casts weight one grain. A cocoon yields 1760 feet of spun silk the ounce of this spun silk is 264,000 feet long. We may conclude, on an average, that the silk-worm, in forming its cocoon, draws a thread of half a mile in length. The full grown worm is three inches long. After four, five or six days each moth will have laid on an average 510 eggs, and 68 egg weight one grain: 180 female moths lay 91,800 eggs, weighting 2S! ozs.[7]

Manufacturers of rich ***taffetas*** in Gujarat and of the famous Sirohi sword blades were directly encouraged by Shah Jahan. But every where one could see "the Crumbling interior" in the otherwise magnificent facade of Shah Jahan' Administration. The corruption of the officials and the greed of the king were paralyzing Indian trade. It never recovered its pristine glory after Shah Jahan's reign.

Internal Trade: Some Features

Internal trade may comprise both inland and coastal trade. Inland trade might be purely intra-local, confined to one particular producing unit, village or town. It is only natural that various types of articles figured in inland and inter-local trade. We refer to a few salient features, without attempting to be exhaustive. These may be grouped in a general way as raw materials, necessitates and luxuries. Villages supplied different raw materials for urban manufacturers (e.g., cotton and silk to textiles). Forest yielded wood for ships, boat and furniture. [8]

The most important items were food stuffs and coarse, cheap textiles. In Bengal, where all kinds of food were plentiful, used to replenish most deficit areas in food grains. Agra got rice, sugar and butter from Bengal and also some wheat from Bengal and Bihar via Patna along the Ganges. Masulipatam in North Coromendel took cheaper Bengal and Orisa rice. Bengal according to "Bowery", absorbed Patna, gain', probably wheat or special variety of rice. But Bengal had to import Rajputana salt via Agra down the Ganges. Gujarat, reputed for her manufacturing and commercial importance, had to import food grains (e.g., wheat and coarse grain) from Malwa, Rajputana and

Northern India via Agra and rice from the Deccan, Gondwana and from Malabar (by sea).[9]

To take a few examples only as regard trade in raw materials the silk industry of Gujarat depended wholly on Bengal raw silk largely replacing Chinese in the 17th century. Again everywhere, textile manufacturers needed indigo and other dyes, grown only in particular areas.

Luxuries included finer varieties of rice, mangoes (e.g., of Bengal Golkonda, Goa and Delhi), finer textiles (e.g., of Gujarat cotton and Bengal silk); Malabar spices including pepper, ginger, cardamom, cinnamon, etc.); Kashmir products (e.g., shawls and woodcrafts). Slaves (usually children and then castrated) procude by the Maghs and the Portuguese were available in Bengal for disposal in different areas. But all these were costly, and evidently meant for the courts and aristocratic circles, and so could touch only a fringe of the internal trade.[10]

Routes and Centres

For the sake of convenience, the principal internal land routes have been shown below as radiating from major emporiums.

A. From Lahore to Sind and Gujarat: (a) to Multan-Bucker-Sucker-Thatta-Lahari Bander-Ahmadabad.

B. From Agra:

a. Northwards to Delhi-Karnal-Sirhind-Lahore;
b. Southwards to Gwalior, via (Malwa-Handia-Burhanpur);
c. Southwest to Ajmer-Bogra-Ahmedabad and then south to Surat via Baroda-Aurangabad and Deccan;
d. Eastwords along the north of the Jamuna to Allahabad; then across the Ganges to Benares and Patna.

C. From Benaras to Patna: one eastward via Jaunpur; and the other southeast across the Son via Sassaram and then north.

D. From Patna to Bengal; via Monghyr, Rajmahal, Kasimbazar, Hughli, Medinipur,

E. Bengal to Orissa: via Medinipur to Balasore.

In Gokonda there were six trunk roads;

i. From Surat to Haidarabad,
ii. From Haidarabad to Masulipatam;

iii. From Haidarabad to Madras via Gandikota;
iv. From Vijaywada (Bezwada) to Madras;
v. From Masulipatam to Srikakulam; and
vi. From Haidarabad to Ramallakota. Golkonda was also connected with Bijapur and Goa. Thus the two seas and two coasts (Masulipatam to Goa) was connected.[11]

River routes: i. From Multan down the Indus to the sea;
ii. From Patna down the Ganges to the Bay of Bengal;

The journey depended on winds.[12]

During the 16th and 17th centuries these inland trade centers passed through, some flourishing, some declining and others rising to prominence. However, taking the period as a whole and proceeding from the east to the west in northern India, the principle emporiums were Sripur, Satgaon, Hughli, Dacca, Calcutta, Patna, Benaras, Lucknow, Agra, Delhi, Multan, Lahore, Qandhar and Kabul, Thatta and Ahmedabad. In South, Burhanpur, Surat, Golkonda and Masulipatam were a few important ones. There was brisk internal (also coastal) trade, between Gujarat, Konkan and Malabar.

Patna and Benares were the important trade emporiums through which Bengal goods, food-stuffs, cloth and silk goods were carried on roads or rivers to northern India and then through Agra, Lahore (the Punjab) and Qandhar to Persia and through Kabul to Samarkand and Kashgar, and through Agra and Burhanpur to Gujarat and Surat. Bihar carried on inland trade with the Uttar Pradesh areas, Punjab, Bhutan and others areas.[13]

Coastal Trade

The hilly hinterland along both the eastern and western coasts of India and unauthorized exaction of the tolls by *jagirdars* and government officials, precluded smooth wheeled traffic on land. This made coastal trade important on either coast. A few of the important coastal routes are noted below:

1. From the mouth of the Indus to Gujarat;
2. From Gujarat ports to the ports along the West Coast; and also to the East Coast; as well as to Bengal ports,

3. The Coromendel Coast ports carried on an established coastal trade mainly in the product of Vivjaynagar empire and Golkonds kingdom, including food stuffs, rice, iron, steel and other metals (zinc, tin), tobacco, spices and the Masulipatam chintz with Bengal, Malabar and Gujarat.
4. Orissa maintained lively coasting traffic with the Coromandel and Malabar Coasts, Khandesh and Gujarat. "Gingelly Coast" oil was an important article exported from Orissa.[14]

Inland Security

Precautionary measures were adopted both by government as well as by the merchants and travellers; guards were furnished by local authorities; caravans; travellers or coachman engaged a special class of guards, ***charans***, as in Malwa and Gujarat, who compounded with the robbers for a sum payable by the party concerned.[15]

The Carrying Agency in Internal Trade

Various agencies transported the articles of internal trade, merchants or ***banjaras***, ***banias***, ***khatris*** and others, on land and water, subject to seasons, floods, draught and inland security. The carriers of inland trade included 'great' and 'small' merchants. They ranged from enterprising 'merchants princes', rich millionaires of Gujarat, Malabar Coromendal, Orissa and Bengal to petty 'pedlar'.

Besides the Indians, there were other Asian merchants, who, besides carrying on their overland trade, also participated largely in the internal trade of India.

Trade in Agricultural Produce

A consideration of the extent and organization of the market for agricultural produce is naturally essential to any serious study of an agrarian economy. The available evidence on the internal trade of Mughal India is by no means small. The closely knit national market of today is clearly the creation of the railways. The most obvious limitations to long-distance trade in our period were set by the means of treansport.[16] Bullock carts, camel and pack-oxen carried goods on roads that were little more than tracks, though distinguished in the case of the major highways, at any rate, by a system of ***sarais*** or walled lodging and store-houses mainly for passing the nights.[17] The traffic passed over some of the small rivers by masonry bridges.[18]

The roads were used by or ***qafilas*** or caravans of merchants carrying articles of higher values. The transport on land of goods of bulk, like food grains, sugar, butter and salt, was organized mainly by the famous cast of ***banjaras*** who practically held a monopoly of this trade.[19] Their method consisted of driving enormous herds of pack-laden bullocks, feeding on pasturages along the routes.[20] The ***banjaras*** were themselves nomads and lived with their families in camps or ***tandas***. A large ***tanda*** might contain as many as 600 or 700 souls and upto 12,000 or 15,000 or even 20,000 bullocks,[21] which would have carried about 1,600 to 2,700 tons.[22] On occasions such as when a large army had to be supplied, the ***banjaras*** might collect 1,00,000 bullocks or more.[23] The costs of transport under this system were obviously much lower than those of other methods of land transit,[24] but the pace was also much the slowest;[25] and the necessity of finding grazing lands along the routes must have sevierly limited the ***banjaras*** operations during the summer and in the drier tracts.[26]

It was the rivers which in fact offer the cheapest means of transport.[27] In Bengal,[28] Sind,[29] and Kashmir[30] goods were mostly conveyed on boats. From Agra, barges of great burthen –of 300 to 500 "tons "- sailed to Patna and Bengal down the Yamuna and the Ganga, performing the downward journey during the rains and taking the rest of the year to come up again.[31] Similarly, Lahore and Multan were river ports from which rather smaller craft went down to Thatta.[32] The capacity of the coasting fleet too, considering the circumstances of the time, was impressive,[33] and it was extensively used for the transport of goods of bulk, including food grains.[34] Eurpean Shiipping now dominated the Indian seas. The broad effects imposed upon trade by contemporary conditions of transport may be best appreciated by a study of transport costs.

For example, the cost of man-load carried on camel's back from Agra to Surat in the early years of the seventeenth century amounted to not less than four times the ***Ain-i-Akbari*** price of wheat of that weight, but only half of that of white sugar.[35] Unfortunately, the cost incurred by the ***banjaras*** are nowhere stated but we can still form some idea of the charges of river transport. The cost by boat from Multan to Thatta in 1639, for the same quantity, was nearly twice the ***Ain-i-Akbari*** price of wheat but only about one-sixth of that of white sugar.[36] But there were also other factors, besides the means of transport, which greatly influenced carrying trade. A series of imperial orders issued by Akbar and his successors declare all such imposts-indiscriminately term Tamgha and zakat abolished entirely or with some exceptions.[37]

It is possible that such prohibitions did result in elimination of a number of tolls and taxes many of them probably inherited from the annexed kingdoms.[38] In the big marts, frontier towns and ports, all goods sent out or in transit had to pay a duty of 2.5 percent ***ad- valorem,***[39] though in some places it was more, in others less.[40] Food grains, like other commodities, were subjected to this duty,[41] though they might be exempted in times of scarcity.[42]

As for the general state of law and order which determined the levels of "protection costs", it is worth noticing that the organization of the ***carvans*** and ***sarais*** of the ***tandas*** of ***banjaras*** who went armed.[43] The protection of the routes was more over regarded as one of the foremost duties of the administration and it was a well-established law of the Mughal Empire that the officer in whose jurisdiction an incident of robbery or theft occurred was bound to either recover the goods lost or himself pay compensation to the victims.[44] The officers met this obligation by pursuing a policy of ferocious reprisal and sacking the suspected villages, methods by no means unprofitable to themselves.[45] In general, however, one gains the impression, from the experience of European commerce in India, and especially from contemporary rates of insurance for goods in inland transit, that whatever dangers a lonely travellers might have to face, caravan trade was normally fairly safe over the larger portion of the Mughal Empire.[46]

The long distance trade became possible only when the price differences in these markets became so large as to accommodate the high costs of transport. There is no doubt that Bengal stood out in this period for low prices[47] and had a large surplus in provisions available for the export. There was a regular coastal trade in rice, sugar and butter, carried to Coromandel,[48] and around Cape Comorin to Kerala.[49]

Sometimes wheat was also sent from its port to southern India and the Portuguese possessions.[50] Opium, long pepper, ginger and tobacco were exported on Indian "Trading Shipping",[51] and gunny bags sent by sea to Persia.[52] Orissa annually exported by sea over 40,000 tons of grain (rice), together with butter and lac to the Coromendel coast included cotton yarn and tobacco.[53]

In the course of the seventeenth century, an important sea-borne trade developed in Bengal silk, notably through the agency of the Dutch who exported it to Japan and Holland. They are said to have taken 6,000 or 7,000 bales yearly (possibly an exaggeration) from the Qasimbazar market. There was brisk trade on and along the Ganga and Yamuna upto Agra. Agra not only imported raw silk and sugar from Bengal and Patna, but also obtained such provisions as rice, wheat and butter from the eastern provinces, without which, it was said, it could not have fed itself.[54] In return, salt was carried down by river to Bengal, where it was very scarce, together with cotton and opium.[55]

From Agra again, sugar, wheat and Bengal silk were carried to Gujarat.[56] As a mart, however, Agra owed much of its prominence to the indigo trade. The European trade became very important in the first half of the seventeenth century, after which it experienced a sharp decline.[57]

Apparently, wheat could be taken to the Lahore market from as far as Muradabad and high-quality rice from Sirhind.[58] From Lahore and Multan, sugar and ginger were sent down on boats to Thatta, whence these returned laden with pepper and dates.[59] Butter for export was brought down by river to Thatta from Bhkkar.[60] Indigo was carried in the same way from Sehwan for shipment to Basra[61] and, occasionally, via Surat to Europe.[62] For some reason, however, the Basra trade decayed,[63] and the English did not succeed in replacing it.[64] Kashmir exported saffron to Agra[65] and other parts of India, entering into competition at Patna with the saffron brought from Nepal.[66] In return, it imported salt, pepper, opium, cotton and yarn.[67]

The most important feature of trade in western India was the position of Gujarat as a great importer of foodstuffs. It obtained wheat and other food grains from Malwa and Ajmer and rice from the Dakhin.[68] Cotton and cotton yarn were sent by sea to the Persian Gulf and the Red Sea ports[69] and down the coast to Kerala.[70] It was also occasionally exported to Europe.[71]

The Indigo produced in Gujarat, especially the Sarkhej variety, was exported to both Europe and the Middle East.[72] A large quantity of opium was shipped to Kerala[72] and tobacco to Thatta,[74] Persia[75] and the Red Sea Ports.[76] Among re-exports, sugar was frequently sent to Europe,[77] silk to the Middle East,[78] and saffron to Malabar.[79]

On the basis of some general statements by Tavernier, the quantity carried by the ***banjaras***, the seventeenth-century specialists in long distance transport, has been estimated at 821 million metric ton miles a year, which may be compared with the Indian railways' carriage of 2,500 metric ton miles in 1882.[80] Over large regions as indicated particularly by the exports from Bengal and the imports into Gujarat-even food crops were affected by the demands of long-distance trade. This was naturally truer still of the cash crops; and in certain tracts specializing in the cultivation of high grade products, such as Bayana and Sarkhej in Indigo, and Pampur (Kashmir) in saffron, the peasant's dependence on trade must undoubtedly have been very great.

Local Trade, the Peasant and the Market

For the mass of the peasantry, the local market must have been of incomparably greater significance; and local trade largely consisted of the trade between town and surrounding country. The towns had not only to be fed, but had also to be supplied with raw materials for their crafts. In respect of food alone, they required a much larger portion of rural produce (in value) than would have been consumed by an equivalent rural population. For one thing, the court and the aristocracy, their dependants, merchants and other richer elements in the towns, required a much higher proportion of the more expensive products more wheat than coarser grains; more fine than ordinary rice; more sugar than ***gur;*** more cattle for meat; more sesame, spices, etc., and similarly more expensive drugs: opium, better-quality tobacco. In addition, the towns had large numbers of artistic who needed raw materials to enable them to work at their crafts, such as cotton, indigo, other dye crops, and silk. If, then, there was an urban population in Mughal India, forming 15 percent of the total, it might well have required for itself as much as 30 percent of the rural produce (in value), if not more.[81]

In most provinces, the peasant was obliged to pay the revenue in cash[2] and there he must have had to sell the produce himself. He must have often done by carting his produce to the local market or the towns.[82] There was the scourge of monopoly and engrossing, ***ihtikar***, alike denounced by moralists.[83] and prohibited officially.[84] When it was a case only a few persons concerning the stocks it was not the peasant, but the townsman, who suffered from it.[85]

In 1633 an imperial indigo monopoly was established, covering the whole empire and due to run for three years. But it was abandoned in the second year, not the least, perhaps, because, "many of the cultivators rooted up their plants in protest.[86] The price paid to the peasants themselves varied, ***arsattha*** documents from eastern Rajasthan show that village, harvest, prices could differ from the mean of such prices in the whole pargana by as much as 5 percent or more.[87] Similarly in Sind and Bayana in the 1640s a slump in indigo prices caused a corresponding decline in indigo cultivation.[88] The most remarkable example of the peasant's readiness to cultivate anything which could sell better is offered by the rapid expansion of tobacco cultivation, where it appeared to a contemporary that the peasants, in fact, anticipated the market.[89] With the exception of the ***sukhdas*** rice, a fine variety with limited market,[90] the prices at Lahor appear to have increased substantially over the century. If the Ain-i-Akbari in prices then represent the ceiling for the prices ordinarily prevalent at Agra before 1586, we may, on that basis, compare them with the prices we have for that city for the years 1637, 1638, 1670 and 1718. The prices for 1637-38 come from the books of the Dutch factory at Agra, stated month by month. For most of 1638 scarcity prevailed, the price rise being duly reflected in the monthly prices. The monthly accounts are complete for the years 1637 and 1638; quotations have also survived for January 1639, which are ignored.

Food Prices: Agra, 1638-1718, all in Rs per man-i-Shahjahani

A'in Annual average of monthly rates...........Feb-April............Aug-Sep ....1637 ....1638................1670................1718

Wheat	0.40	-	-	1.14	-
Wheat flour	0.50	-	-	-	5.71
Barley flour	0.37	1.08	1.72 -	-	-
Gram	0.27	1.05	1.70	0.95	5.16
Moth	0.40	0.97	1.54	-	-
Mung	0.60	-	-	-	6.15
Sukhdas rice	3.33	-	-	2.86	8.00
Ghi	3.50	8.39	9.52	10.00	20.00
Gur I	-	4.32	4.07	-	6.15
Gur II	-	3.41	2.55	-	5.41

A further comparison can be made of the rabi prices (March) of 1637, 1638 and 1670:

	A'in	1637	1638	1670
Gram	0.27	1.00	1.82	0.95
Ghi	3.50	8.46	8.73	10.00

In studying the prices tabulated above, one have to bear in mind the fact that 1638 and 1718 were years of scarcity, while 1670 had a plentiful harvest. The ascent in prices is therefore, unmistakable. By 1637, which seems to have been a normal year, prices were two to three times higher than the ceiling for pre-1586 Agra prices represented by the ***A'in***. In 1670, a year of plenty the prices were about the same as in 1637; and prices of wheat, gram and Ghi now were about three times those of the A'in (the sukhdas variety of rice again forming the sole exception, as in the case of Lahore). Clearly, a great rise had occurred between, 1586 and 1637; and the level attained seems to have continued till 1670.[91]

For Gujarat price data from both halves of the seventeenth century, Van Twist tells that before the 1630-32 famine, wheat ordinarily sold there at a rate equal to Rs. 0.79 per ***man-i-Shahjahani***.[92] This is corroborated by a stray quotation for Surat in 1618 (Rs. 0.77).[93] If it is disregard the high prices reported during the 1630-20 famine and aftermathed one can still find prices at a substantially raised level in the 1640s. Van Santen has collected nine quotations for wheat from the

Dutch records for various months during the four years 1641-4; these range from Rs. 0.87 to Rs. 2.50, but the average is Rs. 1.33 per ***man-i-Shahjahani.***[94] A similar rise is indicated in the case of rice from Van Santen's quotations. It was sold at Surat in 1609 at Rs. 1.15-1.20 and in 1611 at Rs. 1.14 per ***man-i-Shahjahani.*** There are ten quotations for rice at Surat during the years 1641-4, the rates ranging from Rs. 1.32 to Rs. 3.00, the average Rs. 1.61-1.85.[95]

Shah Jahan's strong rule promoted peace but it did not encourage trade. On account of his being a great trader, people were afraid to risk new ventures for they did not know the ***firmans*** in store for them. The disaster famines and the greed of the officials also crippled trade to a great extent. The Dutch, however, carried on their trade in the East, in the South, in Persia, in Sumatra, Macao and Japan. The brightest period of the Dutch prosperity was Shah Jahan's reign. During Shah Jahan's time the French were active on the sea not as traders but as pirates. In 1657, the position of the company was strengthened by reaffirming the monopoly of the company to trade with the Indies and by floating a "New General Stock of **£** 740,000 which was easily subscribed.

B. Trade Centres

Delhi–Delhi was the chief city of India during Shah Jahan's and Aurangzeb's reign. Being the capital of the Mughal Empire during Shah Jahan's reign Delhi grew up out of the ashes of old Delhi into a new and greater Delhi.

Delhi was famous for its skill in the arts and crafts. It was only under royal or aristocratic patronage that the artist flourished; elsewhere the artisan was at the mercy of his temporary employer, who paid him as he chose. The Mughal Emperors displayed a loudable appreciation of the fine arts, which they employed with lavish hands in the decoration of their palaces. A large number of exquisite miniatures or paintings on paper designed to illustrate manuscripts or to form royal portrait-albums, have come down to us from the sixteenth and seventeenth centuries.[96]

Agra

We get a glimpse of Agra in the pages of Mandelso's he describes "Agra in his day as the noblest city of Hindustan, and the one in which the

Mughal most delighted, it was as much as a horse-man could do the ride around the city in a day.

Its streets are fair and spacious, and there are some of them vaulted, which are above a quarter of a league in length, where the Merchants and Tradesmen have their Shops, distinguished by their Trades and the Merchandizes which are there sold; every Trade and every Merchant having a particular Street and Quarter assigned him.' There were eighty caravanserais for foreign merchants, 'most of them three stories high, with every noble Lodgings, Store-houses, Vaults and Stables belonging to them.[97]

Three new facts can be derived from the above description.[98]

a. The distribution of particular streets to particular trades. For instance, Goldsmith would have one particular street. In that street no other trade would be allowed. This specialization of the streets according to the trade that one follows still prevails today in India.
b. The existence of a tax on "Hot-Houses" "which brought in a considerable revenue to the state;" and;
c. The levying of a ten percent, tax on "all the merchandise that are imported into it (Agra) or exported out of it".

A special tax for the capital (Agra) was called ***Hasil.*** It was only one and half percent. Unless they had a rebate system, of which no clear mention is found, goods from Lahore would avoid passing Agra on the way to Surat and Patna. Father Sebastian Manrique in the "Itenerario" published in Rome in 1649 says that the Agra of 1640 stretched for six miles along the Jumna and had a population of six lacs, excluding strangers.

Burhanpur

This city was reputed for the cultivation of opium and the manufacture of transparent Muslins, which were sent out to Turkey, Muscovie, Poland, Arabia, Grand Cairo, and other places. The most beautiful cloth was that of "Gold, Silver, and of silk with flowers, whereof there is no reverse, one side being as beautiful as the other.[99]

Broach

Baftas (pieces of long and narrow calico) were very famous. Custom dues were paid at Broach on all goods, whether imported or exported.

Cambay–Here the industry of cutting agates and turning them into cups, beads, etc. was very important.

Ahmadabad had a considerable trade in silken stuffs, gold and silver tapestries, and ***Kimkhwabs***, Saltpeter, sugar, ginger (both candied and plain), tamarind, myrabolans, and indigo were other important commercial products.

Bengal had a considerable trade in cotton goods raw silk, saltpeter, sugar and rice.

Inter-Provincial and Frontier Trade

On account of famines, the floods, the trade interference of Shah Jahan and his subordinates, and the Indo-Persian wars, inter-provincial trade did not developed much. The 1630 famine was so severe that "children were sold at 12 pence or 6 pence or even free at Dhatia." (Peter Mundy). Agra and Delhi alone could pay for their luxuries, while the rest of the Empire was passing through a severe crisis. There was great demand in Agra and Delhi for the "Bidri pots" manufactured in the province of Bidar.

Bidri pots included the ***pandan*** (for keeping betel, nuts, etc.) ***ab-khora*** (cup of drinking water), ***rekabi*** (saucer), small and large cups, ***hukka*** (hubble-bubble), and candle-stick and other things; different sorts of flowers are inlaid on them with gold and silver by the artisans of this place (Bidar), so delicately and nicely that even a painter cannot picture them in his imagination.[100] Patna trade was important on account of its ***ambatis*** (calicoes), silk, cotton goods and saltpeter.

The Indian merchants brought gold and silver into Patna and purchased what they needed from the Patna Mart. The Deccan was famous for cloth: gold cloth, bordered cloth, turbans, waist-bands had more than a local market for their products. In the territory of the Karnatick ***chhint*** (a kind of cloth) is well manufactured; and a turban, also called ***chhint***, is woven, of which the warp and the woof are made of the hair of the cow. It is very nice, fine yellow and black. Many men make dresses of it.[101] The industry of Kashmir was much developed because Shah Jahan needed a large number of shawls and carpets for the new palaces he was constructing. It thus reached its highest pitch in the reign of Shah Jahan.

The development of Trade and Industry in a country is rather a modern idea and became prominent with the advent of the Industrial revolution. Farman dated 1075 para 21 makes it incumbent upon the people of Ahmedabad neither to burnt lamps on Diwali nor to threw water on the day of Holi (Shah Jahan's period), by the end of the sixteenth century. Ahmedabad neither came to be regarded as the unique city in the whole of India Ali Mohammad Khan the author of ***Mira'at Ahmadi*** called it the beauty of cities (***Zeenat-ul-Bidad***) while ***Abu'l Fazl*** mention as a noble city in the high state of prosperity.

Moreland estimates that between 1614 and 1659 there were 13 famines or period of great scarcity in India of when they occurred during the reign of Shah Jahan.[102] The Mughal Emperor displayed great taste in the building operations, not was a great palace builder, donated huge sums to the members of his family and courtiers as discussed.

The Mughal did not introduce a new revenue system. Only the system consistence with Hindu or Islamic law was adopted. The ordinary Indian was not affected by conquest of foreign Invader. Under Shah Jahan commerce and Industry including agriculture were overburdened with numerous exactions. The wealth of the country was sucked from all parts of the center of the government.[103] The Krori or the collector of a very of dams received 10% of his collection during Shah Jahan's period several instances are received in the reigns of Shah Jahan and Aurangzeb in which harsh and exacting officers were duly punished.

In Shah Jahan's time, saltpeter trade developed. It was required for the manufacture of gun-powder and as such, its trade developed very greatly. Shergarh near Agra, Thatta, Patna and Ahmedabad were in its centers up to 1656, the trade was moderate but the establishment of English, Dutch factories at Patna gave a great impact to this trade. The Mughal officials and the King himself attempted to gain indirectly through this trade. William Foster describes the attempts vividly. The suba of Agra was rich in nominal wealth, it was mined at Perath, and

Singhana, Iran existed in the provinces of Shahjahanbad, Allahabad, and Kabul.

Foreign Trade and the Internal Economy

Though foreign trade indisputably formed an important sector of the Mughal Indian economy, there is a little information of any statistical value on this in either the ***Ain-i-Akbari*** or later Indian sources. Whatever data exists come largely from European records. It is therefore not surprising that studies of Indian foreign trade should have remained so largely Eurocrentic.[104]

The two outstanding items of import into Mughal India comprised treasure (notably silver) and horses, while textile dominated exports. As for the other chief import, the needs of the Mughal cavalry generated an enormous demand for quality horses from Central Asia and Persia. Besides these, there were the horses required by the cavalry troopers. According to Pelsaert, the ***ahadis*** kept 10,736 horses.[105] The effective number of ***tabinan*** of the ***mansabdars*** for which ***daghi*** rates were paid, was 1,41,503.[106] Since these were ***daghi*** troopers, according to the standard formula for the composition of ***mansabdar*** contingents (***3-sih-aspah, 4-do-aspah, 3-yal-aspa***) they should have kept 2,82, 106 horses. On the basis of the ***dagh*** documents from Shah Jahan's reign, we may take it that they maintained hardly any horses of Persian bred, but that 55 percent of their horse or 1,55,158 were Turki.[107]

This might not however, have been true of the ***ahadis,*** who received their first horse from the imperial administration. The horses of the ***ahadis*** were likely to be generally of better breeds; we may, therefore, assume that two-thirds of the horses belonging to ***ahadis*** (7,157) were Turki compared with a component of foreign horses of over 75 percent in the imperial stables.

To maintain such large number of horses of non-Indian breeds, there was need to import horses continuously particularly since these breeds could not be raised well in India.[108] On this calculation, 875 Persian and 927 Turki horses should have been acquired every year to replenish the stables. Horses of the ***ahadi*** and ***tabinan*** cannot, however, be allowed an equal working life span.

They saw action much more frequently, and could not have been so well looked after. We might, therefore, take their average working-life as ten years. On these assumptions, about 16,000 Turki horses must have been required every year as replacement. In addition, there appears to have been considerable demand for horses from Deccan and South India.[109] Many of these were brought across the Arabian Sea from Hormuz,[110] we may see that nearly 1,000 Persian and 21,000 Turki horses must have been brought every year to supply the cavalry needs of Akbar's empire.

We have already offered an estimate of the total amount of expenditure on horses by the emperor, the ***mansabdars,*** the ***ahadis*** and the ***tabinan.*** These are re-stated in Table (A), along with the average price for imported horses by the number of animals. The price of Indian horses is similarly obtained by dividing the remaining expenditure by the number of Indian horses.[111]

Table A

	Expenditure on Imported horses	Implicit price per imported horse	Price per Indian horse
Emperor Mansabdar	34,000 ***muhrs***	44.50 ***muhrs***	25.42 ***muhr***
Ahadis &	24,300 ***muhrs***	22.44 ***muhrs***	7.52 ***muhrs***
Tabinah	2,19,631.5 ***muhrs***	13.53 ***muhrs***	5.61 ***muhrs***

In all probability, the horses of the ***zamindar's*** retainers were generally inferior to those of the ahadis and ***tabinan***; we should thus not be far wrong in taking the average price of Turki horses, imported for the ***zamindars*** as ten ***muhrs*** (just above the average price of the better Indian breeds acquired by the ***mansabdar***s for their stables). The ***zamindars*** expenses on non-country-bred horses, therefore, may well have been about 38,460 ***muhrs.***

The total cost of imported horses thus works out at 3,16,384.5 ***muhrs***; this would be the equivalent of Rs. 28,47,460 at Rs. 9 per ***muhr.*** While bullion and horses constituted the main imports and must have accounted for major portion of the value of imports, there were also imports of certain other articles, namely, precious stones,[112] non-precious metals like copper, quicksilver, tin and lead,[113] amber breads, vermilation, Russian hides, pearls, high quality woolen and silken cloth from Europe, Persia and China;[114] spices from South-East Asia and Ceylon,[115] coral, cloves, coffee and ivory from the east African coast and Red Sea;[116] and dry fruit from central Asia.[117] From across the Himalayas there was the imports of gold, copper, lead, musk, ginger, borax, woollen stuffs, wooden objects, hawks, falcons, etc. This material was carried upon men's backs and on ponies.[118]

According to the estimates then, bullion imports into Mughal India at the close of the sixteenth century probably amounted to roughly Rs. 2,04,71,768; while the value of horses imported annually was around Rs. 28,47,460.5. Bullion and the value of horses thus together amounted to Rs. 2,33,19,228. With the total remaining items (taken at one-tenth the total value), the total value of annual imports would be about Rs. 2,60,00,000.[119] For the maritime trade to the Red Sea and round the Cape of Good Hope we have no data bearing on value or volume of trade. Clearly, both of these channels must have carried far greater quantities of exports than that which went through Khandas and Hormuz. We may however, venture to speak in quantitative terms in respect of indigo. According to Pelsaert's estimate of 1626, indigo production of the Bayana and Doab tracts during favourable years was 884,80 lb. ('4,000 bales') and 21,200 lb. ('1,000 bales') respectively. To these may be added the estimated production of the Sarkhej tract, 3,32,000 lb. (in 1615), and of Sehwan, 1,32,600 lb. (in 1635).[120]

The major portion of Indian exports was accounted for by textiles; their predominant position in Indian commerce has been recognized in almost all modern studies, notably by Moreland.[121] Indian Cotton textiles were also exported by the western overland routes. Babur mentions cotton cloth among the main merchandise brought from India to Kabul,[122] the trade is also referred to at the opening of the seventeenth century.[123] Cotton textiles had an enormous market in the Red Sea countries and Turkey. The English factories at Surat reported in 1630.[124]

The Red Sea trade indeed absorbed very large quantities of Gujarat textiles. In 1629, an English agent reported that the annual 'caphilo of some 800 or 1,000 Cammels' from Cairo returned from Mokha laden with Indian commodities, among which he gives prime place to different varieties of cloth ('shashes, serebasts, allejaes, fine calico, duthy') and only then mentions pepper and cloves. Coarser cloth ('callikeens, coarse calico, chawders) and 'cotton wool' were first among the Indian goods retained in Arabia itself.[125] Even after the fall of Homurz; Persian and Armenian merchants carried 'Cambay' cotton goods on board English ships in the seventeenth century.[126] Indian cotton goods were also shipped to Portugal directly, round the Cape of good hope.[127]

Ceylon and the Maldives Island also imported cotton cloth from Gujarat.[128] The impressive scale of cotton textile exports can be judged equally well if, we change the focus from the importing areas of the world to the exporting regions within the Mughal empire. In the aggregate, Gujarat seems to have exported enormous quantities of cloth during the second half of the sixteenth century. Mughal India also exported some quantities of silk. Although Bengal silk exports were such a striking feature of India's trade in the seventeenth century, Barbosa says that Gujarat silk cloth was exported to East Africa and Pegu.[129]

Varthema too mentions silk alongwith cotton, as an important item of exports from Gujarat.[130] Later on Caesar Fredrick records 'silk of every sort' among the Gujarat exports via Chaul.[131] Alegaes (***alcha***), or stripped silk cloth[132] woven in Sind, had a large market in Persia and Turki. The geographical position of India, projecting southwards from the centre of Asia to the Indian Ocean, not only influenced her history but also determined the directions of her maritime trade.

K.N. Chaudhari observes, 'perhaps the most versatile nation of the time', on account of her geographical, climatic and ethnic diversities. The Europeans came not only for spices but also for textile manufacture (cotton and silk), indigo, saltpeter and other goods. Thus, the Indians trade relations with Europe became more intimate in the seventeenth century than before.[133] Further, besides the European companies, there was the irregular or unlicensed private tradeoff the Europeans. To get a total picture of India's foreign trade, therefore, one has to examine all these four decades, the Indian overseas and overland trade, Portuguese trade European companies' trade and European private trade.

By land: India was linked with the overland trade routes in Asia during 16th to 18th centuries. The inland trade routes of India, which have already been mentioned earlier, were connected with the international highways of commerce. These latter were principally the following:

i. **Agra Lahore to Kabul.** From here one route went north-east to Kashgar and thence to Sucur, Singanfu, Nanking and Canton in China (old silk route), while another route went west to Balkh and thence to Bokhara and Urgenj on the Caspian sea.
ii. **Lahore-Multan.** Via Chotiali and Pishin to Qandhar, India's doorway to West Asia, and thence along the main old silk route to Heart, Meshhed, Yezd, Isfahan, Kashan, Tabrez and Aleppo (connecting with Damascus, Tor, Suez Cairo and Alexandria), and also to Tripoli on the Levant or east coast of the Mediterranean, and again to Trebizond and Brussa on the southern shore of the Black Sea, across which lay Constantinople.
iii. **Lahari-Bandar.** On the Indus delta to Qandhar in the north and Gwador in the West.
iv. Kashmir to Tibet and China.
v. Patna to Central Himalayan states-Tibet (Lhasa)-China.
vi. Awadh to Tibet-China.

Again, the importance of the land route declined at first in the 16th century after the coming of the Portuguese but it revived afterwards. However, in the 17th century after the coming of the northern European powers, the Dutch and the English, the overland route came to be somewhat affected again on account of the competition of European shipping. Indigo carried to the Levant by land from Agra and by sea and land from Gujarat had to complete with that brought by sea, which proved cheaper.

By Sea and Oceans–The principal sea-routes of international commerce during the 16th and 17th centuries were the following.

i. From the mouth of the Indus to Persia, Arabia and occasionally to Ormuz.
ii. From Cambay, Surat and other Gujarat ports to Arabia, Persia, Egypt and the Staraits of Malacca.
iii. On the West Coast, (a) from Goa and Coachin to Persia Arabia and Africa and via Cape of Good Hope to Portugal (Liston); (b) from Goa and Coachin and other Kanarese ports to the Malay

world and the Far East, (c) from Malabar Coast to the Red Sea.

From the above, it will be clear that there were two well-reputed routes to West Asia, Asia, Egypt and the Levant or East Mediterranean coast: one via the Red Sea, Cairo and Alexandria; and second, via the Perisan Gulf, Basra and Baghdad.

iv. On the East Costs (a) from Negapatam, san Thome, Pulicat to Colombo; (b) from Masulipatam to Pegu, Malacca and Far East and also the Near East.
v. From Orisa and Lower Bengal to Europe and the Spice Icelands.
vi. From Bengal ports, i.e. Satgaon, Hughli, Sripur, Chittagong to Burma ports and Far East.
vii. From Pegu to Malacca, Bengal, Coromendal Coast, Orisa, Masulipatam, Red Sea, China and Japan.
viii. From Tenasserim to Bengal and Moluccas.[134]

Apart from the Red Sea and the Persian Gulf trade across the Arabian Sea, and the trade with Arakan, Pegu and the Indian Archipelago across the Bay of Bengal, India's trade with the East Indies and China and Japan to the East, carried on by Indian and Arabo-persian merchants and later on by European powers, as well as the trade with Europe was, principally oceanic. The type and size of ships needed for the seas and the high oceans were different.[135]

Nature and Pattern of Asiatic Trade

During the 16th-17^{th,} centuries India's Asiatic and African trade was conducted both along overland and overseas routes. Three broad points arise; the directions of trade and destination; the source of supply or participating regions; and the merchandise carried both ways.

West–In the west, India had active business connections with West Asia and Africa, though a clear line of distinction is not possible. Among the major maritime regions of India, Bengal traded extensively with West Asia, Persia, Arabia, Abyssinia and Syria (and through it with Europe); the East Coast areas also had brisk trade with Persia, Arabia and east coast of Africa; the West Coast areas including Malabar, Konkan, Gujarat and Sind had active commerce with the Persian Gulf and the Red Sea countries, Persia, Turkey, Syria, Abyssinia and Egypt.

Indian Merchants brought their goods to the Red Sea markets, of which there were two types. One was the ***hajj*** market for pilgrims, where the long distance caravans routes met and from where, Indian goods passed to Europe. The other, the regional market catered to the needs of the town in Hijaz, Yamen and Hadramaut and Red Sea ports on the east African littoral. The Indo-Red Sea carrying trade was controlled but not monopolized by the Karim, a Cairo-based organization (c. 12th –c. 1470). Indian ships could visit the ports in South Arabia and Gujarati ***baniyas*** settled here in 15th century. Indian trade here was also cosmopolitan, Hindu, Muslim and Jewish merchants working in co-operation.

The Red Sea developed as a major overseas market of India by the end of the 16th century. The Red Sea routes were subject to different political authorities, (for the Gulf route trade see later under Ormuz).

East, South-East and Far East

Here the chief customers of India's cotton goods were Arakan and Pegu. The Keen interest taken by China in India's trade is vouchsafed by the fact that China's marine pilots of 15th century used to have maps indicating the principal mercantile centers in Bengal, the Coromendal and Malabar Coasts, Konkan and Gujarat. But cotton goods of India constituted the most valuable exports in this trade in the 16th-17th centuries.

On the Coromandel Coast the local Telugu merchants carried on a brisk trade with numerous ships, exporting cotton cloths of Golkonda, cotton, thread, iron, steel and agricultural products and imported horses from Arabia, gold and silver from Africa, Pegu and China, spices and metals from Moluccas and the Sunda Island, and silk and other goods from China.[136]

International Trade Emporiums in Asiatic Seas

The principal international commercial emporiums in Asiatic seas were the following:

1. The island of Ormuz (Hormuz) in Persian Gulf, then held by the Portuguese, was the center of a small oceanic organization

extending from Basra in the North at the head of the Gulf to Muscat on the opposite coast of Oman in the south.

2. Red Sea ports, As Indian shipping to Malacca declined, as the trade of the substantial Arab merchants like the Karimi or their successors in West Indian Ocean (cf. 'the foreign moors' of Barbosa) suffered and as the Persian Gulf was blocked, all on account of the Portuguese activities, the Indians diverted their trading operations to the Red Sea.

It was an Osmanali Turkish lake. The Turks naturally controlled the ports there. Early in the 16th century, the Red Sea had two unrivalled trade centers, Jedda and Aden. Jedda was imported as an embarkation port for ***hajj*** pilgrims to Mecca with its annual fair where Indian cotton textile sold well. It was also an centre port for the Red Sea transit trade. For Indian ships was the only port of unloading even in the 18th century.

At first Indian ship used to come to Indonesia through the Sunda Straits. As this southern route fell into disuse early in 16th century, the Malacca Starits or the northern route grew to hold the key to the trans-oceanic route from the Far East to Suez. But with the Dutch capture of Malacca in 1641 or the Northern route lost its importance and its trade suffered.

North: Central Asia and Asiatic Russia: During 15th-16th centuries, India had brisk trade along overland routes to Central Asia and western Turkestan. India's cotton goods, spices, etc., reached even Asiatic Russia (Astrakhan) through Bokhara and Samarkand. During the next two centuries, not only did this Indo-Russia commerce develop through Tibet and Bhutan but Indian merchants, Hindu and Muslim, from Gujarat and the Punjab, settled in Astrakhan, a busy international emporium.

Trade with Europe

Before the discovery of the Cape route, i.e. the direct sea route to India via Cape of Good Hope (1497) India's trade with Europe was indirect. It was partly carried by the sea through the Red Sea and the Persian gulf and partly by the overland route, both converging on the Levant or east coast of the Mediterranean where the European merchants came and distributed the India goods to different countries in Europe. The sixteenth century was, in the words of Moreland, a period of unstable equilibrium as regards the organization of oceanic trade in its political and commercial aspects. In the sixteenth century, therefore, both the Muslim and the Portuguese came to dominate the commercial situation. But its nature was undoubtedly changed. Besides territorial ambitions, the Portuguese resolved to dominate the eastern seas, regulate and secure the eastern trade.[137]

The Muslims adjusted themselves to the situation in the areas of trade and permitted other traders of Bengal, Gujarat and Coromandel to hire space and accompany those on their own ships. But the Portuguese made trade a State or Royal monopoly on certain scheduled routes in specific articles, allowed private shipping outside making war prizes (i.e. seizing and confiscating the goods) of all unlicensed ships. This system had different impacts on different ship-owners. Many Muslim shippers, unwilling to yield but unable to compete with the Portuguese, sought to preserve themselves and their trade by adjustment and accepting the *cartazes.* Thus from 1548, Bijapur accepted the system and could send ships from Dabhol to Mocha and later the sphere was extended to Mecca, Ormuz and elsewhere in the Red Sea and the Persian Gulf. The Mughals, too, accepted the *cartazes* for ships from Surat to Mocha. Many ship-owners, fearing Portuguese seizures, suspended their voyages to East Africa, the Spice Island and the Far East or formed indirect partnerships with the Portuguese officials or merchants. Others, still, sought to defy the *cartaze* system, (a) changing the routes, viz., from Malacca to Coromendal instead of to Malabar; (b) preferring shipwreck along the shorter route; (c) sailing to the Red Sea pilgrim ports with *cartazes*; (d) occasionally fighting or pirating the Portuguese ships like the Malabar coastal pirates, whose licences the latter took. In any case, the Portuguese could not very well succeed in completely controlling India's oceanic trade in practice on account of the corruption and laxity of their officers; Indian merchants could thus avail of the loopholes in conducting their commercial activities.[138] The seventeenth century witnessed another commercial revolution more far reaching than that of 16th. The outstanding development in that century was the advent and the activity of the Dutch and the English merchants and the collapse of the Portuguese.

For both the northern companies the reign of Jahangir was a period of experimentation and assessment of the needs and potentialities of this new trade. By 1625, they established the trade in indigo and calicoes. Surat grew to be the chief center of European trade. However, the terrible Gujarat famine of 1630-32 led them to seek alternative fields and supplement the reduced supplies there from. By 1650, the Dutch and the English were not only firmly established in all the principal marts of the coast from Sind to Bengal but they prosecuted their commercial enterprises over Bihar and modern Uttar Pradesh.

Article of Trade of 16 Centuries–Foreign trade is a dependable index of the economic development of a country. The nature of India's foreign trade during the 16th and 17th centuries was fundamentally different from the present time. India's imports consisted of three categories; necessaries raw materials and luxuries. The necessaries included precious metals, horses, bullion was needed for coinage ornaments display and hoardings.The raw materials included raw silk (from China) for Gujarat silk winding; metals, e.g. Copper, Tin (from Malay), Zinc, Lead and quicksilver (from Lisbon via Red Sea); and ivory (from East Africa) coral, amber and dyewoods (from Persian Gulf); other goods for artistic handicrafts.

Luxuries or fancy goods for the king and the upper classes included (i) all sorts of precious stones (from the Archipelago) and pearls (from Ceylon); (iii) spices, (iv) perfume and rose water; (v) fruits, (vi) drugs; (vii) China goods (fine Chinese porcelain, highly prized by the emperor and the Muslim nobles); (viii) Europeans wines (and spirits); (ix) African slaves (x) mirrors glass ware, including coloured glass from Venice.[139] In the 16th century, the principal exports from India were as follows; and their pattern generally remained the same subject to a few changes.

i. **Textile Fabrics:-** including calicoes, muslins and fancy goods formed the major item of export through the 16th centuries.
ii. **Common Food Articles:-** Rice, wheat, pulses, oils, Surplus grain went from Bengal, Orissa and the Konkan Coast, north of Malabar to cities like Malacca, Hormuz and Aden; coconut products and some minor spices like ginger, cardamom, turmeric,

nutmegs, etc.

iii. **Raw Silk:-** from Bengal, and cotton yarn or raw cotton from Gujarat to (pegu).
iv. **Indo:-** Portuguese commerce in the 16th century rested on a single item, export of black pepper from Malabar Kanara. But it was a big business. Pepper lost its primacy as an Asian import because of competition of other goods, especially Indian textiles directly, imported by the Dutch and the English to Europe.
v. Indigo (from Bengal, Coromendal and Gujarat) and some other dyes.
vi. Opium (to Pegu Java, Malay Penisula, China and Peria);
vii. Miscellaneous minor goods, e.g. Bengal wax and lac and Coromendel skins.

Changes in the Foreign Commerce in 17th Century

Of all these exports, cotton goods constituted the most important and extensive. Again of the three principal centers of export of cotton goods, the Coromandel Coast was more important than Cambay of Bengal. It was the left arm of the Moluccas and the Islands round about, because without cloth imports from Coromandel, trade would be dead in the Moluccas (1612).[140] Moreland's view was that at the beginning of the seventeenth century Indian goods were not much demanded in western europe, is either an understatement or ignores the evidence of some Dutch sources.

At first, the English led the race in the cotton trade but the Dutch made up the lee-way in the second half of the 17th century. The demand for cotton goods by the Dutch, the English and the French in Europe also grew in the 17th century as house linen and as calicoes for ordinary use. But the trade was mostly retail and upto 1660 there was practically no demand for muslins and prints for apparel. But by the third quarter of the century Indian textiles became highly popular and the eighties showed 'exceptional' rise in their imports. Then came a setback owing partly to prohibitionist policy and partly to the point of saturation being reached.

Besides pepper and spices, which were older exports, the new items to Europe were the following. ***Indigo*** now became so highly prized in import that it became in Roes's words a "prime commodity' in commerce. It was found to be more advantageous, it was relatively fast and cheap, and hence economical; it was mostly needed in the Mediterranean area. But Spanish, American and West Indian competition reduced its use to a small extent in western Europe in the second half of the 17th century. ***Saltpeter,*** an indispensable raw material for manufacture of gunpowder was in great demand to feed the growing munitions industries in West European countries for their political policies and military developments. It was also a lucrative article of trade. Next came raw silk from Bengal. Mulberry plantations of Kasimbazar and north Bengal yielded silk yarn of all India repute and the area had become famous for its silk-weaving also. The European companies bought at first the finished silk manufactures of the region and then raw silk. By the fifties of the 17th century, Bengal came to supplant Persia, France and Italy as suppliers of silk yarn to Europe's weavers. In the 18th century, it ranked next to textiles in bulk and value among imports.

Demands for a variety of Indian silk goods (taffetas and brocades) and cotton goods grew in Europe now. Raw cotton came to be exported especially to Persia and Arabia but not to England and Europe till the America Revolution. Cotton yarn, however, went to Europe in large quantities for manufacture of wicks. Other items were rice and sugar, both moist and dry (to Persia and France along land routes); lac (to Persia). Iron and steel went from Mansulipatam.[141]

In the second half of the 17th century the principal items of India's direct trade with Europe were four : (i) Madras calicoes, (ii) Bihar saltpeter, (iii) Bengal silk and (iv) Bengal sugar. European goods were as before hardly demanded. But now the rich upper classes got wider opportunities of satisfying their craze for costly novel curiosities, described by Jahangir as 'rarities and antiquities', and mentioned in English commercial records as 'toys' to be presented or sold to them.[142]

The Europeans utilized this weakness of the Mughal ruling classes for gaining vital economic privileges which proved ultimately detrimental to the economic interests of the country.

Problem of Proving Purchasing Power

European merchants trading with India and all countries in the Asiatic seas soon realized that the demand for European goods there, was insufficient. They could, however, easily purchase goods for import to Europe by ready cash. But export of bullion (i.e., gold and silver) was against both prevailing mercantile theory and popular prejudice. The question therefore, arises how they solved the problem of financing their trade.

At first, the Portuguese had to pay for spices in the Archipelago in bullion. Subsequently they avoided this by exchanging goods between India and the Archipelago. By the end of the 16th and beginning of the 17th century, they established a profitable commerce between (i) ***India***, West Asia and Europe, and (ii) China and Spice Islands. Both the Dutch and the English also had to devise methods to solve the problem of financing their imports. They could have paid for these by exporting European goods for sale. But as the Indian demand for these was insufficient, they began to limit such exports. There were three other methods of solving the problem and the commerce of the 17th century was a combination of all these;(i) to carry out precious metals; (ii) to borrow money; and (iii) to invest capital in Asiatic trade and to remit the profit to Europe in the form of spices and other eastern products. Thus, the English company's bullion imports to India steadily grew through the 17th century, from **£** 22,000 in 1601 to **£** 52,000 in 1616; and **£** 80,000 a year by end of 17th century.

Asiatic Export Trade to Other Asiatic Countries: though the quantity of cotton goods handled by the Dutch increased progressively (and more than doubled) during 1625-61, particularly in the markets of south-eastern Asia, there were no signs of a similar development of English trade there. So Moreland doubts whether, the increased Dutch exports represented new business or merely a change in carrying agency. The general facts are that the increase in Asiatic trade was perhaps not much, because goods were sent from Batavia to Europe, Africa and America.

New lines of business, however, were opened specially by the Dutch regarding Bengal silk (from 1650) and Coromandel skins (from 1644) to Japan, export of slaves, provisions (food grains) and other goods for Asiatic trade, build up a capital and recognize the economic life of the Spice Island, developed Indian Export trade. Batavia became a center of grain trade imported from India and elsewhere.

Shipping Industry:- At the time of the advent of the Dutch and the English in the beginning of the 17th century, the overseas and coastal trade of India was shared by the Indian ship-owners and the Portuguese. But now, with the decline of the Portuguese, the Dutch and the English entered the field and soon came to control an increasing share in this trade, not so much by peaceful competition as by terror tactics. The defenseless existing Indian carrying agencies, in backed by their own government were injuriously affected. While Goa declined, Surat and later Bombay prospered.

At Masulipatam, the major part of the shipping was in Indian hands and it is suffered due to foreign competition. But about 1640 the Golkonda officials insisted on preferential treatment for their own ships. Later on (1647) Mir Jumla, the minister of Golkonda converted the preferences into a monopoly and articles could be sent only on Indian ships to Persia, Basra, Mocha and Pegu. This was discounted, when he joined the Mughals. By 1661, the Dutch and the English again competed for freight to Persia.

Moreland has minimized the adverse effects of the advent of the English and the Dutch on Indian shipping. Its declined not as a result of peaceful competition but of a calculated policy of force exemplified in repeated acts of violent piracy.[143]

Establishment of new markets:- the outstanding commercial development' of the first half of the 17th century (1660-60) was the establishment of new markets for Indian goods in England, the Netherlands and France. There were three commercial regions in Europe: Russian, Mediterranean and the Atlantic. The trade in the first region was certainly not as negligible or unimportant as Moreland implies.

Volume of Export Trade to Western Europe–The export trade of the English (i.e. for Western Europe) from Surat passed through several stages. Upto 1620, the main articles were indigo and miscellaneous goods. Then during 1620-30 trade in calicoes rapidly developed. After the Gujarat famine and during 1638-53, the articles increased to calico, indigo, yarn, saltpeter, pepper, sugar, etc. The trade of the English 'East India Company' rapidly increased from 1657 and there was a rapid change in relative importance of the East and the West Coasts. The export of saltpeter as a constituent of gunpowder was a new feature of Indian commerce. It was organized first by the Dutch and then by the English. By the middle of the first half of the 17th century (c. 1625), Surat became the principal port for Europe. The East Coast was contributing little and Bengal was still unknown to European buyers. After the famine of 1630-31, many parts of India including Bengal and Orissa were tapped a fresh to supplement inadequate supplies. After 1650, the eastern coast took a prominent place in European trade.

As the trade of Gujarat declined, then an account of West Indies competition and unfavourable political conditions due to the rise of the Marathas and in the 18th century for political dis-orders in India and Persia, Bengal became commercially more important. A business organization was created with future possibilities.[144]

Chief Sea Ports of India

Bengal mainly exported rice, sugar and muslin; the Coromandel Coast, calico, muslin, fancy goods and dyed yarn; Malabar, pepper; Gujarat, cotton goods, indigo and yarn. Another striking features was that to every important oceanic ports were attached a few auxiliary roadsteads where articles of overseas trade were assembled and distributed.[145]

Gulf of Cambay (or Gujarat) Ports, Collectively forming the most important group in western India. In the 15th century, Cambay (Bandar Khambayat) of the sultanate of Gujarat had grown to be the most important port in India with 2 ports and an income of 34 lakhs. Later on the number of its ports increased to 48, as mentioned in ***Mirat-i-Ahmadi***, dealing with corals and pearls, while that of Delhi depended on wheat and barley. Surat was not only one of the major seaports of Gujarat but the largest port of the Mughal Empire and the port of pilgrimage down to the first half of the 17th century.

The imperial ship, Ganj-i-Sawai, returning from pilgrimage and bringing 52 lakhs of rupees in gold and silver (the sale proceeds of Indian goods at the Mocha and Jedda), was plundered by English pirates (Khafi Kh).[146] The chief export from these Gujarat ports were: silk goods, woven out of Murshidabad silk in Ahmedabad, exported to the

Philippines, Borneo, Java, Sumatra and other neighbouring lands; ***baftas*** dyed in Agra and Ahmedabad and sent to East Africa, Abyssinia and Arabia.[147]

Konkan Ports:–Next came in the Konkan region and in Ahmadnagar Kingdom the Portuguese dominated ports of Bassein, a great ship building center, and Chaul and Dabul (Dabhol), exporting the cotton clothes of painted and of superior quality silk fabrics woven out of Murshidabad (and also Chinese) silk in Ahmedabad and Gujarat and pepper and pilgrim traffic to Red Sea (Mocha) and Persian Gulf areas (Ormuz) and also coastwise to Goa by sea.

Kanarese Ports:–Further south came in Kanarese ports, Goa, Bhatkal (western sea-port of Vijaynagar), Rajpur and Karwar. Goa (passing from Bahmani Kingdom of Bijapur and then under the Portuguese) must be considered alongwith Cochin. If Textiles were the principal export, metals and luxuries were the chief imports to India.[148] Possibly the routes from Konkan and Gujarat were shared by the Arabs with others.

Malabar Ports:–There was also coastal trade to Calicut, Cochin and Ceylon. The advent of the Portuguese in India and their antagonism towards

The Malabar and Konkani Muslim traders adversely affected the shipping of the latter with the middle East and proportionately favoured the Gujarat traders. Unlike the Cambay ports, Malabar group of ports hardly exported local products except pepper. Between Mangalore and Cape Comorian, the most important ports were Calicut (opposing the Portuguese and sheltering the Arab pirates) and Cochin, Calicut was an important center of the Karimi traders in India. Possibly the route from here to Aden was monopolized by the Arab ships.

Bay of Bengal Ports

Coromandel Coast Ports:–From time immemorial India's entire East Coast had maintained commercial and colonial connections with south-East Asian islands and the mainland. In the 16th century the Coromandel Coast Ports, Negapatam, San Thome, Pulicat (Eastern Port of Vijaynagar) in the south and Masulipatam (the chief port of Golkonda) in the north, had already become commercially somewhat important.

In south India, Masulipatam was the most important seaport from which ships sailed to the coast of Bengal, Arakan, Pegu and Tenasserim, laden with all sorts of cotton cloths, glass, iron, cotton yarn, both red and white; tobacco and cowries, used a money in Bengal and Arakan. Other articles of export from the East Coast were iron and steel, diamonds, rubies and perals.[149]

Gineglly Coast–Vizagapatam and Bimalpatam sent out rice and oilseeds to different ports on eastern and western coasts of India for export to foreign countries.[150]

Orissa Ports–Pipli and Balsore became important only during the first half of the 17th century. Cuttack, the capital of Orissa province, at the bifurcation of the Mahanadi and the Katjuri, was an important port.[151]

The sea port of Bengal were not very popular at first because of time factor among other reasons. Even in 1627, the Batavian Governor General considered trade here to be precarious owing to constant wars, rebellions and frequent administrative changes, while the estuaries of the Hughli and the Meghna were full of pirates.

Organization of Commerce-Internal and International

How was this vast internal and international trade of India organized during the 16th to 18th century? On the western coast of India the Muslims concentrated their business especially at Surat and in the ports of Malabar (e.g., Cannanore and Calicut), which became an inter-port of the trade of the Far-East to the Persian Gulf and the Red Sea and hence, a commercial centre of first importance. Besides the Sindhi traders in western India there were the traders of Dabul and Malabar (including the Konkanis, Arabs and other Muslims), referred to as 'Dabulls' and Malabars in English records whose ships traded with the Red Sea ports.[152]

The Persians (including Zoroastrians) and Armenians who traded overland through Qandhar thronged the markets of Agra and Lahore (1620-26). They were in Patna (1632). Tavernier met four of them coming from Danzing and going via Patna to Bhutan to sell yellow amber images. Owing to decline in the trade of Surat after 1664, the

Armenians and Persians left it for Bander Abbas.

The Parsis (Zoroastrians), at first an artisan (weaving) community, developed as traders, money-lenders, middlemen, ship-owners in the 17th century in Gujarat coasting trade, collaborated with the English, and later grew to be the first modern capitalists in India. The Jews, who were at Cochin and elsewhere in the Deccan, were also active on the roads in the interior.[153]

Volume of India's Foreign Commerce

Attempts have been made to estimate the volume and value of Indo-European trade. But in the absence of adequate data, it is difficult, if not impossible, to arrive at any definite numerical assessment of the volume of India's commerce, overseas and coastal and value of her importance and exports.

i. European goods had no market among the poor masses while the rich upper classes had a craze for novelties, toys or dear trifles.
ii. The variety of merchant vessels used on the Indian seas. These were of five broad categories: (a) the largest, the (Portuguese) carracks (1500-2000 tuns) with an average of 1800 tuns (for European voyages) or less (for Far-East); (b) the next largest, the pilgrim ships to and from the Red Sea of 400-1500 tuns.

References

1. William Fosters, ***The English Factories in India*** (1630-1633), pp. xxxiv-xxxv.
2. D. Pant, ***The Commercial Policy of the Mughals***, 1930.
3. ***The English Factories in India (1630-1633)*** by William Foster, p. 21.
4. ***The Travels of Peter Mundy (1608-1667)*** by H.S. (Vol. II). pp. 369-370.
5. ***The Travels of Peter Mundy (1608-1667)*** by H.S. (Vol. II). p. 371.
6. ***The Comercial Policy*** by D. Panth, 1930.
7. ***A History of the British Empire in India and the East*** by Dr. E. H. Nolan (Div.III), p. 404.
8. Mughal Economy, , ***Organization and Working***, J. N. Sarkar.
9. Mughal Economy , ***Organization and Working***, Jagdish Narain Sahay Published, in Jan., 1987, Pub. by Naya Prakashan 306. Printed by Good Associate 16/36 Dixan Law Calcutta, pp.141-142.
10. ***Features***, T. Raychaudhuri, CEH, i. 325-31.
11. Trade routes used by foreign travellers like Fitch, Manrique, Mundy, Bernier,

Tavernier & John Marshall, Van Ravenstien; De: Laet's account, Chahar Gulshan: Sarkar, SAR; Mookerji (observation's on p. 11 very useful): Sherwani, Qutubshahi Dyn; See also CEH. i.

12. For River routes see relevant sub-section in Section II. Mughal Economy Organizal and Working Jagdish Narain Sahay Published, in Jan, 1987, Pub. by Naya Prakashan 306. pp.142-143.
13. Localized markets-Tavernier, ii. 95; Fitch (ETI. 15). Mirat (Supplement)Tr. 12. From Bengal to Bihar: EFI (1618-21), 192-7; Pelsaert, 7; Mundy, ii. 254-9; Master, ii. 135 (Hughli); Wilson, EAEB, i. 379.
14. Moreland, IDA, 240-5;CEH. i. 333. Bengal 16th Century: Barbosa i. 125, 127-30, 137-9; ii, 92-3; Fitch; Linschoten, i. 94-7; Du Jarric, 140, 157; Badauni (Tr)i. 349. 17th Century: Palsaert, 12,27; Moreland, Relations, 59, 68-69; Manrique, i. 56; Bernier, 437-9; Pyrad, i. 327; Baldaeus tr. 163; CEH, i. 331 (Gingelly). Imports to Bengal; Verthema, 151; Fitch, ETI, 18; Baharistan Tr. 5; Manriqueii. 428, 440; Hedges, iii. Pp. clxxviii-ix; Wilson, EAEB, i. 398-400.
15. For Detail, Jagdish N. Sarkar, ***Mughal Polity***, ch 6; CEH i. 356-8.
16. A very effective proof of this lies in how the food grain prices, which earlier had a very large range over the different parts of the country, began to cluster together as the railway network extended during the latter half of the 19th century Zahoor Ali Khan offers an ingenious cartographic exposition of this process in Indian Historical Review, IV (2), 336-53.
17. ***The Agrarian System of Mughal Indian IInd Revised Edition 1556-1707***, Published in India by Irfan Habib, Oxford University Press New Delhi 1st published in 1963. Revised edition in 1999, p.69.
18. Ibid, p.69
19. The English Factories, 1624-29, 270; Mundy, 55, 95; Tavernier, I, 33-34. The classification of the ***banjaras*** by Tavernier into four distinct castes, each respectively carrying corn, rice pulse and salt is entirely fanciful. They took to any region such goods as it was in need of and returned with those of which had a surplus (Mundy, 96, 98-9; c.f, also ***Ahkam-i-Alamgiri***, f. 83 a). They trade largely on their own account, but were ready on occasions to carry goods for others (Mundy, pp.95-96).
20. Peter Mundy, 96. Among the exaction declared illegal by Aurangzeb are listed the fees levied on the ***banjaras*** for grazing their animals (Mir'at, I, 1, 287; Fraser 86, f. 93a; Khafi Khan, I, 87).
21. Peter Mundy, 95-96 Tavernier, I, 32-33.
22. A bullock seems to have normally carried about 4, 2 ***man-i-Shahjahani***, or 310 lb, avdp. (Factories, 1655-60, 63). Mundy, 95, puts the load at 4 ***man-i-Jahangiri***, i.e. 265.5 lb, only, and Marshall, 425, at 4 ***man-i-Shahjahani*** (or 295lb.). Tavernier, 1,32, on the other hand, though it to be as much as 300 or 350 livers, i.e. 327 to 390.5 lb.
23. T.J., 345; ***Ahkam-i-Alamgiri***, f.83a.

24. This may be deduced for instances, from Factories 1618-21, 102 and 1655-60, 63. The low costs were not primarily due to the use of bullocks. Pack oxen hired in the ordinary way were more expensive in terms of weight carried than carts (Marshall, 117-118).
25. Not above 6 or 7 miles a day at most (Mundy, 96). Otherwise pack-oxen provided the quickest transport (Tavernier, I, 33). A laden cart normally took 35 days to reach Agra from Patna in the dry season (Factories 1618-21, 191, 199), and both carts and camels 50 days to perform the journey between Agra and Surat (Lett. Recd., IV, 237-8).
26. The whole subject of banjaras has been discussed by me, with use of further evidence, in James Tracy (ed.), Rise of Merchant Empires, 371-79.
27. This may be illustrated by the transport charges quoted in 1639; "Freight or cartage of goods" from Agra to Multan was Rs. 2½ per "mean"; but from the Multan to Thatta, a slightly longer distance, the freight by boat amounted to only Rs ¾ "per mean" (Factories, 1637-41, 135-6).
28. ***Ain-i-Akbari*** I, p. 389.
29. ***Ibid.***, it is States that were some 40,000 boats "small and big" playing in the Sarkar of Thatta or Sind below Bhakkar. See also Tarikh-i-Tahiri, Or. 185, f. 58a-b; ed., 130.
30. ***Ibid.***, 563; T.J. 298 Abu-l-Fazl says there were 30,000 (rect, 3,000?) boats in Kashmir (A.N., III, 550), while Jahangir, ***op. cit.*** gives the number as 5,700 for the city (Srinagar) and the Parganas.
31. Jourdain, 162; Mundy, 87-88, Moreland puts the"tun" of the English records of the time at 4/10 to 6/10 of the net registered ton of the modern shipping (India at the Death of Akbar, 310-12). Bowery, 225, speaks of "great flat bottomed Vessels of an Exceeding Strength .... .called Patellas", playing between Patna and Hughli, each of which brought down 4,000 to 6,000 "Bengala maundus" or about 130 to nearly 200 tons in weight. Cf. also Hamilton, II, 20-21.
32. ***The Agrarian System of Mughal India IInd Revised Edition 1556-1707***, Published in India by Irfan Habib, Oxford University Press, New Delhi 1st published in 1963. Revised edition in 1999, pp. 70, 71.
33. The Agrarian System of Mughal Indian, IInd Revised Edition 1556-1707, Published in India by Irfan Habib, Oxford University Press, New Delhi 1st published in 1963. Revised edition in 1999, pp. 70,71.(Factories, 1646-50, 190). Cf. Moreland, India at the Death of Akbar, 227ff. and Akbar to Aurangzeb, 81ff.
34. ***Ibid.***, p.71. (Mir'at, I, 354.).
35. ***Ibid.***, p.71. See A'in, I, 60, 65, for prices of wheat and white sugar.
36. ***Ibid.***, p.72. (Khulasatu-s-Siyaq, f. 90b; Or. 2026, f. 57a.).
37. ***Ibid.***, p. 72.
38. ***The Agrarian System of Mughal Indian IInd Revised Edition 1556-1707***, Published in India by Irfan Habib, Oxford University Press, New Delhi 1st published in 1963. Revised edition in 1999, pp. 72, See Tavernier, I, 31; Factories, 1646-50, 192-3;

and Waqa-i-Ajmer, 12-13, 196.

39. ***The Agrarian System of Mughal Indian, IInd Revised Edition 1556-1707***, Irfan Habib, Oxford University Press, New Delhi, p. 73.
40. ***The Agrarian System of Mughal Indian IInd Revised Edition 1556-1707*** , Irfan Habib, Oxford University Press New Delhi, p. 73.
41. Cf. Khulasatu-s-Siyaq, ***op.cit.*** Fraser 86, f. 74a-b.
42. Khafi Khan, II, 88, Or. 6574, f. 33b; Mir'at, I, 309, 315.
43. Mundy, 262. For their readiness to fight, see Tavernier, I, 33.
44. ***The Agrarian System of Mughal Indian, IInd Revised Edition 1556-1707***, Irfan Habib, Oxford University Press New Delhi. p. 75.
45. ***Ibid.***, p. 75.
46. ***The Agrarian System of Mughal Indian IInd Revised Edition 1556-1707*** , Irfan Habib, Oxford University Press New Delhi. p.76.
47. Linschoten, I, 94-5; A'in, I, 389 Bowery, 193-4***; Kalimat-I Taiyabat,*** f. 50a. An English factor declares in 1650; "At Hugli may be procured beeswax, pepper, civet, rice, butter, oil and wheat; all at about half the price of other places" (Factories, 1646-50, 338).
48. ***Relations,*** 40, 60; ***Factories,*** 1634-36, 41; Bernier, 437; Early Annals, I, 399.
49. Fitch, Ryley, 185, & Early Travels, 44; Relations, 60. And also to the Portuguese possessions on the western coasts, for which see Fitch, Ryley, 110, & Early Travels, 24, 28;; Lett. Recd., IV, 327.
50. Lett. Recd., IV, 327.
51. ***Ibid,.*** II, 17 ("Gunnies for embaling goods").
52. Bowrey, 121-2. Cf. also Cascar Frederick, Purchas, X, 112-13; Relations, 54; Hamilton, 60.
53. ***Relations,*** 60.
54. Pelsaert, 4-5, 9; Mundy, 95-6, 98-9. The Imperial court obtained its supply of ***sukhdas*** rice from Bahraich (A'in, I, 53).
55. Jourdain, 162; Pelsaert, 9. For the dearness of salt in Bengal, see, ***Ain-i-Akbari*** I, 390. it was scarcer still in Assam (Fathiya-i- 'Ibriya, f. 32b).
56. ***Factories,*** 1618-21, 102; 1624-29, 235-6; Pelsaert, 19; Tavernier, II, 2. As Pelsaert and Tavernier tell us, there was a large silk-weaving industry at Ahmedabad which was wholly dependent upon Bengal Silk.
57. ***The Agrarian System of Mughal Indian, IInd Revised Edition 1556-1707***, Irfan Habib, Oxford University Press, New Delhi. p. 80.
58. See the account of the dues levied at Shahdara-Lahore in Khulasatu-s-Siyaq ff. 90a-92b, Or. 2026, ff. 57a-59b.
59. Pelsaert, 31-2; Factories, 1637-41, 136.
60. ***Factories,*** 1637-41, 36. The butter produced in Sind is praised by Linschoten, I, 56, and A'in , I, 556. Hamilton, I, 126, speaks of "great Quantities of Butter" exported from Sind; and Manucci, II, 427, says it was exported to Mustaq.
61. ***Factories,*** 1637-41, 136-137.

62. For trade in it by the Portuguese, see Roe, 75; for trade by the English, Factories, 1637-41, 274; 1642-5, 203, etc.
63. ***The English Factories***, 1642-5, 136.
64. ***Ibid.***, 203; 1646-50, 12-13, 29, 33.
65. Pelsaert, 35.
66. Marshall, 413. Cf. also Fitch, Ryley, 116, & Early Travels, 27, for "saffron like the saffron of Persia" produced in Bhutan.
67. T.J., 300, 315; Pelsaert, 36.
68. ***Ain-i-Akbari*** I, 485. And also from Agra, as we have seen.
69. Fryer, I, 282.
70. Van Twist, 76; Factories, 1665-6, 101.
71. ***The Agrarian System of Mughal Indian IInd Revised Edition 1556-1707***, Irfan Habib, Oxford University Press, New Delhi, p. 81.
72. ***A'in*** I, 486; ***Factories***, 1630-33, 19-20; Fryer, I, 282.
73. Linschoten, II, 113; Van Twist, 76; ***Factories 1661-64***, 355; 1665-67, 99-101. (Tavernier, I, 19).
74. ***Factories***, 1646-50, 60.
75. ***Ibid.***, 1637-41, 126.
76. ***Ibid.***, 1618-21, 63.
77. ***The Agrarian System of Mughal Indian, IInd Revised Edition***, 1556-1707, Irfan Habib, Oxford University Press New Delhi, p. 81. Lettd. Recd., V. 115; VI 280; ***Factories***, 1618-21, 102; 1624-29, 235-6, 270. Cf. also Akbar to Aurangzeb, 138-9.
78. Fryer, I, 282.
79. Van Twist, 76.
80. I. Habib in Tracy (ed.). ***Rise of Merchant Empires, 376***-77. Cf. Tavernier, I, 33-34.
81. Cf. I. Habib, Essays, 200-13, esp. 202-3.
82. ***The Agrarian System of Mughal Indian, IInd Revised Edition, 1556-1707***, Irfan Habib, Oxford University Press, New Delhi, p. 84-85,
83. ***The Agrarian System of Mughal Indian, IInd Revised, Edition*** 1556-1707, Irfan Habib, Oxford University Press, New Delhi, p.85.
84. Badauni, ***Nijatu-r-Rashid***, 349-51. See also ***A'in***, I, 291, where it is declared to be the meanest of all occupation.
85. ***The Agrarian System of Mughal Indian, IInd Revised, Edition 1556-1707***, Irfan Habib, Oxford University Press, New Delhi, p, 87. ***Insha'-Abu'l Fazl***, 65 (Mir' at, I, 169-70); ***A'in***, I, 284.
86. ***The Agrarian System of Mughal Indian, IInd Revised Edition 1556-1707***, Irfan Habib, Oxford University Press, New Delhi, p. 87.
87. ***The Agrarian System of Mughal Indian, IInd Revised Edition, 1556-1707***, Irfan Habib, Oxford University Press, New Delhi, p, 88.
88. See table 3 in S.P. Gupta, ***Agrarian System of Eastern Rajasthan***, 85. The prices are for the years 1664 and 1730 in ***parganas*** Chatsu and Malarna.

89. ***The Agrarian System of Mughal Indian, IInd Revised Edition, 1556-1707,*** Irfan Habib, Oxford University Press, New Delhi, p. 89.
90. Sujan Rai, 454. See also Moreland, ***Akbar to Aurangzeb,*** 190-192, on the general tendency of the peasant "to follow the markets.
91. ***The Agrarian System of Mughal Indian, IInd Revised Edition 1556-1707,*** Irfan Habib, Oxford University Press, New Delhi, p. 91. The sukhdas variety, praised by Sujan Rai, II, cnnot now be identified.
92. ***The Agrarian System of Mughal Indian IInd Revised Edition, 1556-1707,*** Irfan Habib, Oxford University Press, New Delhi, p. 93.
93. Van Twist, 68.
94. ***The Agrarian System of Mughal Indian, IInd Revised Edition, 1556-1707,*** Irfan Habib, Oxford University Press, New Delhi, p. 93.
95. van Santen, 93.
96. ***Ibid.,*** 92.
97. ***Mediaeval India Under Mohammedan Rule*** by Stanley Lane-Poole, pp. 367-370.
98. ***Ibid.,*** p. 204.
99. ***Commercial Policy of the Mughal*** by D. Panth.
100. ***Travels in India*** by Tavernier. Edited by Ba;;, p. 51.
101. ***Chahar Gulshan*** by Jadunath Sarkar, (Book I), pp. 160-161.
102. ***Chahar Gulshan*** by Jadunath Sarkar, (Book I), p. 161.
103. Moreland, ***India from Akbar to Aurangzeb,*** p. 208.
104. ***Shah Jahan Nama,*** Inayat Khan per, Mss (S.B.U.) pp. 199, 205-7 C.H.Z. Vol., p. 520.
105. ***The Economy of The Mughal Empire*** by Shireen Moosvi 1987. Printed by All India Press, Kennedy Nagar,Pondicherry Pub., by R. Dayal Oxford University Press, YMCA, Building, Jai Singh Road New Delhi, p. 375.
106. ***Chronicle,*** tr., p. 35 see also Chapter II.
107. ***Ibid.,*** Chapter 9.
108. Cf. R.A. ***Alvi's*** data in Medieval India- A miscellany, II, p. 73.
109. See for Example p. Della Valle, II, p. 334.
110. Nuniz in the 1530s puts the demand from the King of Vijaynagar alone at 13,000, thought all of these were not imported (R. Sewell. ***A forgotten Empire,*** 2nd Indian ed. Delhi, 1970, pp. 61-2).
111. Tom Pires, I, p. 58; Caesar Frederick in Purchase, X., pp. and 99.
112. It will be seen from the Table the implied prices for the ***mansabdars*** horses (imported) fall under the maximum price of Rs. 300 set for a horse which was given from the Imperial Establishment to a ***mansabdar*** in Deccan in 1639 (Selected Documents of Shah Jahan's Reign, p. 74).
113. Linschoten, I, pp. 45. 917; II, pp. 140, I.
114. Tom Pires, II, p. 20; Remonstrantie, tr., p. 23; for quicksilver from China se Factories, 1618-21, pp. 54-55.
115. Remonstrantie, tr., p28; Pyrad, Ii, p. 239.

116. Tom Pires, II, 270; ***Principal Navigations***, III, 206.
117. Linschoten, I, pp. 33 & II, p. .34; Carletti, 220,221; Purchase IX, 559; for coral imported from the red sea, see also Khurram's Nishan, A.D., 1618 Harl. Roll, 43 A. 4; Factories, 1618-21, pp. 54-5 for ivory, Principle Navigation, III, 206.
118. ***Ain-i-Akbari***, p. 67 Bernier, 204.
119. ***Ain-i-Akbari I***, p. 434.
120. ***The Economy of The Mughal Empire*** by Shireen Moosvi 1987. Printed by All India Press Kennedy Nagar-Pondicherry Pub. by R. Dayal Oxford University Press, YMCA Building, Jai Singh Road, New Delhi, p. 381.
121. ***Ibid.***, p. 382.
122. Moreland, ***From Akbar to Aurangzeb***, p. 54.
123. ***Baburnama***, I, tr., p. 20.
124. ***Letters Received***, IV, p. 202.
125. ***Factories***, 1630-33, pp. 124-5.
126. Factories, 1624-29, p. 350.
127. Factories, 1630-33, pp. 124-5.
128. ***Carletti***, 202.
129. ***Barbosa***, II, pp. 117, 164, 177; Tom Pires, I, p 86; Pyrad in Purchase, IX, p. 561.
130. ***Barbosa***, I, pp. 7-8, 15,28,126-7, 153-4, 198.
131. ***Verthema***, p, III.
132. ***Principal Navigations***, III, p. 210.
133. ***Atlas of the Mughal Empire***, p. 69.
134. General: Moreland IDA, ch. VI; FAA, Chs 1 an 2 are based on various sources; Mukerji, chs. 4 and 6; Chicherov, ch. 3; K.N. Chaudhari, TWA, 193-94; ch,xiii (i): CEH, I, 382-407; A. Dasgupta, op., cit., Ch. xiii (2).
135. ***Mughal Economy, Organization and Working***, J.N. Sarkar published by Maya Prakash, 1987, p. 152.
136. ***Influence of Wind pattern and Risks of Storms***, TWA, 201f; Sarkar, SAR; Moreland, IDA, 198, 218f; FAA, 57-8; Mukerjee, 117.93, Passim; Chicherov, 105f; Dasgupta, ***op. cit.***
137. ***Mughal Economy, Organization and Working***, J.N. Sarkar published by Maya Prakash, 1987, p. 154.
138. ***Barbosa***-353-358, a Journal of the first Voyage-1947-99
139. Cartaze, Moreland, FAA. 9f; Steengaard, 84; Chaudhari, 383-5; CEH, I, 381-2.
140. ***Mughal Economy, Organization and Working***, J.N. Sarkar published by Maya Prakash, 1987, p.161-62.
141. IDA, Ch; BN, 52; Srivastava in Mughal Empire, ed. R.C. Majumdar, 731; CEH, I, 413-6.
142. Mughal Economy, Organization and Working, J.N. Sarkar published by Maya Prakash, 1987, p.165.
143. See f.n. 20; ***Toy trade***, LR, i. 33; Roe, 383; EF (1618-21), 111; (1624-26), 134; (1637-41), 183, 184; (1642-45), 81.

144. ***Mughal Economy, Organization and Working***, J.N. Sarkar published by Maya Prakash, 1987, p.171.
145. Moreland, ***op., cit.***, 96-141.
146. Moreland, IDA, 203-18; FAA, 57-58 (Chart Valuable); Mukherjee, Ch. 6; CEH, i. 413.
147. ***Mughal Economy, Organization and Working***, J.N. Sarkar published by Maya Prakash, 1987, p.176.
148. ***Mirat-i-Ahmadi***, 38,29; ***Bird Hist., of Gujarat***, 13; ***Verthema*** 111; ***Barbosa***, I, 146; Commissariat, i. 264-5;CEH, 412-13 Chaudhari, TWA, 195; Arab Shia Merchants traded ontheir own ship in spices, silks, musk, porcelain and other goods with Melacca, China, Tenasserim, Pegu, Sumatra. For Bombay see Holden Furber.
149. Linschoten, c, 10; Pyrad, ii. 259; Jourdain, 198; Srivastava, in Mughal Empire., ed. R.C. Majumdar, 751; Sewell, Forgotten Emp, (old), 156, 210; Groups of ports, Moreland, IDA, 19, 208.
150. Coromandel-Pegu, Purchase, II, X.. 1718, 1733, 1739; Dutch Letters Reed, (1607-8), No. 961, quoted in Brij Narain, 54. Masulipatam described in my Life of Mir Jumla (2nd edn.), Ch, I, Methwoid, Relations, Ed. Moreland, 36-7; TWA, 198.
151. Srivastava, ***op. cit.***, Mukherjee, 125.
152. Mukundaram quoted in Mukerjee, 122; Caesar Frederici (1567) Purchas, x, 113, 114; Campos, 57; Fitch (ETI), 26; TWA, 198.
153. ***Mughal Economy, Organization and Working***, J.N. Sarkar published by Maya Prakash, 1987, p.185.

9. Architecture

Building Projects

There appears on the Indian scene that superb combination of drama, pageant and historical era, known as the empire of the "Great Mughals", staged amidst an environment of surpassing splendour, under the patronage of this Mohammedan dynasty. The architecture developed by the Mohammedans in India, was itself in a relatively late phase of the Islamic movements as a whole and the Mughal style typifies its most important final manifestation. The monuments therefore, produced during this period may be regarded as representation of "Indian Summer" of Muslim art and architecture. And it was a summer more than ordinary brilliance and fertility. For previous advent art of the country was showing distinct evidences of decline, especially under the waning influence of the imperial rule at Delhi, although it still continued to flourish with varying vigour in the provinces. At this stage, the Mughals began to assume control over northern India bringing with them the fresh blood of their progenitors, the Timurids, an infusion which stimulated exceedingly all forms of intellectual activity, and notably the art of building. During the early years of the Mughal domination the country was too unsettled to produce any work of distinction, but gradually a form of the building art emerged expressive of this ruling dynasty and which in the course of time developed into one of the most important architectural styles in India. The type of building thus, evolved was no provincial or even regional manifestation. On the contrary, it was an imperial movement, affected only in its architectural character as well as in its structural principles in whichever part of the empire it was introduced.[1]

In comparison with the ceaseless architectural activity that was maintained during the greater part of Akbar's reign, the period of the rule of his son and successor, Jahangir, was, in the field of the building art relative uneventful. It was who patronized so enthusiastically the school of miniature painting that is associated with the Mughal regime, and whenever constructional work was contemplated, it more frequently took the form of laying out large formal gardens and similar ornamental retreats rather than the erection of the architectural monuments.

Mughal architecture begins with Humayun's tomb, in Delhi, which is essentially an Indian stone version of an Iranian tiled mausoleum, and the first major example in India of an ornamental tomb garden, the great mosque and tomb that followed experimented with formal relationships of building elements particularly the ***iwan***, courtyard domes and minarets. Fortress and places were also built, echoing the caravan serais and tent cities of the Mughals nomadic ancestors.

At the end of the 16th century, Akbar conceived the new royal city of Fatehpur Sikri, outside Agra, where free reign was given to the skills of Hindu craftsmen. The red sandstone architecture of this period gave way in the early 17th century architecture of Shah Jahan, whose masterpiece, the Taj Mahal, is the ultimate, during the reign of Jahangir, to the white marble expression of Mughal architecture.

Shah Jahan resolved to find a new capital city at Delhi; he was partly influenced by the fact that the summer heat of Agra can be particularly trying. The location of the seventh city of Delhi, Shahjahanbad or old Delhi as it is now universally called was just north of Kotla Firozshah and included within its limit part of the area formerly belonging to Firozabad, the fifth Delhi was built by Firozshah Tughlak in middle half of the 14th century. From the ruins of Firozabad, as well as from buildings in the neighbourhood of the Purana Qila, Shah Jahan obtained much of the material for the walls and gateways of his new city.

The principal artery of Shahjahanabad was the famous Chandni Chowk, which extended front the open ground in front of the Red fort to the west of the Fatehpuri Masjid (constructed in 1650 by one of

Shaha Jahan's wives) and then along one side of the mosque to the Lahore gate of the city. In the seventeenth century and indeed up to the British period, Chandni Chowk was lined with trees and in the center was a channel of running water so that in appearances it must have closely resembled the Chahar Bagh in Isfahan, laid out a few years earlier.

When however, Shaha Jahan decided to restore Delhi to its former importance he commissioned his Persian favourite Ali Mardan Khan who had experience of canal system at Kandhar and on the Ravi near Lahore to repair Firuz Shah Tughlaq's canal and to enlarge it by bringing a new branch from Karnal to Shahjahanabad, thereby providing the city with and alternative to its existing supply of water from the Jumna. .These works were later incorporated into the 19th century Rohtak and western-Jumna Canal system.

Some way south of Chandni Chowk Shah Jahan constructed the imposing Jama-i-Masjid (1644-58) which must rank only a little behind the Taj Mahal itself as one of the finest monuments erected during his reign. Built upon a lofty platform commanding a magnificent view of the surrounding city and the Red fort to the east the Delhi Jama-i-Masjid is the largest congregational mosque in Northern India. Its central courtyard is 325 feet square and is surrounded on three sides by cloisters and on the fort by a decorated prayer hall flanked by two tall minarets and supporting three cupolas similar in shape to the dome of the Taj Mahal.

When Shah Jahan favourite wife Mumtaz Mahal died, the bereaved emperor assembled designers and craftsmen from all over India, Iran and Central Asia to construct a tomb that was to prove the ultimate achievements of Mughal architecture. The Taj Mahal harmoniously combines the great building traditions of Central Asia, Iran and India, all of which placed great emphasis on the government relationship contained within a building.[2]

Shah Jahan's memorial to his beloved wife took twenty two years to build (1632-54) Tajmahal. The Legend was that Mumtaz Mahal herself had previously chosen the site as the result of a dream. She died following the birth of her fourteenth child, in Burhanpur in 1631 and the following year, work on the tomb began. Her body, brought back to

Agra was buried temporarily in the gardens, until the actual sculpture should be ready.

Tavernier describes how he himself saw both the commencement and the completion of the work and that about twenty thousand workmen were employed throughout the whole period of building. The finest materials were utilized for its establishment and the quality of the craftsmanship available in northern India was probably superior to that of any previous period. He records, Shah Jahan's intention to build for himself a second tomb. The Taj Mahal which in style is in direct line of decent from the tombs of Humayun and the Khan-i-Khanan in Delhi, stands on a white marble platform 22 feet high and 313 feet square at the far end of large formal garden enclosed on three sides by lofty walls and gateways. On the fourth flows the river Jumna. Structurally, the Taj Mahal is built on shape of a square with each of its four sides dominated by a deep recess 63 feet high but with its four corners beveled to form what is, in fact, an octagon. Above this rises the graceful dome-drum capped by a 'Tatar' dome, modify to satisfy the taste to the period. The total height of the building including the metal pinnacle surmounting the dome is 243 feet.

This is an un-mistakably architecture in the Safavid style perhaps the greatest single achievement of Safavid art and it is therefore, ironical that it should soften be regarded as the quintessence of the Mughal spirit. It (Taj Mahal) is a work of the finest Safavid taste except for the use of the most immaculate Makarna marble which translate the gray and gaudy Persian taste into the dreamy, languid spirit of later Mughal art, there are in Taj Mahal only a few other deviations from Safavid orthodoxy the four Rajput ***chattris*** around the dome; some differences in the proportion of the dome and dome drum (common, however, in the Deccan), and also the minerates, probably inspired by Muhammad Khilji' tomb at Mandu. It is one of the freaks of history that this "Wonder of the World", which is the least characteristic of Mughal art, has become the classic representative and emblem of Mughal civilization.

In Agra itself the renovation of the interior of Akbar's great fort was a major undertaking, of which the Moti Masjid or Pearl Mosque (1646-53) (cf. pl. 112), the Diwan-i-Khass of Hall of private Audience and the adjoining apartments reserved for the use of the imperial family rank among the most exquisite achievements of the century. The Taj Mahal stands on the land which was once a garden belonging to Raja Jai Singh of Amber to whom Shah Jahan gave four royal mentions as compensation. The brilliant architectural master piece is built by Turk Ustad Isa, Ustad Lahori and Haji Begam, Geronimo Veronio completed some 60 years before at Humayun's tomb in Delhi by his wife. Taj has been elovised as a monument in memory of love, yet it was planned as a Rauza (Tomb) and Urs (pilgrimage center and therefore, the complex includes the garden, Baazar and service quarters all enclosed by boundary walls). It was along the river flowing at the back that Shah Jahan used to visit the Taj from Agra fort. The gateway to the Taj is built in red sandstone with white marble inlay and calligraphy containing verses from the Holy Quran. On entering a gateway one can see the garden beyond which is the tomb build in and to detached subsidiary edifices, a mask on the west and ***Mehman Khana*** on east for symmetrical balance or answer (Jawab) the approach channel has elevated pool in the center called Hauz-e-Kausar and flanked by marble path lined with long row of cypresses from the central pool the water channels flow in the four directions dividing the garden at right angles into four in a form of Charbagh or four portioned garden planned.

The splendid mausoleum is 57 meter square with canted angles to form and eight side structure which like facets on a gem stone catches the light in all directions. The superfine treatment in elevation lies in the gracefully shade onion dome 25 meter high, 18 meter in diameter supported over a high drum rising to a height of 64 meter above the ground. There are remarkable proportions in the beautiful building Taj.

No wonder that Shah Jahan rightly observed, "the builder could not have been of this earth for it is evident the design was given him by Heaven". The truth of his saying can be observed by comparing his unique master piece with the Bibi ka Maqbara the grave Rabi Durrani, the wife of Emperor of Aurangzeb under whose reign the glory of mughal architecture came to vane. Built in red sandstone just forty year later Bibi ka Maqbara is a mere travesty of the immortal Taj.

No architectural account of Muslim style is complete without the reference to the Mughal gardens. For example, Kabul Bagh at Panipath built by Emperor Babur and the famous garden of Kashmir such as Shalimar Bagh or Garden of bliss and Nishat Bagh built by Emperor Shah Jahan in 1637.

Shish Mahal

It is so named because the walls and ceilings of the two halls adjoining each other are covered with small fragments of looking glass set in plaster and arranged in most beautiful designs.[3]

The Shish Mahal is situated on the north-eastern corner of the Anguri Bagh on the exact west side of the Musamman Burj just below the hall of the Diwan-i-khas. It is made up of extra thick walls and ceilings to ensure undisturbed coolness within. The Shish Mahal is composed of two large halls of equal size, each measuring 36'7' by 21'. Both are connected in the center by a broad arched opening and on the sides by two narrow passages. The arches and doors of the hammam have with Aleppo added to the beauty of the other wonders." This magnificent Hamam-i-Shahi which has been referred to by the European travellers of the 17th century as Ghusl-Khana, is now in complete ruins. Denuded of all its one-time wonderful decoration. Glass mosaic work in the fort of Agra has only survived in the Shish Mahal but that, fortunately, on the grandest and the most sumptuous scale. The mural glass decoration in its interior, "Aina-bandi namuda and" in the words of Lahouri.[4]

The Khas Mahal of Under Ground Chambers

Under the platform of the Khas Mahal there are underground chambers known as the Teh Khana, where the fair damsels of the court retired at noon from the terrible summer heat of Agra and passed the long hours of the day in pleasant jokes and merry-making. Some of these underground chambers were also used as cells for offenders.[5]

Art

With the reign of emperor Shah Jahan golden period which found expression in style of architecture of exceptional splendor and carried to the highest degree of perfection. In the sphere of the building art it was an age of marble, this material in its most refined form taking the place of the sandstone hitherto largely employed, so the architecture received a new impressiveness during the regime. The preference of Shah Jahan for buildings of this kind is graphically shown by the fact that he caused to be dismantled many of his predecessor's sandstone edifices with the sole objects of substituting others of a more polished type. Here one may pass in stride from sandstone buildings of the later half of the sixteenth century as exemplified by the Jahangiri Mahal, to the marble pavilions of the first half of the seventeenth century as represented by the Khas Mahal, in other words from the robust production of Akbar to the voluptuousness of Shah Jahan.[6]

The alternation of the group of palaces within the fort of Lahore were similar to those effected at Agra, a number of Akbar's sandstone structure being swept away to make room for pavilions of a more approved type. In their place rose mostly of the building towards the northern side of the enclosures such as the Diwan-i-Am, the Khwab Gah, the Shish Mahal, the Musamman Burj, and the Naulakaha, but some of these have again been subjected to modifications and elaborations at the later date.[7]

The Chini Ka Rauza

One of the masterpiece of glazed tile decoration is the mausoleum of Mulla Shukrullah Shirazi, entitles Afzal Khan Allami. The tomb is popularly called Chini Ka Rauza and is situated on the left bank of the Jumna at Agra. He came from Shiraz (Persia)[8] and serve under Abdur Rahim Khan-i-Khana. Later he was patronized by Prince Shah Jahan made Shukurullah his Diwan and bestowed upon him the title of Afzal Khan. He was a noted poet in Persian and composed under the pen name of 'Allami'. He was with the rebel Prince Shah Jahan for a considerable time, and the latter sent him to the Imperial Court in A.D. 1626 to plead and represent his case, but Jahangir detained him and made him his Khan-i-Saman (Steward).[9]

On accession to the throne in A.D. 1628, Shah Jahan conferred upon him the mansab of 4000 *zat* and 2000 *sawar*. Next year (A.D. 1628-29) he was made Diwan-i-Kul (Wazir of Chief Diwan or Head of the Department of Wizarat). In the eleventh year of Shah Jahan's reign, he was promoted to the mansab of 7000 ***zat*** and 4000 ***sawar***. He died at the age of seventy on 12 Ramzan 1048 A.H. (7 January 1639) at Lahore with which he was closely associated throughout his career and where, as it seems, he made the necessary arrangement of men and material for glazed decoration upon his proposed mausoleum. He died childless and it is likely that he constructed his tomb during his own lifetime.

This grand sculpture stands between the Tomb of I'timad-u-Daula and Ram Bagh, on the right bank of the river Jamuna. When Carlleyle saw and surveyed it in A.D. 1871-72, it was enclosed by high walls within a compound measuring 462'9 x 232'11" with a gateway on the eastern side, two three storied octagonal towers on the river side. The mausoleum is a square with 79 feet side. A square chamber has been provided at each corner, with 12 sides. The interior of the central hall has been exquisitely painted, on a vault which has been designed on stalactite or honey combed from and soffit, with conventional and inscriptional patterns in rich colours chiefly turquoise and pink. Some painting has been efficiently restored by the Archeological department of the Government of India.[10] The most important feature, however, is the glazed tile work with which the whole exterior of the building is covered and which has given its present name Chini Ka Rauza.

Mosaic Inlay and Glass Mosaic Alleged Italian Origin of Mughal Inlay

Shah Jahan (A.D. 1628-58) was one of the greatest patrons of architecture in Indian History. He preferred white marble for the construction of his architectural projects, so much so that he demolished some of the red sandstone pavilions of his august grandfather in forts of Agra and Lahore and replaced them by palatial; mansions of white marble.

With the adoption of white marble, new aesthetic values were brought to light; norms of architecture changes the structural and decorative features were diverted into new channels. Percy brown very aptly remarked 'Marble, provides its own decorative appearances owing to its delicate graining and any ornamentation requires to be most judiciously almost sparingly applied, otherwise the surface become fretted and confused.

Shah Jahan greatly loved pure white surface decorated with gold and other beautiful colours. At times when marbles could not be used the red sandstone the impression or white marble. The Diwan-i-Am in the Agra Fort stands as a testimony to his proverbial love of pure white colour. The Diwan-i-Am of the Delhi fort also had originally been stuccoed over with this shell-plaster, [11] which was all scrapped off during the British period.

Musamman Burj or Jasmine Tower

It is known both as Musamman Burj, Jasmine Tower or Saman Burj, Octagonal tower. It was built by Shah Jahan for his beloved wife Arjumand Banu Begum. It was here that Shah Jahan closed his eyes in death in January, 1666, gazing steadfastly on the tomb of his beloved Arjumand, the Taj Mahal visible at the distance of a mile of down to Jumna. His dying eyes fed on the beauty of the Taj was enshrined his once priceless possession on the earth and whose memory he was cherishing with all the depth of his first love for the last 36 years. The Saman Burj is enclosed by highly artistic screens of marble, while the octagonal were above, delicately inlaid with patterns of jasmine flower Andover topped by a cupola, greatly adds to the charms of its beautiful surroundings. In front to the Burj the pavement is made up into squares in coloured marble for the Emperor to play the game of ***pachisi.*** They moved from point to point as the game proceeded, affording a fund of merriment and laughter to the Emperor and the lovely women folk of the palace. This seems to have been one of the most favourite games of the Mughal emperors as we come across the same sort of chessboard arrangement in the palace at Fatehpur Sikri also.

Shah Jahan transferred his capital from Agra to Delhi in 1638 and constructed the new fortress-capital of Shahjahanabad. The Red fort to the east of the city was laid out in a series of squares surrounded by massive, red sandstone, fortified walls and gateways. Progression into the center of the fort was through bazaars, a music pavilion gatehouse and a large garden, at the back of which was set the Public Audience Hall (Diwa-i-Aam) a single storey pavilion of red sandstone with cupsed arches. On either side were gardens, flanked by white marble constructions overlooking the Jumna River. These open single story pavilions were built as inter connecting courts linked and cooled by channels of water flowing though them under delicately carved dividing screens into shallow marbles basins such as the lotus shaped pool of the Rang Mahal. Cusped aches, curved cornices, bulbous domes and highly decorated flat ceilings, in gilt overlaid with sinuous serpentine patterns and naturalistic flower designs, were features of this architecture.[12]

The Red Fort Delhi

Bernier,[13] describing Shah Jahan's decision to develop a new city at Delhi, says that the emperor considered the summer heat and humidity of Agra made it unsuitable for his capital. In Bernier's time, the walls, not the river side, wherein circled by a moat filed with water and well stocked with fish. Beyond this lay garden and the royal square's so that the whole vast red wall set off by the rich colour of flower and trees. Centered on the Lahori Gate was the Chandni Chowk the main street of the city, with trees and canal of running water forming an introduction to the palace in which irrigation a vital part. There were two major gardens, the Hayat Baksh or Life giving garden, and the Mahtab Bagh or Moon Light Garden combined to form one grand design. The later no longer exists but much of the Hayat Baksh still remains. Design at water garden, the central pavilion stood in a pool full of fountain. From this ran four canals, which terminated at south in small water pavilion, the Sawan and Bhadon. The Mahtab Bagh by contrast was planted with pail flowers only. Jasmine tuberoses, lilies and narcissus, while both gardens were enclosed by rows of cypresses. Here the emperor appear daily at dawn to his people gathered on the river bank below and here in Diwan-i-Khas, the hall of private audience, stood his peacock throne. The same inscription appears as at Shalamar and at its zenith, the Red Fort at Delhi must indeed have seemed a paradise on Earth.

Jama-i-Masjid

This was the royal mosque for the new Shahjahanabad and is one of the largest courtyard style mosque in India. It is raised on a high plinth with its surroundings arcades open at the sides linked by gateways and kiosks. The prayer hall advances into the main courtyard and is independent from the surrounding arcades. Its front elevation is framed between two four stage minarets. Three bulbous white marble domes with red sand stone stripes are raised on their central ***iwan*** to avoid any imbalance caused by the close proximity of ***iwan*** and dome, as seen in Iranian and earlier mosques in India. The decoration is simple with alternating areas of red sandstone and white marble used to emphasize the domes and minarets. Inside simple niche and arabesque patterns in white marble are set in the red sandstone walls.[14]

Fortress of Delhi

The Delhi city was the capital of Mughal Empire. It had a commanding position and thereof was made as the capital over a period of thousand years. Hence there goes the popular saying. "He who holds Delhi, holds India". The city Delhi was protected by high fortified wall 945'm long and 5'm wide. There are two gateways, the one on the southern side intended for private entry while that on the western side is known as Lahore Gate, which is the main entrance and therefore designed elaborately with nobles ramparts on its sides, in red stone. The Lal Qila or Red Fort represents the might and splendor of the Mughals. It has certainly witnessed in plenty, romance, conspiracy, violence, tragedy, debauchery etc.

The colour of the majestic fort itself seems highly symbolic.[15] The Lahore gate facing Chandni Chowk consists of a huge vaulted arcade forming the imposing ceremonial entrance. This fortress city consists of many splendid edifices, a few of which are Qutub Minar, Jam-i-Masjid, Humayun's Tomb, Moti Mahal, Tang Mahal, etc.

The Diwan-i-Khas or hall of Private Audience

It is an exquisite work of art, erected by Shah Jahan in 1637, by the side of the Jumna during the same time that the Taj was being built. The artistic marvels of Persian style-the flower beds, the flowers, the twisted leaves and branches are so tender and delicate that one can clearly see here the hand of the architects of the Taj which was begun in 1631 and completed in 1648. The building consists of two halls and measures 65 feets long and 34 feet wide. It is made of white marble and the beautiful carving and artistic inlaid workplace its among the best architectural productions of the age. One of the arches towards the river side of the Dewan-i-Khas was struck by a shell from the cannon of 'Lord Lake' in 1803 and was partly broken. Its marble flooring is said to have been dug out and carried away by the Jats.[16]

The Machchi Bhawan or Fish Palace

It is situated at the back of Diwan-i-Aam and is connected with it by a communicating door. It consists of a courtyard measuring 200 feet by 150 feet which is surmounted by a roofed gallery in the upper storey on the north, west and south. On the east there is a terrace in front of the Diwan-i-Khas and there is reason to believe that formerly it had marble carried off to Deeg and Bharatpur by jats as building material for their own palaces, the place is known as Machchi Bhawan as during the time of Mughal Emperors there were tanks of marble for fish in the courtyard below, to which water was conveyed by artificial changes from the jamuna these tanks were carried of by Raja Suraj Mal of Bharatpur

They were filled with gold fishes which provided merry sport to the emperor and the Zanana of the palace. On the terrace or raised platform in front of the Diwan-i-Khas are placed two thrones, one of black slate and the other of white marble, the former having been used by Jahangir at Allahabad in 1602 as his own royal seat when he rebelled against his father. It is said Akbar subsequently became reconciled with his son and invested him with the full powers of an emperor before his death.[17]

The Nagina Masjid or the Gem Mosque

It was a private mosque chiefly for the female worshippers of the palace and is connected with the Zanana by a screened passage along the roof of the Diwan-i-Aam. It is built of white marble with three domes supported by arches resting on rows of pillars. The place is certainly a secluded book for devout worshipper and rightly deserves the name of Gem from the artistic delicacy it reveals in small miniature.[18]

The Khas Mahal

The Khas Mahal was built by Shah Jahan in 1636, the eighth year of his reign. It is a beautiful blocks of three marble pavilion standing on an elevated platform on the side of the Jumna. The emperor with some of the chief ladies of the court used to resides here. The central pavilion measuring 70 feet by 40 feet is joined to the two side one by means of doorways. The Burj mentioned above is separated from the side pavilion on the north by a marble screen. The walls which are elaborately carved in relief are still seen in their original artistic grandeur, but the beautiful golden painting on the ceilings has all disappeared. An idea of this Mughal painting with beautiful golden floral patterns in gold may be gathered from the part which was sought to be restored under the orders of Lord Curzon. The pavilion on the south was the residence of Shah Jahan's eldest daughter, Jahanara Begum, who shared her father's captivity within the fort from 1658-1666. This palace contained the portraits artists, which were removed by Raja Suraj Mal of Bharatpur. On the space below, under the windows of the central hall of this palace, elephant fights were held, culprits condemned to death were executed. Death sentences, however, were very rare.[19]

Anguri Bagh

It is situated in front of the Khas Mahal in a big courtyard measuring 235 ft. by 170 ft. It was made by Akbar for his harem women, with sets of chamber on three sides. The garden is laid out in artists flower-beds with a central tank and fountain, and is divided into four parts by means of pavements. It is said that the soil for the garden was brought from Kashmir for the purpose of growing luscious grapes for the imperial household.[20]

Lahore Wazir Khan Mosque

A separate and distinct style of Mughal architecture evolved in the Punjab influenced by Safavid Iran. Buildings were constructed in baked brickwork and used glazed tiles for decoration. Unlike Safavid buildings, which were totally covered in glazed tiles, the decoration of the mosque is subordinate to the architectural elements. Octagonal minarets and walls, kiosk and gateways are divided into rectangular panels framed by bands of plain brickwork. These panels are filed with mosaic tile work forming floral and geometric patterns in vivid greens, oranges, blues and browns. Inside, the walls and ceilings are entirely covered in sinuous patterns and floral designs, painted in tempera in rich shades of magenta, dark green ochre.

Tatta Friday Mosque

It was built by Shah Jahan as a memorial to his stay in Tatta, this courtyard mosque with its four inward facing ***iwans***, brick construction and glazed tile decoration reflects the strong cultural tiles that Sind shared with Iran. The great east gateway and twin courtyards were added in 1658. The main chamber has three features unusual in Indian Islamic buildings; a domed ***iwan***; light admitted into the central chamber through screened openings at floor level in the Qibla wall; and some supported in a series of interesting arches forming squint nets. The wall arches and dome of the central chamber are totally covered in glaze tile work.

Inlay in the Building of Shah Jahan

Other example of inlay work in the Fort of Delhi are in the Diwa-i-Khas, Rang Mahal, Shahburj and in other marble pavilion on a smaller scale. At the Diwan-i-Khas carnelian, corals and other precious stone were used for inlay in floral pattern on the dados and the massive piers.[2] The art of inlay have however, been presented most beautifully at Agra in the marble palace of the fort, e.g, Musamman Burj, Diwan-i-Khas and the Taj Mahal. The dado border of the Taj Mahal which are appreciated more because they are more popular and better known are similar to the borders in the Diwan-i-Khas.

Some necessary features of this embellishment were the extra thick massive wall and ceiling to ensure coolness in the interior and also to provide adequate depth of different layers of the plaster backgrounds, the opening were minimized to necessitate the use of artificial light which was an unavoidable requisite to obtain the superb colour effects of the glass mosaic work.

The four most characteristic elements of the Islamic Architecture are as follows:

1. The Arabesque
2. The Stalactite.
3. Geometrical.
4. Calligraphies

The Arabesque: has been defined [21] as a particular and exclusively Islamic form of denaturalized vegetal ornament consisting of shoot or split or be furcated leaves on inorganic tendrils. The Arabesque was used by the artisan of Akbar on a large scale of Agra Fort and at Fatehpur Sikri. The Delhi Gate pavilion of Agra Fort have beautiful Arabesque design in stucco on soffits and arched niches, the best example of the Jahangiri Mahal in same fort. The Arabesque is used in panel decoration in an extremely graceful format. The technique, i.e., the incised stucco in gesso style, presenting a beautiful play of light and shadow, as much as the rhythmic flows of the design, presents a wonderful mural surface.

The Arabesque was employed in the building of Shah Jahan in carved and inlaid marble. The spandrels of portals and arched alcoves at the Taj Mahal have inlay design marvelously floralized. The **Chini Ka Rauza** at Agra which is one of the best examples of glazed tile decoration in the world had arabesque in the coloured tiles

The Stalactite: like the Arabesque the stalactite also owes its growth and development to Islam to beautiful mask of Delhi of the First half of sixteenth century each representative of its own class viz., the Bara Gumbad Majid situated in the Lodi Garden and Qila-i-Kohna Masjid in the Old Fort have stalactite design in the phase of transition. The Qila-i-Kohna Masjid is entirely a stone construction. There are beautiful squinch arches in the nave.

The stalactites used at the springing of the Dome of Humayun's Tomb at Delhi is ornamental. It is more the design than the method of Dome construction which worked wonders in the imagination of Mughal builders and he used this design on the Capital of his pillars on cornices, on the semi-soffits of alcoves and portals and on the soffits of domes and cupolas, almost universally from Akbar to Shah Jahan. [22]

A beautiful form of the stalactites can be same in the entrance chamber of Jahangiri Mahal in Agra Fort. The stalactite used in the building of Shahjahan Mahal in Agra Fort in the main hall and all around the east room and the vaults have a stalactite design in stucco. The pillars of Musamman Burj have stalactite capital. The soffits of alcoves and the overlapping cornices in the Diwan-i-Khas also have stalactite. It is popularly used for the ornamentation the arched and vaulted soffits of alcoves and portals at the Taj Mahal. Noteworthy however, is the fact that in both stucco and white marble, except for few exception the stalactite is used ornamentally i.e., as a design, in the building of Shah Jahan and its structural implication is not much in view. It was the aesthetic effect of the stalactites, rather than its suggestions of fantasy which was so, spontaneously understood by the early Islamic builders who developed it, that served as the guiding principle for its use by the Shahjahanian artisan.[23]

Geometrical: the age of Shah Jahan marks the decline of their popularity. His architect did not seek the assistant of traditional decorator and primarily depended on the architectonic effect. The use of pure ornamentation was minimized.

Even when ornaments were employed the Shahjahanian artist relied on his own scheme of decoration which was largely composed of typically Mughal Design, i.e., some floral combine with stylized motif. Very little use of geometrical design has, therefore, be made in his palatial mansion and mosques. The trend of art thus, changed from Akbar to Shah Jahan. Naturalistic florals become the exception after the tomb of Itmad-ud-daulah and their use in the building of Shahjahan is extremely rare, the emphasis now being laid whole heartedly on the stylization of these forms. Even when florals were indispensable, e.g., in the dado centers of Taj Mahal.

Painting

Akbar encouraged painting to such an extent that "over a hundred artsist, worked in the school organized by Akbar.[24] During Jahangir reign that Mughal art attained its highest perfection. Jahangir was an all round patron and art critic and there are ample evidences in his memoirs of his gift of thinking pictorially.[25] One of the best portrait of Jahangir as a prince is in the collection of M. Cartier Paris.[26] A beautiful picture of Jahangir as a prince is in the album of Shah Jahan is the Chester Beatty collection London.[27] It shows the Prince leaning against a pillow in an open garden and indulging in his favourite pastime drinking.[28] An excellent picture of Jahangir shooting a large tiger is in the Indian Museum, Calcutta.[29] The advent of Shah Jahan on the Mughal throne of India also witnessed the advent of those forces that contributed to the fall of the Mughal art in India.

To give justice to Shah Jahan it cannot be said that he was against art; on the contrary, Shah Jahan loved art very dearly. This love however, was directed in a different sphere for Shah Jahan loved to see exquisite buildings rather than exquisite painting. He patronized great architects rather than renowned painters. Hence forth Mughal art had to reckon without a patron and in the words of renowned art critic "there must be patronage or there will not be art".[30]

Shah Jahan's reign from point of view of Mughal is noticeable are one thing. Individual portraiture had begun to be the fashion of the day in Jahangir's time and this fashion was developed to it's utmost limit by painters during Shah Jahan. In the picture Shah Jahan wears a turban decorated with jewels. The trouser of Shah Jahan in the portrait of made up of a cloth with floral pattern, the material of the trouser in the second portrait is the muslin of stripped design. Both pictures shows Shah Jahan in the prime of life, but the most noticeable object in these pictures is the throne accused by Mughal Emperor. In general design the two throne are very much similar but a careful comparison brings out many differences.

For instance, the mounting stool attached to the throne is a very plain peace, the first picture, but a work of art in the second, the shape of the legs of the throne vary in the two pictures and so do the supports of the canopy overhead. The setting of the jewel in the two thrones differs absolutely. The top of the canopy of both the throne show two peacock with spread out tails, but each of the peacock the present picture had a large silky in front of the breast from whence hangs a peer-shaped pearl of 50 carrot and of some of yellow water.[31] This part of description by Tavernier tallies with what is in the present picture, but what follows does not agree at all with the picture. Tavernier says "upon the forfeit which are very massive and from 20-25 inches high are feast the four bar which support the base of throne and upon these bars are arranged 12 columns, which sustained the canopy on three sides, there not being any on that which faces the court.[32]

These columns are not visible in both the pictures. The columns have attracted more than ordinary attention from 'Tavernier', for latter on his description he mentions, which in my opinion is the most costly things about his magnificent throne is that the 12 columns supporting the canopy are surrounded with beautiful rows of pearls which are around and of fine water and weight from 6 to 10 carats each.[33] In other respects the description given by this French Traveller tallies with the description of the throne in the second picture.

Tavernier, no doubt, in this description alludes to the famous peacock throne, and in the light of this account of an eyewitness, the opinion of Percy Brown that the throne shown in the second picture is the famous peacock throne is unacceptable. Again, Tavernier describe another part of the throne which is not at all in the present picture. According to him both sides of peacock, there is a large bucket of the same height as the bird and consisting of many kinds of flower made of gold inlaid with precious stones.[34]

Another fine portrait of Shah Jahan was exhibited in the coronation Darbar exhibition at Delhi in 1911.[35] The picture shows Shah Jahan in his early life, mounted, but the hints to final colourings are very faintly indicated. Both the rider and the horse are drawn with same force. The Prince of Wales Museum, Bombay has in its collection a very good portrait of Shah Jahan,[36] but in this portrait the emperor is depicted as conquered by age and, no doubt, by worries. The emperor, as usual, holds in his left hand the Mughal symbol of sovereignty, the rose, dressed in plane white, the Emperor has a few necklaces round his neck, and a few jewels in his turban. There are only a few flowers round about the Emperor, but these are drawn great delicacy, while the clouds the background indicate a bright day. However, not even the beauty of the flowers is the brightness of the sun seems to take away the expression of care and worry from the face of this noble emperor. Perhaps he is thinking too much about Aurangzeb, perhaps he remembers his beloved Mumtaz. There is another fine portrait of Shah Jahan[37] showing him in middle light, with all the sternness of the Mughal Emperor depicted in his face. The portrait painted against a dark background, and shows the emperor simply dressed in white, with two rows of necklace round his neck and a katar in his belt the emperor stands barefooted. Balchand, Shah Jahan court painter, has drawn a portrait of the emperor[38] showing him standing in full straight dress; he holds a fly whisk in his left hand and a sword in his right. He has profuse jewellery around his neck, and some more in his turban and in his belt. The emperor is dressed in plain white, and his features are those of a middle age man. Two birds of paradise grace the sky, whilst the foreground is decorated with a few delicately painted flowers. The painting which had a brought border is rather stiff and there is nothing particular about it worth noticing.

British museum processes an excellent picture of Shah Jahan consulting a holy man.[39] The Mughal Emperor very plainly and simply dressed, is seated before the holy man who is equally plainly dressed. The seen is laid in the simple countryside, and the emperor and the holy man are sheltered from the burning sun by a very crude canopy over head. The Mulla is seen offering a rose to the emperor who is attended by one of his warrior squatting a little behind him. The background shows four women busy drawing or carrying away water from a well. Whilst, the foreground shows three other persons, only one of whom seems to be interested in the emperor. The storks beautify the picture in the right foreground, and so do 2 or 3 birds seated on the branches of the tree in the background. The middle of the picture is occupied by a poor farmer, he too busy drawing water from a well with the help of his bullocks. The whole seen is bathed in charming simplicity, not even overlooking the emperor who looks to be advanced in age.

The picture shows the three Mughal emperors, Akbar in the centre, Jahangir on his right and Shah Jahan on his left, all the three seated on three identical thrones accommodated under a graceful canopy. The decline in Mughal art which was a bit unnoticed in Shah Jahan' reign was clearly marked in the reign of Aurangzeb. This puritanical monarch was to zealous a Musalman to ever think of patronizing art, let alone think of along it to continue. He did it utmost to discourage art, and never cared to extend his patronage to an art that was so tenderly nourished by his four predecessors.

Gardens of Shah Jahan

Like Akbar, Jahangir took his son travelling with him to Kashmir and both made their contributions to the gardens at Shalimar and Vernag.

Dara Shikoh and Peri Mahal -Kashmir

Dara Shikoh had inherited his father's gift for splendour, his grandfather's love of nature, and he is remembered by two gardens in

Kashmir. The first at Bijbehera was planned to extend on both sides of the Jhelum River. Traces have been found of the parterres and canals, but the garden fell into ruin, and is today marked only by the great chenars, and by the remains of a pavilion and a bridge. His other garden, near Srinagar, shows him to the grandson of Jahangir. Peri Mahal, the 'Fairies' Palace is on the hill immediately south-east of Lake Dal. There is a suggestion of a Greek temple in its sitting, for it lies across a spur of rock, thrown into relief against the darker, higher mountain behind.[40]

Chasma-Shahi the Royal Spring in Kashmir

It was built in 1632; an early inscription at the gateway attributes this garden to Shah Jahan himself. It seems more likely that the actual builder was 'Ali Mardan Khan, working to the emperor's instructions. In its present form the garden combines the work of many hands and various periods. The design derived from a powerful spring at the top of the garden renowed, for the excellence of its water, which bubbled up through a marble lotus basin, now vanished, set in the floor of the upper pavilion. The Mughal work is to be seen in the cascade, the plinths of the two pavilions and the complex of canals, tanks and fountain. The two pavilions themselves are Kashmiri and the upper garden has been widened into a broad terrace.[41]

The Island of the Four Chenars, Kashmir

The two Islands in Lake Dal, the Rupa-Lank and the Sona-Lank (the silver and the golden Lanka) are of considerable antiquity. Entirely artificial, their early names derive from a tradition that silver was buried upon the one and gold on the other. The northern island (the Sona Lank) in particular has been for century's irresistible attraction to travellers. Lying midway across the lake, it is a mere half acre in size, with carefully squared boundaries. It lies just above the water level, so that the trees seem to be floating in the water. The present name is ***Char Chenar*** dates from Shahjahanabad' visit, when he planted a plane tree symmetrical in each corner.

Shalimar Bagh, Delhi

Lying to the north-west of Shahjahanbad close by the Grand Trunk

Road, near Badli Sarai was once yet another great pleasure garden, comparable to those of the same name at Lahore and Srinagar. It was laid out by one of the Shah Jahan's favourite wives, Azizun-Nisa and evidently the Shalimar Bagh in Kashmir had been her inspiration. Its remains are recorded in a plan showing a garden of considerable size, its main feature being a central canal about 18 feet wide, which ran the length of the garden. According to a contemporary historian Muhammad Salih, it was originally even longer.

The upper terrace stood nine feet above the lower, and at the change of level was a complex of tanks and buildings with rose of pearl showering fountain and marvelously adorned halls. Some distance below lay an octagonal reservoir, similar to that vernag, and from the records it would seem that this reservoir originally marked the middle of the garden, with a third and even larger below it. It took four years to build, and was opened ceremonially by the emperor in September 1650, the occasion be marked by a festival. Bernier, visiting it, describes it as regal and beautiful but a mere shadow of Fontainebleau or Versailles. It was to figure notably in the reign of Aurangzeb, but later fell into ruin and decay. It played its part in the downfall of the Mughal Empire, for the during March 1739, the Persian Nadir Shah camped there, a prelude to the massacre of Delhi and seizure of the throne. By the end of the eighteenth century much had already been destroyed, the most valuable materials plundered.

Shalamar Bagh

The first great undertaking had been the construction of a canal to bring the water of Ravi river up to the garden in Lahore. By 1633 the canal was ready and Shah Jahan celeberated its completion by giving instruction for the creation of garden on a grand scale with tank and fountain, a bath house and several pavilion. About 1642, the work was completed and he paid the garden a ceremonial visit after consulting with his astrologers as to an auspicious date. The design comprises three terraces, dropping down from the south the changes in level being about 15 feet. The first and third terrace are ***Char Bagh*** of similar proportion and design; the middle one contain the great reservoir which is the principal feature of the garden. Fedai Khan's Pinjore

Graden were one of the few exceptions to this rule. The upper terrace of Lahore was known as the Farah Baksh (the bestower of pleasure). While the middle and lower terrace forming the more public part of the garden were known together as the Faiz Baksh (the bestower of planty) Ali Mardan Khan as a former governor of Kashmir was likely to have been familiar with the Shalamar Garden there which had receive similar name. Shah Jahan is said to have ordered fruit tree from Kabul and Kandhar. Historian refer to continuous flower bed with plane trees and aspens at interval and the emperor is recorded as having himself planted aspen between two planes. Abdul Hamid Lahori describes the cascades with in innumerable Chini-Kanas or Pigeon holes, beneath them in which where placed golden vases of flower by day and camphorated was candles at night. The original number of fountains have been estimated 450, many of which still survive. In the canal the water throne up in jets 12 feet high.

All these palaces (Delhi Agra and Lahore) are full of garden with running water, which flows in channel into reservoir of his stone jasper and marble in all the room and hall of these palaces there are ordinarily fountains and reservoirs of the same stone of proportionate size. In the garden of these palaces there are always flowers according to the season. There are no large fruit trees of any sort, in order not to hinder the delight of the open view. In these palaces are seats and private rooms, some of which are in the midst of running water. In the water are many fish for delight.

References

1. ***Indian Architecture (Islamic period)*** D.B. Taraporevala Sons & Co. Pvt. Ltd., 210, Dr. D. Narozi Road Mumbai 40001, Copyright 1956, 90, 92, 97, p. 88.
2. ***Architecture of the Islamic World,*** by George Michelle, p. 266.
3. ***Architecture of the Islamic World,*** by George Michelle, p. 270.
4. Percy Brown, ***Mughal Architecture.***
5. ***The Great Ages of World Architecture*** by G.K. Hiraskar, p. 318.
6. ***Imperial Agra of the Mughals*** by K.C. Mazumdar, IInd Ed. Pub. by Gaya Prasad & Sons, Agra, p. 145.
7. ***Imperial Agra of the Mughals*** by K.C. Mazumdar, IInd Ed. Pub. by Gaya Prasad & Sons, Agra, p.146.
8. ***Ibid.,*** p. 147.
9. ***Imperial Agra of the Mughals*** by K.C. Mazumdar, IInd Ed. Pub. by Gaya Prasad &

Sons, Agra, p.146-147.

10. ***Architectures of the Islamic world,*** by George Michelle, p. 273.
11. ***Architecture of the Islamic World,*** by George Michelle, p. 273-74.
12. ***Colour Decoration in Mughal Architecture*** by R. Nath, p. 72-74.
13. ***Imperial Agra of the Mughals*** by K.C. Mazumdar, IInd Ed. Pub. By Gaya Prasad & Sons, Agra, p. 151.
14. ***Indian Architectural Islamic Period*** by Percy Brown, Pub, D.B. Taraporevala Sons & Co., Pvt. Ltd., Bombay 40, 0001, p. 99.
15. ***Indian Architectural Islamic Period*** by Percy Brown, Pub, D.B. Taraporevala Sons & Co., Pvt. Ltd, Bombay 40, 0001, p. 102.
16. ***Colour Decoration in Mughal Architecture*** by R. Nath, pp. 31-33.
17. ***Ibid.,*** pp. 30-33
18. ***Colour Decoration in Mughal Architecture*** by R. Nath, pp. 31-32.
19. Percy Brown, ***op., cit.,*** p. 104.
20. Sanderson A.S.I. ***Annual Report 191-1912,*** p. 15, Brown, ***op., cit.,*** p. 104.
21. Cf. E. Kuhnel, ***The Encyclopedia of Islam,*** Vol, I (1960 Ed.), p. 538.
22. ***History of Decorative Art in Mughal Structure*** by R. Nath, p. 68-69.
23. ***Ibid.,*** pp. 72-73
24. P. Brown, ***Indian Painting under the Mughal,*** p. 108.
25. ***Victoria and Albert Museum Portfolio, Thirty Mughal Paintings of the School of Jahangir,*** p. 2.
26. P. Brown, ***Indian Painting under The Mughal plate,*** XVII.
27. ***Loan, Exhibition of Antiquities Coronation Darbar*** 1911, Plate XXXV, (a).
28. ***Loan, Exhibition of the Antiquities Coronation Darbar,*** 1911, plate XLI.
29. P. Brown, ***Indian Painting Under the Mughals,*** plate XLIT
30. ***Ibid.,*** p. 10
31. J.B. Tavernier, ***Travels in India,*** translated by v. Ball, Vol, I, p. 383.
32. ***Ibid.,*** vol, I, p. 384.
33. ***Ibid.,*** Vol, I, p. 283.
34. ***Loan, Exhibition of Antiquities, Coronation Darbar,*** 1911, Plate XLV (a).
35. W.E. Gladstone Salomon, ***Essay on Mughal Art,*** Plate XIII
36. P. Brown, ***Indian Painting,*** Plate, 13.
37. ***Victoria and Albert Museum Portfolio, Thirty Mughal Paintings of the School of Jahangir,*** Plate, 9.
38. L. Binyon and T.W. Arnold. ***The Court Painter of the Grand Mughal,*** Plate, XVII.
39. ***The Gardens of the Mughal India,*** Vikas Publishing House, Pvt. Ltd., Ist Pub, in India 1973, pp. 135-137.
40. ***Ibid.,*** pp. 138-140.
41. ***The Garden of the Mughal India,*** Vikas Pub. House, 1973.

10. Conclusion

The Mughal dynasty was like a number of other dynasties in central Asia and Iran, a Timurid, one, descended from the great figure of the Lord of the conjunction (Sahib-I-Quran), Amir Timur Gurgan, who had created a huge empire ranging over central Asia, West Asia and even a part of South Asia, from the fragments of the Chingiz Khan dispensation between Timur's death in 1405 and the definitive installation of his direct decendants Zahir-ud-din Babur. This century and more did not affect the Timurid legacy, which in fact remained a crucial pole of orientation for the self-definition of Mughal dynasty as late as the reign of Shah Jahan (whose literature significantly includes the claim to be the second Sahib-i-Quran).

In the Mughal system of government the emperor was no more figureheads, his personality and activity performed all the functions of government. He was responsible for concerning plans and he saw to their executive, as he was the head of the civil as well as military administration. The emperor was regarded as the 'Shadow of God'.

It is noteworthy to mention here that Shah Jahan's reign makes a reaction against the liberal policy of Jahangir. Muslim chronicles describes him with pleasure as Shahanshah Din-i-panah and speaks of his measures against Hindu orthodoxy. One considerable weakness which was always present in the Mughal system of government, was that it did not provide any machinery of a constitutional nature to settle any dispute that might arise from time to time between the ruler and his grandness. There was no legally constituted body of men who could point out the emperor without caring his displeasure, any defect in his administration and persuade him to correct them the absence of any such body, always left the door open for an armed rebellion.[1]

The empire for which the brothers fought so furiously, was yet to grow to its fullest extent in the reign, but it can certainly said to be that it was never more prosperous than during the thirty years (1627-57) of Shah Jahan's rule. Inspite of the early rebellions, foreign wars of aggression, famine in the Deccan and Gujarat, the age of Shah Jahan showed much that was glorious and many unanimous sign of unique prosperity. To justify this period described the golden age of the empire Rai Bhara Mal, in his ***Lubb-ut-tawarikh*** records with admiration: "the means employed by the king (Shah Jahan in these happy times to protect and nourish his people, his administration by honest and intelligent offices, the auditing of accounts, his care of the crown land encouragement of agriculture and the collection of revenue all tended to the prosperity of the empire)".[2]

European critics, partly judging by modern standards, partly reluctant to acknowledge that India was above most prosperous than in the modern times. Thus we come across the following statements: "The reign of Shah Jahan which covers nearly thirty years from 1627 to 1658, is usually regarded as the golden period of Mughal rule. It is drawn present research, that it was outwardly a period of great prosperity. Foreign wars were few and not unimportant. Yet despite the vast treasure which Shah Jahan had inherited from his father and grandfather, despite the growth of large trade between India and western Asia which was rendered possible by the existence of a strong government in Persia, despite the establishment of the export trade with Europe, which certainly brought some profit to the Mughal empire, and inspite of other apparent advantages, the reign of Shah Jahan rounded the knell of the empire and of its economic system.

It is not sought to extenuate the crimes and short-comings of Shah Jahan's reign, but it is necessary to admit the undoubted prosperity of however, short a period without mixing up with its matters of an extraneous nature.

To cite another e.g. of the undue severity of biased criticism, Smith observes-"Shah Jahan has received from most modern historians and specially ELPHINSTONE, treatment unduly favourable. The magnificence of his court, the extent and wealth of his empire, the comparative peace which was preserved during his reign, and the unique beauty of his architectural masterpiece, the Taj have combined to dazzle the vision of his modern biographers, most of whom have slurred over his many crimes and exaggerated such virtues as he passed."

In this research it is concluded that Smith has different views and slurred over his many virtues and exaggerated such crimes as he was guilty of as a brother, as a father and finally as a widower. In affairs of state he was cruel and unscrupulous. Then he has little skill as a military leader the organization and command of his army was inefficient.

Shahjahan's justice was merely, the savage, unfeeling exercise without respect of person and without the slightest tincture of compassion.

PETER MUNDY's another traders bear similar testimony to the misgovernment of the country.'

BERNIER- observed that as he speaks of the actual state of the country at the most brilliant period of Mughal rule. The periodical expenditure and unexampled splendour of the court, which occupied so prominent place in most of the current descriptions of Shah Jahan rule had therefore a dark background of suffering and misery seldom exposed to view." Then perhaps follows a painful vividness from the pen of the official historian ABDUL HAMID LAHORI- who contrary to the frequent practice of writers of his kind, makes no attempt to disguise the honour of the calamity."

SMITH denies the various kindness and bounty of Shah Jahan described by the same writer so far as MUNDY is concerned he had seen nothing to help the sufferings of the people was done by the government," though meantime the camp of Shah Jahan at Burhanpur was filled with provisions of all kinds. No statistics are recorded but we are not without imagination SIR-RICHARD TEMPLE, the editor of Mundy's work, has good reason for saying that–"it is worth while to read Mundy's in impassioned matter of fact observations on this feline, in order to realize the immensity of the defense in the conditions of life as existing under the rule of the Mughal dynasty when at the height of its glory and those prevailing under the modern British government.

ELPHISTONE describes the age of Shah Jahan as the most prosperous ever known India... together with a larger share of good government than often falls to the lot of Asiatic nations.

KHAFI KHAN, the best historian of those times gives his opinion that although Akbar was prominent as a conqueror and a lawgiver, yet for the order and arrangement of his territory and finances and the good administration of every department of the state no prince ever reigned in India that could be compared to Shah Jahan.

Focus is now on the cities of the Shah Jahan's times Mundy's describes Agra as least twice at large as its ***farman*** (then in its greatest glory with fine streets, good shops, and numerous baths and caravanserais.) nor was this prosperity confined to royal residencies all travellers speak with admiration of the grandeur of the cities even in remote provinces of the fertile and productive countries in which they stood.

Those who look on India in its present state may be inclined to suspect the native writers of exaggerating its former prosperity, but the deserted cities ruined palaces and chocked the aqueducts which will see with the great reservoirs proves the evidence of contemporary travellers.

TAVERNIER who had repeatedly visited most parts of India says that Shah Jahan reigned not so much as a king over his subjects but rather as a father as a friend and as children.

BRINIER writes of the prosperity of Bengal under Shah Jahan in the fallowing terms: "Bengal abound with every necessity of life and it is this aboundance that has induced so many Portuguese and other fertile kingdom.

In regard to valuable commodities of a nature to attract foreign merchants. Besides the sugar there is in Bengal such quantity of cotton and silk that the kingdom may be called the common store house merchandise, not of Hindustan or the Empire of great Mughal only but of all the neighouring Kingdoms of Europe. Lastly it is said that from this fruitful kingdom that the best lack, opium are kippers various drugs are obtained.

Administration of justice of Shah Jahan is concerned. BERNIER has also observed that in Hindustan every acre of land is considered the property of the king's the Spoilation of the peasent would be a robbery committed upon the king domain. In the light of these statements Rai BHARA MAL observed. Notwithstanding the great area of this country, complaints were so few that only one day in the week that is Wednesday was fixed upon for the administration of justice and it was rarely even then that twenty plaintiffs could be found to prefer suits, the number generally being much less.

If offenders were discovered, the local authorities used generally to try them on the spot (where the offence had been committed) according to law and in concurrences with the law officers, and if any individual, dissatisfied with the decision passed on this case, appealed to the governor or Divan, or to the Qazi of the suba, the matter was reviewed, and judgment was awarded with great care and discrimination lest it should be mentioned in the presence of the king that justice had not been done. If parties were not satisfied even with these decisions, they appealed to the Chief Diwan or to the Chief Qazi on matters of law.

MORELAND has indeed pointed out that the reign of Shah Jahan was a period of agrarian tranquility though the condition of the peasant became worse towards the beginning of the next reign. This prosperity under Shah Jahan was largely due to his "careful administration", which raised the income of the state beyond all precedents. The testimony of RAI BHARA MAL, already cited in confirmation of this, is sought to be disparaged by some on the ground that the actual orders of Shah Jahan on matters that is referred to are not traceable.

MORELAND is certainly not correct in describing the author of the LUBB-UT-TAWARIKH as "a letter written" for the Rai himself speaks of the "writer of this historical sketch on more than one occasion, being honoured with an audience of the king (Shah Jahan). His account unmistakably points to the efficiency benevolence and undoubted prosperity of Shah Jahan's Empire.

It is not possible to make an accurate estimation about the extent of his prosperity. Few of its visible indications are given below.

(1). In 1647, Shah Jahan sent, as a thanks offering, jeweled and candlestick to the revered tomb of the Prophet (on whom be the greatest favours and blessing) on account of which is here given.... having selected out of the amber candle sticks that he had amongst his private property, the largest of them all which weighted 700 to lacs and was worth 10,000 Rs. He commanded that it should be covered with a network of gold ornamented on all side with flowers and stud with gems. Candle stick costs 2 lacs and 50,000 was the price of the diamond.

In the course of years many valuable gems had come into the imperial jewel house, each one of which might serve as an eardrop for Venus or would adore the girdle of the sun. There were some changes in Mansabadari system; the mainframe work of the whole system took shape in the later half of Akbars reign. In the literature, the transition from single to double rank occurs in the first year of Jahangir reign, but as a matter of fact it was also existing under Akbar's reign.

When the mansab has taken evidence from the narrative of the 1st decade what strikes us is the moderate scale of promotions granted by Shah Jahan *zat* promotions in the first two years of his reign inspite of his considerable political difficulties in the beginning. Shah Jahan granted only 39,90 in the net increase in *sawar* mansab (46,200) in Shah Jahan's first two years did not fall much beyond the net increase of *sawar* granted by Aurangzeb.

The comparison of the lists of 20th and 30th years shows that there were net *zat* enhancement of 1,33,350 as against 53, 625 sawars. It is difficult to explain why Shah Jahan mansab's policy changed in the third decade.

Now we have drawn our attention towards the trade in Shah Jahan's reign in this period when Gujarat and North India had yet to recover wholly from the disastrous effects of the famine of the early 1630, but one needs to go beyond this, as the policy in Shah Jahan, period where trade was concerned has a coherence that transcends regional imperatives.

During the 16th and 17th centuries these inland trade centers passed through, some flourishing, some declining and others rising to prominence, by the end of the 16th and beginning of the 17th century Portuguese established a profitable commerce between India, West Asia, Europe and China.

Shah Jahan was a great builder and the buildings at Delhi and Agra are standing monuments of his achievement. Taj Mahal was the most admired mausoleum in the world. The architectural style of Shah Jahan's buildings was different from that of his predecessors. It was characterized by elegance either than by strength and by the lavish use of extraordinary costly decoration. Shah Jahan used marble instead of red stone whereas there was a mixture of Hindu- Muslim style in the building of Akbar and Jahahngir but there was no such thing in the architecture of Shah Jahan. He built a large number of buildings in Agra and Delhi; a few buildings were built at Ajmer. Peacock throne cost Rs. 19 crores, it was solid gold studded with costly jewels.

He laid the foundation of Shahjahanabad. The Tomb of Nizamuddin Aulia was built of pure white marble, a few buildings was also built at Ajmer. There was decline in the style of Shah Jahan too much use of gold pigment which reflects Emperor liking for pomp and show. Painting lacks of proper blendings of colour

For the safety of the travellers, Shah Jahan did lot of work and he did all in power to render travelling within the empire as safe as could be one of the means he adopted was to provide caravan serais with proper equipments. Mannuchi writes that throughout the realm of the Mughal on every route there were many sarais they are like fortified, places with the strong gates, most of them are built of stone or brick.

The measures taken by Shah Jahan for the relief of the famine stricken in the earlier part of his reign LAHORI writes–"The emperor in his gracious kindness and bounty directed the officials to Burhanpur, Ahmedabad and the Surat to establish soup kitchens for the benefit of the poor. Emperor takes amount nearly to 70 lacs of rupees were rebutted by the revenue officers–a sum amount nearly to eight krores of dams, which amount to one-eleventh part of the whole revenue.

Smith declares while the people were dying of starvation, the camp of Shah Jahan at Burhanpur was filled with provisionary of all kinds and so far MUNDY saw nothing to help the suffering of people was done by the government. At least two instances of the construction of canals to improve agricultural prosperity are on record. ***Badshah Nama*** states that Ali Mardan represented to his majesty that all of his followers were an adept in the forming of canals. Emperors gave to the Khan 1 lac of Rs. A second canal was called Nahar-i-Bahisht.

Shah Jahan's patronage was not confined to architecture alone. Both Persian and Hindi, prose and poetry, music, painting and dams, mathematics and medicines flourished equally. There were both Hindu and Muslim writers, scholar and artist. Translation of great Sanskrit works were also made. The Prabodh Chandrodaya by Munshi Banvali

Das and the Ramayana by Ibn Har Karan; Mulla Farid Munajjim the greatest astronomer of the period, prepared the astral chart entitled Zich-i-Shahjahani; Ataullah wrote a treatise on Algebra, Mensuration and Arithmetic and dedicated it to the emperor and Dara while Abdur Rashid translated Bij Ganit Sanskrit. The Hindi poets who were connected with court were Sunder Das, Chintamani and Kavindra Acharya.

Shah Jahan was an excellent singer, particularly in Dhrupad style and was adept veena player. Emperor delighted Tansen son in law, Lal Khan Gunasamudra, singing the Dhrupad tune, which was the emperor's favourite Jagannath, the best Hindu musician of the age was favoured by Shah Jahan and received from him the title of Mahakavi Rai. Sukhsen was a master player on the Rubab or Guitar and Sur Sen on the vin of zither

In the field of literature there were both Hindu and Muslim writers scholars and artists. Translators of great Sanskrit works were also made. Mulla Farid Munajjim, the greatest astronomer prepared the chart entitled Zich-i-Shahjahani which is described as the most brilliant epoch in the development of different kinds of literature and languages.

Inspite of all that has been stated above even Shah Jahan still remains a paradox in some respect. The minute details of his daily routine of which we have contemporary evidence show him to have been a man of strenuous activity and great command but legant whispers of extreme self indulgence verging on scandalous depravity of which however, there seems to be little foundation.

The character of Shah Jahan is very controversial. Indian chronicles point him as the very ideal of a Muslim monarch.[3] They style him the pillar of Shara, the defendant of religion and the restorer of the warning fortunes of ISLAM in India. They praise his piety, his religiousness with subjects, they condemned his faults, and justify some of his darkest deeds on the grounds of the public and political morality of the time. Thus according to their picture Shah Jahan appears as a virtuous and affable sovereign with hardly blemish in his character worth mentioning. Shah Jahan was very fond of music and dancing. The names of Kavindra, Chitra Khan, Lal Khan Sriman are mentioned as court musicians.

There was a big staff of dancing girls attached to the court.

BERNIER praises their supplements and grace. It may be that Shah Jahan some times indulged in frivolities with them, but to presume that his life was one unceasing round of bestial sensuality in erroneous. It is doubtful if Shah Jahan was addicted to drinking. MANUCCI says that the emperor was not a drinker himself thought he did not care to remedy the evil.

Shah Jahan was orthodox in his religious attitude the practice of desecrating and destroying Hindu temple revived in the reign of Jahangir and became systemic under Shahjahan. The abolition of sijda and prohibition of the wearing of the emperor's portrait in the turban are cited as instances of his religious outlook. But more important thing was his attitude towards the non-Muslims including the Hindus and the Christians.

He first ordered in January 1633, the demolition of the newly built temple in his whole empire especially at Benaras and this order was followed by a total prohibition for the erecting of a new temples or the repairing of the old one. The Hindus were forbidden to dress in Muslim style, to sell or drink wine openly or privately to cremate their dead or burn the safis near Muslim grave yards; and to purchase Muslim slaves of war.

After the sixteenth year of his reign his vigour nature began to decline. The Ulemas issued a fatwa to excuse him from the Ramzan and permitted him to give alms untied imprisonment shattered his health completely. He fell ill in January 1666 as the effect of rubbing himself with medicated oil.

He was seized with fever which was soon complicated by stranjury and gripping of the stomach. Although the surgeon Brindaban removed the obstruction often nine days, the emperor could no longer fight against nature and began to sink. On January, 22 his condition became hapless. He fervently thanked God, prayed him to forgive his sons uncle his will to his concubine and gave up his life in full view of the Taj amidst the waiting of the women's and sons of his attendants. Thus in kingly career which opened with the tragedy ended also in tragedy.

References

1. Ram Prasad Khosla, ***Mughal Kingship and Nobility***.
2. Lanepoole, ***Contemporary Sources***, p. 110.
3. ***Qazvini*** f. 302 A.H. Lahouri, Vol. 1, p. 139.

Bibliography

Primary Sources

1. A'in-i-Akbari of (Abul Fazl), Translated by H. Blochman, Vol. II, 1891.
2. A.H. Lahuri Badshahnama, Vol. 1.
3. Akbarat-i-Darbar-i-Mualla (Court Diary Manuscript) Department of History, Aligarh Muslim University, Aligarh.
4. Akbarnama of Abul Fazl Translated by Henery Beveridge.
5. Dastur-ul-Amal, B. M. ms, or 2026.
6. Farhang-i-Kardani By (Jagat Rai, Sagal Kayasth Saxena), Manuscript 85/315 Abdul Salaam, Pub. by Maulana Azad Library, Aligarh Muslim University, Aligarh.
7. Jahangir (Tuzk-i-Jahangiri), Translated by Rosers and H. Beveridge, II, London 1909.
8. Khan Khafi (Muntakhab-ul-Lubad), Pub. by Kabiruddin Ahmad, Biblioca India , Calcutta, 1911.
9. Khan Mutammid (Iqbalnama-i-Jahangiri), Translated by Elliot and Dowson, 1865.
10. Kaifiyat-i-Subajat-i-Mumalik-i-Maharusa-i-Hindustan.
11. Ma'asir-i-Jahangiri of Kamgar Khan.
12. Minhaj-us-Siraj (Tabqat-i-Nasiri), Translated by H.G. Rawat, London, 1881.
13. Muntakhab-ul-Lubab Muhammad Shahi of Muhammad Hashim Khafi Khan.
14. Padshahnama of Qazwini.
15. Selected Document, Shah Jahan's reign, by the Daftar-i-Diwani,

Hyderabad, 1950.
16. Tarikh-i-Farishta (Mohd. Qasim), English Translation by Col. Briggs, Vol. II., Longmans 1829.
17. Tarikh-i-Rashidi (Mirza Haider), English Translation by Elias and Denison Ross, 1895.
18. Tazkirat-ul-Waqiat Jauhar.
19. Tuhfat-us-Salatani Amir Shahi.

Secondary Sources

1. Abdul Aziz, ***The Mansabdari System in the Mughal Army,*** Delhi 1972.
2. Bamber Gascoigne, ***The Great Mughals.*** B.T. Publication New Delhi, 1971.
3. Banerjee, S.K., ***Humayun Badshah,*** O.U.P. 1938.
4. B. Ahmad, ***The Administration of Justice in Medievial India.***
5. Beni Prasad, ***History of Jahangir,*** Allahabad, 1930.
6. Elliot and Dowson, ***The History of India as told by its Own Historian,*** 1877.
7. Firdaus Anwar, ***Nobility Under the Mughal,*** Manohar Publication, 2001.
8. Gavin Hambley, ***Cities of the Mughal India,*** Vikas Pub. House, 1977.
9. George Michelle, ***Architecture of the Islamic World with Complete Survey of Key Monuments over 700 Illustrations,*** 112 in colour.
10. Hiraskar, G.K., ***The Great Ages of World Architecture with Introduction to Landscape Architecture.***
11. Ibn-i-Hasan, ***The Central Structure of the Mughal Empire O.U.P. 1936.***
12. Irfan Habib, ***Agrarian System of Mughal India,*** Delhi, 1963.
13. Irfan Habib, ***Mansab Salary Scale under Jahangir and Shah Jahan,*** (Art No. 383). Pub. by Islamic Culture, Hyderabad, Vol LIX. No. 3.
14. Irfan Habib, ***The Currency System of the Mughal Empire,*** Reprinted from Medieval India Quarterly, Vol. IV, Nos, 2.
15. Irvine William, ***The Army of the Indian Mughals, Its Organization and Administration,*** Luzac, 1903.

16. Irvine William, ***The Army of the Indian Mughal***, Euresia Publishing House, 1962.
17. Jafar S. M., ***The Mughal Empire from Babur to Aurangzeb***. Ess. Ess. Publication 1936.
18. Khosla, R.P., ***Mughal Kingship and Nobility***, Qasimjan Street, Delhi, 2001.
19. Lnae-poole, ***Babur Rulers of India Series,*** O.U.P. 1899.
20. M. Athar Ali, ***Provincial Governor Under Shah Jahan***, An Analysis. Center of Advance Study, Department of History Aligarh Muslim University, Aligrah.
21. M. Athar Ali, ***Mansab and Imperial Policy under Shah Jahan.***
22. Moreland, W.H., ***The Agrarian System of Muslim India***, Pub, CSI Oriental Book, Comp, Reprint. 1968.
23. Muhammad Yamin, ***A Special History of the Mughal (1526-1658).*** Bom, 1973.
24. Naqvi, H.K., ***History of the Mughal Government and Administration***, Kanishka Publishing House, Delhi, 1990.
25. Naqvi, ***H.K., History of the Mughal Government and Administration***, Kanishka Pub., House 1990.
26. Naqvi, H.K., ***Histroy of Mugal Government and Adminitsration***, Kanishka Pub. House, Delhi, 1990.
27. Nath, R., ***Colour Decoration in Mughal Architecture.***
28. Percy Brwon, ***Indian Architecture (Islamic Period)***, D.B. Taraporwala Sons and Company Pvt. Ltd.
29. Pant, D., ***Commercial Policy of the Mughal***, Taraporwala, Bombay, 1930.
30. Qaiser Ahsan Jaan, ***Distribution of the Revenue Resource Among the Mughal Nobility***, ISC, ALlahabad Session, 1965.
31. Qanungo-Kalikaranjan, ***Sher Shah***, Calcutta, 1921.
32. Quraishi, I.H., ***The Administration of Mughal Empire***, N.V. Publication.
33. Rajkumar, ***Administrating Law and Justice in Medieval India***, Anmol Pub. Pvt. Ltd., New Delhi, 2000.
34. Rajkumar, ***India Under Shah Jahan***, Arbab Publication Pvt. Ltd. 2000.
35. Saran, P., ***Provincial Government of the Mughal***, 1526-1658. Pub.,

Kitabista, Allahabad. 1945.

36. Sarkar, J.N., ***Mughal Administration IV Ed.***, 1952.
37. Sarkar, J.N., ***Mughal Administration,*** Calcutta, 1924.
38. Sarkar, J.N., ***Mughal Economy and Organization,*** Naya Prakashan, 1987.
39. Sarkar, J.N., ***Studies in Mughal India,*** Calcutta, 1922.
40. Saxena, B.D., ***History of Shah Jahan,*** 1934.
41. Sharma, S.R., ***Religious Policy of the Mughal Empire,*** New Delhi, Bombay, 1962.
42. Smith, V.A., ***Akbar the Great,*** Oxford, 1917.
43. Smith, V.A., ***Akbar the Great Mughal,*** Oxford, 1917.
44. Siddiqui Noman Ahmad, ***Land Revenue Administration under the Mughals,*** Asia Publishing House, 1970.
45. ***The Garden of the India,*** Vikas Publishing House, 1972.
46. Tripathi, R.P., ***Some Aspects of Mughal Administration,*** Allhabad 1936.
47. Uday Chand, ***Datur-ul-Amal-i-Sarishtahjat,*** Oriental, ms 83. Edenburg.

European TRAVELLER'S Account

1. Bernier Francois, ***Travels in the Mughal Empire,*** 1656-68. A Constable Translation V.A. Smith (Ed.) Delhi 1989.
2. De Laet, ***Description of Indian and Fragment of Indian History,*** J.S. Hoyland tr. An Annotated by S.N. Baerjee, ***The Empire of Great Mughal,*** Bombay, 1928.
3. Foster, W., ***English Factories in India,*** Oxford, 1926-27, C. Foralt, Oxford, 1936.
4. Manucci Nicolao, ***Storia Do Magor,*** 1653-1708, William Irvine, tr, Calcutta, 1965.
5. Mundy, Peter, ***Travels,*** Vol II, Travels in Asia 1630-34, R.C. Temple, Ed., II Series London. 1914.
6. Pelsaert, ***Jahangir's India,*** Geyl and Moreland tr. Cambridge 1925.
7. Thomas Ray, ***The Embessy of Sir Thomas Ray,*** W. Foster, 1926.

Periodicals

1. ***Journal of Asiatic Society of Bengal***, Calcutta
2. ***Journal of Indian History***, Allahabad, Madras.
3. ***Medieval India***, Quarterly, Aligarh.
4. ***Oriental Miscellany***, Calcutta.
5. ***Proceeding of the Indian History Congress.***
6. ***Encyclopedia of Islam.***
7. Barbosa, ***The Journal of the First Voyage.*** 1947-49

Index